The

IVORY DOMINO

Gary Henson

Charleston, AR

COBB PUBLISHING

2018

Published in the United States of America by:
Cobb Publishing
704 E. Main Street
Charleston, AR 72933
(479) 747-8372
CobbPublishing@gmail.com
www.CobbPublishing.com

At their request, some names have been changed to protect the privacy and rights of the individuals outlined herein.

All Scripture references and quotations are from (as noted) the Douay-Confraternity Version, or the King James Version

1st Edition, February, 2018

ISBN-13: 978-1947622074
ISBN-10: 1947622072

The Ivory Domino is dedicated to the person I most adore.
My friend whose touch thrills me;
My counselor whose wisdom guides me;
My encourager whose words lift me;
My companion I love to love…
My wife
Sheila (Gamble) Henson

THANK YOU

To the many who whole-heartedly encouraged me
in the writing of this book, so that you, the reader,
may also know what I had learned.

To the beloved Christians I live among in El Reno, Oklahoma,
for their patience and faith in me during this volume's production.

To the gracious proofreaders and reviewers:
James Cudd, Bill Howard, Garrell Kidd,
Wayne Price, and Ray Rose.
Their willingness, time, and suggestions prove invaluable
to every person who reads this book.

To Michael Shank and his *Muscle and a Shovel*,
who inspired me to write this book.

To Roy Young for locating manuscripts of some of his
sermons he preached during the challenge I faced.

To Bradley Cobb, whose editorship, help, and friendship
was, and is, simply priceless.

To God-fearing, soul-loving Christians
who invite their family and friends to read
what I am unable to tell them in person.

FOREWARNING!

If you are like the rest of us, you face challenges. Some challenges are brutal and unshakable. This story is based upon my fierce ordeal and the victory I achieved.

I feel morally obligated to caution you though: you may not like what you are about to read. You may get mad, even furious—either at the book, or at what the book will set before you. So, for you, I went back and documented everything I learned, in order that you can see for yourself that *it is all true!*

[If you have stress-triggered health issues, keep yourself monitored. I assure you, I am not joking.]

If you have what it takes to finish the book, you will see how I was able to be victorious over my trial—and, if so challenged, how you can too. You will even get answers to questions you stopped asking a long time ago, because you thought the world had no answer.

The story that awaits you presents the grievous test of my faith and honesty. And I promise you, it will also test yours! So, take a look in the mirror; when you have finished the book, you may not be the same person you are now!

Galatians 4:16

*Have I therefore become your enemy
because I tell you the truth?*

CHAPTER 1
MISTAKEN PERFECTION

I sat on a small bench in the dimly lit closet. With my back against the wall, I gazed at the door three feet away. A porous screen covered the one-foot square window by my right shoulder. The prolonged wait heightened my dread as my heart thumped against my front ribs.

I heard the panel on the other side of the screen slide open. That was my cue.

"Bless me Father, for I have sinned."

Through the dense screen, I could make out the priest tracing the sign of the cross toward me while he said, "The Lord be in thy heart and upon thy lips, that thou mayest confess thy sins rightly in the name of the Father, and of the Son, and of the Holy Ghost."

"It has been four weeks since my last confession, in which you absolved me of my sins, and for which I performed the penance you required. I confess to God Almighty, and to you Father, that I have since sinned."

Now came the stomach-knotting part. I never felt comfortable confessing my sins. Not even to a priest who couldn't see me. But I did, nevertheless. I wanted my sins forgiven, and this is how God said to do it.

One by one, I choked through the list of my transgressions. Then, as my chest relaxed, I recited the final words the nuns taught me in Catechism School: "For these, and all the sins of my whole life, I am most heartily sorry, because by them I have offended God, the Supreme and Most Amiable Good. I detest all my sins, and am firmly resolved to amend my life and to sin no more."

"Is that all?" the priest asked with suspicion in his voice.

"Isn't that enough? And Father, why do you always ask me that?"

"My son, only three sins in four weeks is far from normal. Maybe you have forgotten some? Or perhaps you are embarrassed to mention others?"

"Oh no, Father. I want to go to heaven. So I strive to do right, and when I don't, it stands out and I can't forget it."

"Well then, bless you my son. Bless you indeed. I absolve you from your sins. Your penance is two 'Hail Marys.' Go and sin no more."

I squinted as I stepped out of the dark booth into the sun-lit sanctuary. Kneeling on the fold-down kneepad of a nearby pew, I pulled my black rosary out of the left front pocket of my slacks —not that I needed to keep count of just two prayers, but it felt comforting. With my head bowed, eyes closed, and rosary clutched, I prayed.

> *"Hail Mary full of grace, the Lord is with thee.*
> *Blessed art thou among women*
> *And blessed is the fruit of thy womb, Jesus.*
> *Holy Mary, Mother of God, pray for us sinners,*
> *Now and at the hour of our death. Amen."*

After the second "Hail Mary," I made the sign of the cross and slid back onto the pew in the quiet sanctuary to think upon what lay before me—the challenge to my faith. I knew what I was up against from personal experience. My previous years in school as a teenager proved quite trying, and my senior year would be worse. *Not only will my good Catholic morals continually get tested,* I thought with dismay, *so will my Catholic beliefs when students talk religion. But I'm fortifying myself. Confession today, Mass tomorrow (as always), and weekly Catechism School. I'll be ready for any challenge!*

Bold words for someone who had no clue just how monstrous the trial lying in wait would be.

The school bell rang and the doors swung open. The 1969-1970 Putnam City West Patriots (1,350 of us) funneled into the school like sand in an hour-glass. Senioritis officially began!

"Spoiled brats"—that phrase in no way described us, yet, we knew about the rare—very rare—privilege we enjoyed. Putnam City West (PCW) reigned as the newest high-school in Oklahoma and came loaded with the latest advancements a building could boast: central heat and air, a second gymnasium with tartan flooring (a hard rubber-like substance), a theatre, all kinds of equipment, and on and on. Plus, it was all new. I mean, unused, unworn, and un-scratched. Yet, it lacked the most important item…well, at least to some of us. A football stadium. Instead, we shared the stadium located at the other Putnam City high school. But, like I said, "spoiled-brats-'R'-not-us," so we made the every-other-Friday, five-mile bus trip with no complaint.

In the previous year, PCW began with only juniors and sophomores, which presented a clear-cut pro and con. The pro: my class ruled as the upper classmen for two years. The con: we got beat to a pulp in every athletic event that first year. To save embarrassment, when asked in public what the letters PCW stood for on my letter jacket, I would tell them, "Ponca City West." But this year would be different. And we knew it. Every starter was returning. We were bigger, faster, and experienced. This year we would repay the beatings. With interest.

The new building on the western edge of Oklahoma City nestled into an area saturated with tall oak trees, and laid only three blocks from beautiful Lake Overholser, or, as some called it, Lake Hold-her-closer.

Everything, even the intangibles, paved the way for a remarkable year. All summer we anticipated these nine months, and our excitement electrified the very air as we passed through the halls to our first class. When I walked by the full-length glass panels that housed the main office, David Cotton, our student council president, organized his notes for his morning intercom welcome to the student body. He spotted me, charged to the door, and hollered, "Gary, you footballers going to give us a win next week?" David possessed an amazing knack for stirring school spirit, and stood head and shoulders, even chest, above other leaders. Last year, when he and I represented PCW at Oklahoma City's Inter-City Student Council Meeting, he decided—just moments before the election for the '69-'70 president—to run. I introduced him, and he gave a spontaneous speech and won. Amazing guy.

"Put an 'X' in the win column, Mr. President," I yelled back.

I turned my head just in time to avoid a nasty collision with a teacher struggling to unlock her classroom door, her arms laden with books, satchels, and a purse.

"Here, let me help," I insisted.

I removed one book, stepped back and grinned.

She glared back with squinting eyes and shook her head.

As I took hold of all the books and satchels, I jested, "Too bad I'm not in your class. I could use some bonus points."

To this she quipped, as she tilted her head down to look over her glasses, "You mean, demerit points, do you not, Mr. Henson?"

I laughed (I hoped she was joking), turned the corner, and went up the staircase to my locker.

As I spun through the lock's combination, a voice behind me ordered, "Hey, big-un, don't forget to be at practice as soon as possible."

I knew the voice. Bob Wilson was our right tackle, senior class president, very intelligent, and one of my closest friends.

"Yep. Picture day," I acknowledged. "Be sure you put on a gladiator face."

"You go last, though. Your mean face will melt the lens."

I rolled up a thin paperback and turned to bop his head, but a hand bolted from beside us and the firm grip halted my swing in mid-air. "I got him, Bob. Run for your life while you can."

"Yeah," I added to the playful sparring, "I don't want to knock any more sense out of the small amount a lineman has."

The firm grip belonged to another best friend, my locker-mate, Cole Newby. If an award was given to the best dressed male student, he would win it. (There was, and he did.) Cole shined as a defensive back and ran as my teammate on the 440 relay. Alike in attitude, confidence, and viewpoints, we hung out a lot together. From sports to socializing. From double-dating to watching John Wayne.

"Had a big breakfast?" I asked.

"Yeah. Keeping to the plan."

"Good. Then we'll load up at lunch—man, I hope it's not the Chinese spaghetti today—and then drink as much water as we can."

"How much heavier do you think we will be?" he asked hopefully.

4

"Oh, maybe four to six pounds. Unless we burst."

"That's not enough. Today's weigh-in will be in every game program this season. Our weight must be heavy and our mug-shots mean."

"You're not thinking about bribing the coach, are you?"

He slapped my shoulder. "Here's what we can do! Slip a rope through a couple of five-pound weights and tie it around our waist under our gym shorts."

"No can do, good buddy. That's like lying and I'd have to go to confession. Can you imagine everybody hearing the priest laugh while taking someone's confession?! Why, for embarrassing him, he would make me say the entire rosary ten times. Huh-uh. Besides, Coach Webb is sure to catch you." (And he did).

Indeed, the outlook for my senior year was perfect on that first day of school. I had the best friends in the world, in the finest facility in the state, at the most envious location, and predictions of championships in every sport—especially football. That isn't to say the year would be without its challenges. Yet, we would fight our athletic and academic challenges together.

But, there was a monstrous challenge I would face alone. And I didn't even know it was approaching.

CHAPTER 2
THE WAGER

Was I a loyal Catholic? You better believe it. Pure Catholic bred. My immediate ancestors hailed from deep south Louisiana where Catholics controlled and temples towered. My grandparents, great-grandparents, aunts, uncles, and cousins—all of whom I cherished and tried to make proud of my Catholic faith—stood unmovable in the Church. During the early immigration years of this country, our family came from Catholic France. Knowing the ancient Catholic heritage of France, it would be absurd to think anything other than my family tree being Catholic all the way down to its roots in the second or third century. Indeed, my very being cried "Catholic."

Until the eighth grade, I grew up in Bellaire, Texas—a suburb swallowed up on the southwest side of the growing giant, Houston. Even in this environment, the vast popularity of Catholicism swayed that massive metropolis to serve fish on Fridays at public schools to accommodate the multitude of Catholic students. The powerful influence of Catholicism engulfed me, confirming to my young mind the rightness of the Catholic Church.

Mom's parents lived fifteen minutes away, and we attended St. Vincent De Paul, the archdiocese[1] of Houston-Galveston. Of course, I don't remember my baptism, being only six weeks old, but I easily recall my Confirmation (the strengthening by the Holy Spirit) at seven years. In a big to-do, a seemingly endless procession of kids my age filed down the middle aisle of St. Vincent's to, one-by-one, face the archbishop. As though in a wonderful dream, I stepped up to the God-like man who then laid his hand upon me, dipped his thumb in the Chrism Holy Oil (bishop-blessed olive oil and balsam), traced the sign of the cross upon my forehead, and said, "Be sealed with the gifts of the Holy Spirit" (courage, piety, wisdom, understanding, etc.). He concluded when he gave my cheek a mild slap to remind me of my duty to endure all kinds of trials—including the beast I soon would encounter.

I took my Confirmation seriously. As taught, I was a follower of

Jesus and property of the Church. I persisted in Catechism school-ing, even into high school. My religion went with me outside of Mass—I did not steal, cuss, cause trouble, talk back to Mom and Dad or teachers. I believed and trusted in the Church, priests, nuns, and pope. Whatever they taught stood true and right. After getting my driver's license, when Mom didn't make it to Mass, I would still go. Catholicism was not merely my Mother's religion, it was *my* re-ligion.

I knew that every non-excommunicated Catholic would go to heaven, eventually. But Purgatory still troubled me. I wanted no part of the punishment after death to pay for sins before I could go to heaven. So I strove to do as the Church taught me.

I didn't bother to read the Bible. Didn't need to. God told the pope what He wanted; the pope told the hierarchy; and the priests told the Church. God sure made it easy for us to know what He wanted.

Something else molded my character, but I don't know if it was for the good or bad. Some of both, I guess. Mostly good, I hope. I must have inherited it from Dad, a semi-perfectionist. It was this: I wanted to be in the right. I don't mean I wanted to be right in every argument (although that would be included), but I mean I wanted to be a part of only that which was in the right. That is what kept me in the Catholic Church. It was the original Church begun by Jesus and His apostles, it has the pope, and we were 660 million strong. It was the right church, and if I had not been in it, I would have joined it. I wanted to be in the right!

The Friday night celebration commenced, courtesy of the Patri-ots football team. The awaiting cheerleaders and numerous students applauded, cheered, and whistled as we entered Bevo's Restaurant, our after-the-game hangout. And they had every reason. An hour earlier, they beheld our assault—four touchdowns before the John Marshall team made their lone score late in the game. Offensively and defensively, our opening game made a statement, and the ex-citement level rocketed off the scale.

Cole and I grabbed a four-person booth in the middle of the fes-tivity. We each took opposite sides and sat at the end of our benches in order to leave the inner space vacant. It was our carefully conspired strategy. As numerous students hopped from table to table to chatter about the game, Cole and I held our position on the bench seat to keep the 'hoppers' standing in the aisle. But, when a dating candidate appeared, we scooted over.

A couple of guys, each with a chocolate shake covered with cream and a cherry on top in one hand, patted our backs with the other. "Terrific game! You think we will go 10 and 0?"

"Don't know," I replied as I snatched off one of the cherries and popped it in my mouth. "Hope so, but that's hard to do."

"How did you like Andrews' 85-yard punt return for a touchdown?" Cole asked as he went for the other cherry, but was slapped away by our anticipating friend.

"Absolutely sensational! The blocking was amazing, and when he got in the open, man, he was gone!" said one.

"What did coach say about the game?" asked the other.

The entire school liked Coach Webb, and the seniors enjoyed a close bond with him. Before PCW opened, he coached us for two winning seasons at Western Oaks Jr. High School. This made it our fourth year with him as head coach. He impressed me (with an ever increasing admiration) the first time I saw him as I walked onto the junior high practice field. He stood nine feet tall (so it seemed), muscular, trim, and handsome. While in high school at the original Putnam City building, he won All-American as a lineman. Recruited by the University of Oklahoma, he was destined to become an OU legend with a career in the National Football League. A blown knee changed all that. Slowed, but not stopped, he played at Central State College in Edmond, Oklahoma, and helped win the 1962 NAIA National Championship. Coach Webb's mere presence and his genuine concern compelled us to excellence on every play, whether in practice or game.

"Coach was pleased," answered Cole as he reached for a menu.

"But he said don't get the big head," I added as I snatched the menu from Cole.

The table-hopping and congratulations kept going, but you can only talk so much about anything, including the football game. So, with some, the chitchat turned to church and the extending of invitations to worship. Most knew about me and didn't bother to ask. However, three timid girls adorned in their blue pep-club sweaters (meaning they were sophomores and didn't know better) walked up to the table. (We did not scoot over.)

"Great game guys," said one, while the others showed their pearly whites and nodded.

"Thanks," replied Cole.

"We'll see if we can't do it again next week," I added.

The spokesman of the trio went on with her pitch. "This Sunday, our church is…"

"Sorry, I'm busy that day," Cole interjected, tossing their invitation totally in my lap.

I gave him an under-the-table kick.

All three now stared exclusively at me. She started over. "This Sunday, our church is having a special day. You will really like it, and we would like for you to come. It's…"

"Girls, thank you, but I'm a firm, unmovable Catholic."

They got the message and left. Cole lit up. "Hey! I might try that. Just tell them I'm a firm Catholic."

"Be my guest. But then you would have to go with me on Sunday!"

As we chuckled, I noticed over Cole's shoulder one of the gold-outfitted cheerleaders walking toward us.

"Cole!" I whispered, "Here comes a scooter."

While he casually turned his head to see who it was, I scooted down my bench, leaving him no chance. As she sat down next to me, I winked at Cole. He sneered back.

A returning cheerleader from the previous year, Sheila was well-liked by everyone.

"Great game!" she said with as much flair as though the game ended only a second ago.

"Oh no, it was great cheerleading! You and the others cheering is what prodded us on."

Cole rolled his eyes.

"Tell me," she asked, "what does it feel like to be on the field in front of all those people in the stands?"

"Well, believe it or not, we don't notice it. We're so focused on what we're doing, we withdraw into our own little world out there."

"Oh?!" She asked with a touch of humor in her voice. "What about, now how did you put it, 'your cheering is what prodded us on'? Rather remarkable, wouldn't you say, that our cheering, which you didn't notice, prodded you on to win the game?"

Cole tightened his lips and his shoulders shook from suppressed laughter.

I scrambled to reply. "Uh…it was subliminal. Your cheers reached our subconscious."

"Nice try, but you lose. And just for that, you need to come to church with me."

POW! My balloon burst into a hundred pieces. *Just when I thought I had something going*, my heart cried.

"Sorry, but I am a firm, unmovable Catholic."

"That's okay. You can go to an early Mass, and then make it where I worship. You won't miss a thing."

Whoa! I thought. *What happened to my goofproof reply?*

"Besides," she continued without so much as a hint of mercy, "visiting somewhere else will broaden your knowledge of religion and expand your culture."

I had no other rehearsed replies. I never needed them. I had to wing it. "But, if I have the right church, and I do, then I don't need to visit others."

"Then," she fired back, yet with a face beaming in cheeriness, "coming to my church will make you appreciate your Catholic Church more."

Yeow! I thought. *Is she also the captain of our debate team?* I looked at Cole. He read my mind and shook his head, meaning, "You're on your own." He even had the nerve to excuse himself to hop to another table, leaving the two of us to battle it out. And I was losing.

Then my mind shouted, *I got it!*

"Sheila, I'll go to your church if we don't win next week's game." I knew we would win. Last year we only lost by one point. So this year we would run all over them.

"Make it a win by two touchdowns—fourteen points," she bartered while holding up two fingers in my face and sporting a smile.

"Done."

She left, finally. My lungs thrust forth a whoosh, and then I whispered to myself, "Smooth move, Gary. You got out of that one."

Or did I?

CHAPTER 3
THE LEGITIMATE REASON

Cheerleader or not, I kept my eyes peeled for that pesky girl and avoided her at all costs. Maneuvering around the hallways between classes like a thief eluding a policeman proved difficult enough, but, unless I wanted to skip lunch, the cafeteria left me wide open.

I took a seat with Cole, Bob, our right-end and another close friend, Randy Thomas, and others at our usual table. "Hey, champs, what's good?"

"Not the yellow-mellow" (the cook's attempt at imitating Jell-O), snapped Randy. "Tart lemon with no sugar."

"The McGuinness coach must have bribed our cooks," I retorted.

Cole, sitting across from me, focused above my head, then at me and gave a single, slight nod. I knew what that meant.

It's her! I shrieked to myself. *She cornered me again!* I awaited her voice to say…who knows what.

But it never came. I glanced over my shoulder pretending to look at the wall clock. She sat directly behind me with eight to ten other girls. Although it was only mid-week, they soon engaged each other with invitations to their respective denominations. I guess their pastors pushed attendance drives or something. Then I heard Sheila ask in a volume just loud enough for all the girls—and me—to hear, "All of us here believe God inspired the Bible. But, when you invite someone who doesn't believe that, what do you tell them so they can see that it is?"

The lively table chatter came to a halt and the lingering silence indicated no one had given it much thought.

Boy, she's going to have more than me trying to avoid her, I chuckled to myself.

Finally, one of the girls responded. "Because it says it is."

"Yes it does," answered one of the girls, "but if a book is inspired by God just because it says it is, then, since the Book of

Mormon says it is inspired by God, does that make it so?"

"Of course not," insisted another. "And that which proves too much, proves nothing. So, what's a *real* reason?"

Another girl proposed, "Well, millions of people have believed it was written by God for centuries."

"The same thing can be said about the Koran," came another voice. "So, does that mean it is written by God? No."

A third girl, in a frustrated voice steaming with firmness, blurted, "I know it's inspired because I get a good feeling when I read it."

Someone in the group countered, "That's exactly what the Mormons claim for the inspiration of the Book of Mormon. What a person *feels* doesn't prove anything. What we need is a true, legitimate reason that really does prove the Bible is from God."

A worried voice in the group asked, "Is there one?"

"Yes," Sheila answered with assurance. "My Bible class teacher taught it to us. Would you like to hear it?"

I heard a jumbled mix of affirmative answers.

Just at that moment, the guys rose to go shoot baskets in the gym until the next class began. However, I was not about to miss what she had to say. "You guys go ahead. I'm going to eat this yellow-mellow and show you who's the man among us."

"Well, here, make sure we will never forget it. Have mine," Cole insisted as he slid his mock Jell-O onto my plate.

"Mine too," added Randy.

Soon, a hill of yellow, square, hockey pucks jiggled upon my plate.

"If you eat all that," Bob hooted, "I'm not blocking you at your belly in today's practice. I don't want yellow goo all over my back."

"Wilson, I'll make it a point to collide with you first." As they left laughing, smiling, and shaking their heads, I thought, *Well, this is just great! Sitting alone with a mound of yellow-mellow. So much for being inconspicuous.*

As I poked at the mountain of imitation Jell-O, I listened to Sheila.

"Let's start with an illustration: is it possible for a one-year-old baby to be the author of our library's 3,000 page, unabridged dictionary?"

I again heard a jumbled mix of answers, this time in the negative.

"Why not?" Sheila asked.

"Because they can't even talk."

"They can't spell."

"It is beyond their ability."

"Exactly," she concurred. "Writing a dictionary is beyond the ability of a baby, and so we know babies did not write it. Rather, someone with a much greater ability had to have written it. Likewise, if the Bible contains information that is beyond the ability of man to have known and written, then we know that men did not write the Bible. Instead, there has to be a God, and He wrote it."

One in the group asked, "Does the Bible have that kind of information in it?"

"Yes," Sheila replied. "And it too begins with an illustration. Everyone think of a number between 1 and 100."

Let me see. I played along. *I'll use Cole's jersey number: 12.*

"Nine," she said. "Anyone pick nine? No? Try it again. Choose another number."

Maybe Randy's number is luckier. 86.

"Seventy-one. Anyone select 71?" she asked.

"I did," responded one.

"Let's do it one more time. Pick a third number."

Okay, Bob ol' buddy, your turn, 74.

Sheila announced the last number. "Fifty." She waited for a response, but none came. "Don't be surprised that not a one of you even came close to guessing the right number all three times. The chance of someone doing that is one in one million. And, if we would have tried it five times, the chances are one in ten billion! So, based upon that figure and the fact that none of you even guessed the right number twice, tell me this: is it possible or impossible for a person to guess the correct number between 1 and 100 two-hundred

14

times in a row without missing even once?"

"Impossible!"

"No way."

"Can't be done."

As I listened, I had to agree with the girls. If none of us could even do it twice, we sure couldn't do it 200 times.

Then Sheila asked, "Since getting 200 correct answers in a row is impossible for people to do, what kind of being would have the ability to do that?"

A unanimous blend of voices replied, "A Supernatural Being"; "God."

She resumed with their full attention. "Now that you've seen for yourselves that God is the only one who can do that, let's see how that applies to the Bible. Of course, the Bible is not a book about guessing numbers, but it does the same thing, with an even greater degree of difficulty. The Old Testament contains a large number of prophecies—predictions about nations, people, and events. More than 300 of those prophecies have been counted that predicted various things about the life of one man named Jesus. So, just as you tried to predict certain numbers, the Old Testament predicted certain things about Jesus."

"But," one of the girls asked in a sincere tone, "how do we know these prophecies were written *before* Jesus lived, not after?"

Sheila did not hesitate. "My Bible class teacher answered that. He explained that the last of the Old Testament's thirty-nine books was written near 400 B.C. Still yet, the famous translation of the Old Testament into the Greek language, the Septuagint, was made by about 250 B.C."[1]

That seals the deal, I thought as I fork-slapped the yellow-mellow mound to watch it jiggle. *All those prophecies are guaranteed to have been written at least 250 years before Jesus was even born.*

I heard her fumbling around in her purse, then the sound of a book plopping on the table, and then the rustling of pages. "Here is the first one, Micah 5:2."

But thou Bethlehem Ephratah, though thou be little among the thousands of Judah, yet out of thee shall he come forth unto me that is to be ruler in Israel; whose goings forth have been from of old, from everlasting.

"This verse," she explained, "predicted the town where someone who has always existed would be born."

"That would be Jesus," said one.

Sheila carried on. "This prophecy was made in 700 B.C. How many towns and villages do you think existed at that time? I mean, you chose a number from 100 possibilities, but how many possibilities did Micah have?"

I could hear the group talking among themselves, but, like me, they had no idea. Their consensus was, "Since the verse says there were thousands in the land of Judah, then, throughout the world, there must have been several hundred thousands of towns."

"Of all those hundreds of thousands of towns," she asked, "which one did Micah pick?"

"Bethlehem," several answered.

"Was Micah's prediction right?" she asked.

Of course, I proudly thought. I knew the Christmas song. "O Little Town of Bethlehem…"

"You may want to read Matthew 2:1-6 sometime," Sheila suggested. "Not only does it tell us that Jesus was born in Bethlehem, it also refers to this very prophecy of Micah."

No doubt about it, I thought. *Micah nailed it.*

Then she asked, "Which is more difficult, to guess the correct number out of a hundred possibilities, or the correct town out of hundreds of thousands?"

The answer was obvious. After all of our misses with only 100 possibilities, Micah's accurate prediction astonished me.

Sheila brought up a second prophecy. "Another, Jeremiah 23:5, was made around 600 B.C. and it predicts who Jesus would descend from. I'll read it."

Behold, the days come, saith the Lord, that I will raise unto David a righteous Branch, and a King shall reign and

> *prosper, and shall execute judgment and justice in the earth.*

"How many males," she asked, "do you think were living in 600 B.C.?"

Again, no one had any idea.

"I didn't know either," she said, "until I was told. It was around 100 million. So, from out of 100 million choices, who did Jeremiah predict to be the man from whom Jesus would descend?"

"David," several answered.

Sheila then responded, "Now listen to Romans 1:2-3 and see if Jeremiah got it right."

> *Which he had promised afore by his prophets in the Holy Scriptures, concerning his Son Jesus Christ our Lord, which was made of the seed of David according to the flesh;*

"Wow," I whispered, "out of 100 million possibilities, Jeremiah got it right!"

Sheila asked again, "Which is more difficult, to guess the correct number out of 100 possibilities, or the correct man out of 100 million possibilities?"

No one needed to answer, and no one did. Like me, they were all dazzled at what Jeremiah did.

But, what Sheila said next absolutely flabbergasted us. "Do you remember, the chances of picking the right number out of 100 possibilities three times in a row is one in a million? Well, the chance of Micah and Jeremiah both getting their prophecy right is one in 100 trillion!"

The oohs, ahhs, and wows of the group drowned out those of mine.

Sheila pressed her point, "Are you beginning to catch on that the prophecies in the Bible are beyond the ability of people? And these are only two! I wrote in my Bible some others my teacher showed us. Old Testament writers accurately prophesied about a friend betraying Him,[2] for thirty pieces of silver,[3] that were thrown to the floor of the temple,[4] and then used to buy land for a cemetary.[5] He

17

had false witnesses at His trial,[6] was spit upon and struck,[7] hands and feet pierced,[8] crucified with thieves,[9] lots cast for His garment,[10] and many, many more. As I said, someone counted more than 300, and not a single one was wrong."

I caught on to what Sheila, or her teacher, was saying. So did the group of girls.

"Sheila, you made this so easy to see," said one of the excited girls.

"Yeah," said another. "The predicting of numbers is just like the prophecies, and since the accurate predicting of numbers is impossible for people to do, then, even more so, the 100 percent accurate prophecies are definitely impossible for people to do."

A third added, "It's like that baby and the dictionary…"

A fourth butted in, "Why, of course! The dictionary is beyond the ability of a baby, so we *know* the baby did not write it. Instead, someone with far greater ability had to. The Bible is beyond the ability of people, so we know people didn't write it. Rather, it had to be written by an amazing Supernatural Being."

"And that," emphasized Sheila, "is a true, legitimate reason that really does prove the Bible to be inspired by God. And no other religion in the world has anything like it. Not Mormonism, Buddhism, Hinduism, Islam, or whatever. Everything in their 'holy books' is something people could have written, and it is because their authors were just that, merely people—not deity."

Sheila's tutorial thoroughly impressed me. *Her teacher put together a convincing proof of the inspiration of the Bible,* I admitted to myself as I, through a crowd of staring schoolmates, took the mound of yellow-mellow to the trash. *Too bad her teacher is not in the right church and believes a bunch of false doctrines. Anyway, tomorrow is the big game and Sheila and her church will be off of my back.*

But first, we had to win it…by 14 points.

CHAPTER 4
YOU WIN SOME;
YOU LOSE SOME

Friday night football arrived. So did my wager with Sheila. And I'll admit, my confidence at winning the bet quivered after I heard McGuinness was ranked 5th in the state.

The bus arrived at the stadium an hour before kickoff. Forty pairs of metal-tipped cleats clattered upon the concrete and through the gate. PCW's loyal crowd of hollering, waiving, horn-blowing students packed the area between the fence and the field with the pep club girls lining a path through which we would pass. At the end of the tunnel leaped the pom-pom-waving cheerleaders. I spotted Sheila. She smiled and gave me a thumbs-up.

Hmmm, I wondered. *Does she mean we'd win the game, or, she'd win the bet?*

After going through pre-game warm-up drills, we regrouped in the locker room for Coach Webb's fiery pep-talk, and then charged onto the field before 3,000 cheering fans.

I always thought we had the best looking uniforms: Columbia-blue jerseys with white numbers and three-inch wide gold (which could pass for rich yellow) stripes lining the outer edge of the shoulder pads; white pants with blue and gold stripes extending down the outer leg; Columbia-blue high-rise socks encircled by three gold stripes; and a white helmet with a blue stripe extending over the top from front to back. We set out to win and look good doing it.

McGuinness looked every bit of their 5th rank, holding us scoreless in the first quarter. But we held them scoreless, too. The wind was ferocious that night, so we attempted only one pass the entire game. In the second quarter, McGuinness ran off 21 plays to our eight, but our stout defense kept them out of the end zone and also gave us the break we needed. With 6:50 left in the half, we intercepted a pass at their 42 yard line. A few plays later, in a 21 yard scamper, we punched it in. At half-time, the score stood: 7-0, Patriots.

With the game still up for grabs—as well as my 14 point wager with Sheila—we began the second half. Both defenses flexed their muscles, but ours bulged bigger. We held them to minus three yards rushing in the second half, and only allowed 25 for the game. Both the opponent's punter and myself punted nine times each, but mine averaged eight yards further per punt, giving us 72 yards of field advancement by the kicking game.

The Patriots and the Irish fought intensely as the game clock ticked down—they, trying for a score; we, trying to shut them down. Everyone in the stadium knew it took only one fluke play for McGuinness to score, go for two, and win the game. The crowd, both Patriot and Irish fans, roared, and our pep club bellowed encouraging cheers. Once again our heroic defense forced them to punt. Like a raging bull, a Patriot burst through and blocked the punt with such force the ball ricocheted 30 yards back into their end zone. One of our linebackers, Jim Hall, raced to the ball and fell on it for the score. The game was ours! And the escape from Sheila's church would be mine when I booted the ball through the goal-post. But, with the gale-force blowing straight at me, a mere boot would not do. It required an explosion.

We broke huddle. Cole positioned the kicking tee. I took three steps back, two steps left. I kicked soccer style—an oddity in those days. Influenced five years earlier when watching Pete Gogolak, the first NFL soccer-style kicker, I immediately adapted his style (in spite of the laughter and finger-pointing) to become, no doubt, the first prep-school soccer-style kicker in the state, and perhaps the nation.

On one knee, Cole looked up to me. "Ready?"

"I was born ready."

He turned to the center, held out his hands for a target, and called the signals. "Down, set, hike!"

The ball spiraled perfectly and slapped into Cole's hands. He placed it without a flaw. Right, left, *PUMPH!* The ball shot end over end high above the outstretched Irish arms and toward dead center of the uprights. The ball knifed through the wind, then struggled, yet passed beyond the cross-bar. The referees began to raise their arms to signal "good." But, on the way down, the wind pushed the ball back on the near side of the bar!

"Kick no good," signaled the refs.

I stared at the goal post in disbelief. "Are you kidding?!"

Cole stood beside me. "From the thrill of victory, to the agony of defeat. Tough luck, buddy." He knew what that one point meant to me. But the others did not.

"That's okay, Gary. We got it won," said one.

"Lighten up! We didn't need it," said another. "Besides, on any other day, that was yours."

"Gary," laughed a third as he slapped the top of my shoulder pad, "you gave us something to tell our grandkids "

The game ended. Tomorrow's newspaper, in bold, three-quarter inch letters that stretched fourteen inches across the page, read: **West Stuns McGuinness, 13-0.**[1]

Frenzied students, teachers, and parents poured out onto the field to bestow well-earned congratulations and hugs. Out of the crowded Mardi Gras, Sheila found me. Instead of joining in the victory celebration—including merriment for her personal win of our wager—she appeared quite reserved, with one hand holding her blowing hair out of her face and her head tilted slightly down with an expressionless look.

"You don't have to come to our worship service. If it wasn't for this wind, you would have easily made it. I just don't feel right to hold you to our deal."

Wow, this girl has class! Well, so do I.

As my cheeks bulged under the eye-black grease, I replied, "I guess *you* don't have to hold me to our wager, but *I* do. A person's got to keep his word. Otherwise, he is nothing. I'll be there Sunday."

I would soon want to kick myself for that. And I could kick mighty hard.

CHAPTER 5
TRAPPED AGAIN!

Up earlier than usual, my integrity cornered me into keeping my promise of attending Sheila's church. After completing the routine of preparation for public presentation, I slid into my parents' 1966, sky-blue with white top Cutlass Supreme Oldsmobile. Athletes, unable to work, suffered through high school by driving a parent-chosen family car. Fortunately, Ol' Blue, adorned in our prominent school color, passed my peers' acceptance standard.

As each of the four miles rolled over the odometer, my dread intensified. Then I saw it—"the haunted house." I surveyed the hostile environment and spotted Sheila making a bee-line to my car. Hoping I would keep my promise, her radar screen blipped my arrival. Not wanting to navigate this uneasy place alone, her presence eased my anxiety like a dentist saying, "No cavities today."

Several friendly people greeted me, but I remembered even Hitler's Nazis could smile. Things went sour from there. I looked for the basin of Holy Water to bless myself before entering the sanctuary—and how I needed it—but there was none. When she and I took a seat in a pew with her parents, two sisters, and two brothers, I noticed the absence of fold-down knee pads. *Don't these people pray?*

Inconspicuously as possible, I scanned the building. *This is a place of worship?!* So plain. So very plain. Just walls. No statues of saints. No images of angels. No stained-glass windows. No candles. No cross. Just walls. Plain walls. The atmosphere left me feeling very irreligious.

Worship began with singing. Yes, just that, singing. No piano, no guitar, no nothing. *Well, I guess that's okay. They probably don't have enough money to buy them.*

After a few songs their priest stepped up to the pulpit. *What, no robe? Just plain clothes? A suit and tie like all the other men?* I later learned they called him preacher, not priest, nor Father. And he was married! *Good grief! How messed up can they be?!*

Roy Young was his name, and for such a young guy (early to mid-twenties) he used a lot of big words and spoke with spunk. But I had no trouble understanding him to say in his sermon, *The Communion*, that the Catholics' teaching of the priest's blessing the bread to transform it into the actual body of Christ was wrong.

Are these people crazy?! Are they some kind of cult?!

Sheila quickly wrote upon a piece of paper, "I am so sorry. I did not know the sermon would be on this."

Well, I thought, *I'm okay. They're the ones that are off.*

I tried not to listen to anything else he said. Instead, I replayed the McGuinness game in my head. But, eventually my failed kick came to mind.

If only the wind had let up just a little, I wouldn't be in this warped place!

An abrupt quietness in the auditorium pulled me back into reality. The pulpit stood empty, and four men positioned themselves behind a wooden table with several chrome-like trays for the communion.

If they don't bless the bread to turn it into the body of Christ, I'm sure not taking it. Well, they couldn't do it anyway. Roy's not a Catholic priest, and they're not the Catholic Church.

One of the men lead a prayer, and then, unbelievably, instead of everyone walking down the aisle for one of the men to place the bread on their tongues, the four each took a tray to the pews, handed it to the person on the end who then passed it on down the aisle with each person taking a piece *with their own fingers!* My mind exploded.

What an abomination! Only the consecrated hands of the priest may touch the Sacred Host! We must never touch it with our fingers! This is too much! I'm among spiritual savages!

Then another oddity occurred. The four men next passed out trays containing small, individual cups filled with grape juice. But, instead of feeling repulsed, curiosity perked me. Only our priest drank of the cup, not us.

Why do they do that? I wondered. Or, why don't we? Oh, well. Whatever. We're right and they're wrong.

But I still wondered.

At last, the agonizing hour ended. *I've been brain-scarred for life,* I moaned, *but I paid off my wager and learned my lesson: no more bets!* I put into action the plan I earlier devised to escape that torture chamber. I told Sheila bye (but did not thank her for anything), rushed for the door, and locked myself in the car.

"Wow!" I gasped. "I think I condemned myself. I feel like I need to take a shower with lye and go to confession!"

THAT EVENING

After watching True Grit for our third time, Cole and I pulled into Bevo's for a hamburger.

"John Wayne was at his best," Cole stated.

"Yeah," I agreed. "He could win the Academy Award."

"Hey, how did it go this morning at Sheila's church?"

"Ohhh!" With elbows resting on the table, I dropped my face into my hands. "You just ruined the evening. I'm done with that. As in, f-i-n-i-s-h-e-d, done."

"Look," Cole pressed, "we can always go watch True Grit again to lift your spirits. So tell me about it."

"Okay, but you pay for the movie tickets. And the popcorn."

Cole was not Catholic, but like a true friend he listened and relived every moment with me as I rehearsed the visions of my nightmare. From the building's bare walls to the touching of the communion, I unloaded my dump-truck.

"Also," I added, "they drank the grape juice in the Lord's Supper."

"And Catholics don't do that?"

"No. And I wonder why they do."

"Why don't you ask Sheila?"

"Told you. I'm done with it."

"Afraid you are wrong? Look, if you are right…"

"We are."

"…then you have nothing to fear by asking and listening to her explanation."

I had no answer for that. Mainly because, he spoke the truth.

The waitress approached with our hamburgers and Cole got in the last word. "You know what John Wayne says, 'A man's gotta do what a man's gotta do.'"

THE NEXT DAY

"Gary!"

I turned to see the editor of our school yearbook trotting up the gym hall with two cameras bouncing on the straps around his neck.

"Whoa, Nick. You're going to hurt yourself with those two flying bricks. You need to see Coach Webb about a helmet."

"Here." He handed me a yellow paper slip.

"What's this? It's only Monday. I'm not in trouble already, am I?" I joked.

"It is a release slip from your third hour class. Give it to your teacher, then meet me at the parking lot. I'll wait for you in my car at the door."

"Cool, Nick. But, you haven't told me what this is all about."

"Oh, yeah," he yelped and popped his forehead with his palm. "At the beginning of the yearbook, I'm putting a full-page picture of one guy and one girl overlooking Lake Overholser that will represent all the students anticipating a great year. Neat idea, huh?"

Nick, turned and trotted to the exit door with cameras swinging.

"And who's the girl?" I hollered.

He didn't hear me.

A large tripod hogged the passenger seat, so I hopped into the back, slapped on the seatbelt, and turned to see who Nick selected for "Miss Anticipation."

Can't be! I shrilled to myself. Looking face to face with a lion would have produced no greater shock. It was Sheila! And I was trapped!

Immediately, I engaged in a non-stop conversation with Nick

about cameras (about which I knew nothing) in order to keep her from talking to me about the previous day. But, when at the lake, and while Nick concentrated on preparing the camera for the shot, my strategy of immunization from her uneasy questions expired.

She saw the opening. "I didn't get to thank you for coming, you left so quickly."

There's step one, make me feel like a heel.

"And I do apologize for the preacher saying something against the Catholic Church. Really, he wasn't trying to be mean. Neither was I."

Step two. Take away my complaint. Now comes the big question.

"What did you think about your visit with us?" Her face lit up in hopes of a favorable reply.

"Sheila, I'll admit, your people are amazingly friendly. You seemed like one, big happy family."

"Thank you," she said with delight as her hopes increased.

"But, honestly, what you said at Bevo's was right, it made me appreciate the Catholic Church more. Much more. Catholic I am and Catholic I'll be. Like I told you, there's just no sense in my visiting any other place."

Her crumbled countenance signaled her dashed hopes. With victory mine, I should have left it at that. But I still wondered about something, and I remembered Cole prodding me, "You have nothing to fear by asking." So I did.

"Sheila, could you tell me though, in your communion, why do all of you drink the grape juice?"

After a couple of moments of gazing into the blue lake, she said, "I don't think I have a good enough answer for you at the moment. But I tell you what; we have Bible classes on Wednesday evening. I will ask my teacher, and then get back with you. Okay?"

"You just made yourself a deal," I said, relieved she didn't ask me to her Wednesday class.

"Hey, you two," called out Nick, "let's shoot that picture."

THURSDAY

"Do you know what is special about today?" Cole asked me as he pulled a book out of our locker before our first class.

"Joe Namath coming to see you?" Cole also wore number 12 and white shoes (all high-schoolers wore black shoes then), and pulled double-duty as our back-up quarterback.

Ignoring my joke, he answered, "It's the day before our game. So, easy practice today."

"You wimp," I chided him and gave him a friendly shove. But, within the space created between us, you-know-who stepped in with her optimism fully recovered.

"You appear to have gotten my answer," I invited, expecting a quick answer to bring the ordeal with her church to an end once and for all.

"Gary, I have good news. My Bible class teacher for teenagers said he would teach this Sunday's class lesson on why we serve the grape juice."

"Now look, that's not part of the deal," I spat back. "You were going to get the answer and bring it to me, not bring me to him."

"But, compared to him I am very inadequate to explain it good enough. And, you *do* want to know, don't you?"

I just looked at her as I hoped a good reply would come to mind. Nothing did.

"Besides," she poured it on, "it is only Bible class, not worship. You can leave right after class. You have nothing to fear by listening."

Cole stood behind her and glared at me. I read his facial broadcast: "A man's gotta do what a man's gotta do."

If I say "no," I reasoned, *it will shame me in front of Cole; I'll have to dodge Sheila all year; others will know about my cowardice; and worst of all, I'll know I am a coward.*

I'm trapped again!

CHAPTER 6
ON ENEMY GROUNDS

During the easy drive north to Sheila's Bible class, my thoughts wandered to last Friday's football game. An away game, and this our first, always presents a threat to the win-loss column. In the pre-game locker room, Coach Webb, with the firmness of a military sergeant, ordered the starters to report to an adjacent room for ankle taping. We all tried to avoid Coach Sanders. His tight taping made our toes swell into little red balloons. Being the punter who must extend his foot downward in order to attain proper ball contact—something a taped, L-shaped foot could not do—I devised a plan. While the coaches focused on taping, and as my teammates struggled among themselves to maneuver their order in line to avoid Coach Sanders, I slipped off to the side, quickly slid on my socks, and then walked away faking stiff ankles. Nervy, but it worked!

The game was completely ours. Rugged defense gave us the football, after a Western Height punt, on our 37 yard line. We then methodically marched over the goal line in eleven plays. Patriots, 7-0. In the second quarter, my punt from the 44 yard line was downed by Cole on their one yard line. Unable to move the ball, the Jets punted only to their 28. Four plays later, we scored a second touchdown. Twice in the game, Cole halted Western Heights' scoring threats. Once, on fourth down near the end zone, he flew like a dart on a safety blitz and slammed the Jet's quarterback for a 13 yard loss. Later, again on a fourth down, a Jet ball carrier blasted through the line to head for the score, but Cole nailed him with a perfect head-on tackle. We took over on downs, and in six plays we punched in a third touchdown. For the extra-point, the center spiraled the ball to Cole; in a heart-beat he positioned the ball on the tee; I kicked; 21-0. Cole put on a clinic that night. If game-balls were given, he would have obtained it. I was proud of my buddy.

"I'm here?" I whispered to myself as I awoke from my five-star day-dream, not remembering a thing about the drive. "That's scary!"

As she promised, Sheila waited for me by the front door.

In response to, evidently, my apprehensive face, she said with light-hearted laughter, "Don't worry, he won't bite."

When we entered the classroom for teenagers, my antagonist, Mr. Babbitt, was easy to detect. His immaculate grey suit and red tie complemented his neatly combed light-grey hair. Early 70's, I figured. He stood straight with head up and shoulders squared and presented himself even taller than his six-foot stature. My evaluation advanced to puzzlement. *Why is such an old man teaching teenagers? Doesn't he realize there's a double generation gap? He can't relate to teens.* As I continued to observe him when I took a seat, a partial answer came quickly. Mingling with one or two students at a time, he pursued their welfare and their activities at school. This old man, as comfortable, encouraging, and witty as Bob Wilson, our high school class president, didn't know what a generation gap was. And neither did his students.

"Hello, I am Loral Babbitt," he smiled as he extended his hand to shake mine. "Without doubt, you are Sheila's guest. I am honored you are here." Then, he leaned closer and whispered, "I hope I will be able to answer your question."

"It is time to begin our class," Mr. Babbitt announced, ending his socializing. "This morning, before we begin our regular study, we will consider a question Sheila asked of me during the week."

Smooth move, Mr. Babbitt, I conceded, grateful he concealed with whom the conflict really laid. Although I was right and they were wrong, I did not relish being Daniel in the lion's den. *But,* I reminded myself, *acts of kindness are no substitute for religious truth.* Suspicious of non-Catholics, I already prepared myself for explanations like: "Since most people believe and practice the Lord's Supper this way, it must be right"; or, "Some of the most popular preachers teach it this way"; or, "We just prefer doing it this way"; or some other self-falsifying appeal that does not even consider what God said and demands.

He went on as he casually moved three or four steps to his left. "The question is this: 'During the Lord's Supper, which is also referred to as the Communion, why do we both eat the bread and drink the fruit of the vine?' Splendid question. The answer is found in several verses, but let us turn to Matthew 26. Kent, would you read verses twenty-six through twenty-nine?"

A Bible verse?! We're going to look in the Bible for the answer?! That's not what I expected, I thought as I turned through the pages in the King James Bible Sheila slipped me.

Kent, finding the passage, read so all could hear.

> *And as they were eating, Jesus took bread, and blessed it, and brake it, and gave it to the disciples, and said, Take, eat; this is my body. And he took the cup, and gave thanks, and gave it to them, saying, Drink ye all of it; For this is my blood of the new testament, which is shed for many for the remission of sins. But I say unto you, I will not drink henceforth of this fruit of the vine, until that day when I drink it new with you in my Father's kingdom.*

"Now," Mr. Babbitt began, "in verse twenty-six, what did Jesus tell the disciples to do with the bread?"

"Take and eat it," answered a younger teenager named Christie.

"And who was He telling to take and eat? Only certain disciples, or all of them?" came his follow-up question.

"Well, 'disciples' means all of them," answered Terri, keeping up with her sister, Christie.

"So, are you saying that when Jesus tells all of His disciples to eat the bread, then *everybody* is to eat the bread?" Mr. Babbitt asked a self-answering question, driving home the truth as everyone, including myself, nodded our heads.

"Now then," he asked, "in verse twenty-seven, what did Jesus command those same people?"

Richard, Sheila's younger brother of three years, replied, "Drink from the cup, which, verse twenty-nine informs us, was the fruit of the vine."

"And, who was He saying this to?" Mr. Babbitt worded the follow-up question identical to his question with the bread.

I tilted my head down to look at the verse, and it kicked me like a mule: "*all of you*"! My Catholic-protected mind shook. Where did those words come from? If the Catholic laity does not drink of the cup, what are those words doing there? And, since both of Jesus' commands to eat the bread and to drink the cup are identical, then why do we do one but not the other? I saw that consistency demands both to be done.

Mr. Babbitt, without using worthless "most-people-believe-it-this-way" type reasons, went right to the Bible, and, instead of telling us what to believe, he guided us to easily discover its teaching for ourselves. The words, phrases, and verses presented no difficulties, doubts, nor deceptions. The logic was impeccable. The conclusion was inescapable: *We Catholics were not doing what Jesus told us to do!*

"Surely, my priest must know the reason," I whispered, trying to settle myself. "After today's Mass, I'll ask him."

CHAPTER 7
BATTLE WOUNDS HEALED

"A hhh. This is more like it."

The soothing security of St. Patrick's Catholic Church wrapped its comforting arms around me as I sank into a pew to await the start of Mass. Our building, erected only seven years ago, received the Architectural Gold Medal due to its unique structure and design—one sanctuary inside another. It thereby acquired the slogan, "A Church within a Church." The walls of the Tabernacle-like outer church—fifty massive, rectangular-shaped, concrete slabs with wood-like textured surface, each of which contained a 36 foot tall, by 16 foot wide, by two-inch deep, imprinted angel—provided us a complete encirclement of huge angels. Each one identical and with wings uplifted and heads turned toward the altar, seemed to be singing, "Holy, Holy, Holy."

Within these majestic walls, and separated by a courtyard of about 30 feet on all sides, loomed the inner church—a sanctuary of clear glass. This transparency permitted the inescapable presence of the majestic angels. The ceiling covered us with a series of twelve, enormous, freestanding architectural umbrellas. The pews—handcrafted solid oak—rested upon the floor of cut stone. The altar of marble, perched upon five pyramid-type platforms of stone, rose as an island above all else. Above the altar hung three tiers of encircling sprays of delicate, golden spears and appeared as the brilliant glory of God shinning approvingly from heaven upon us. The altar's background wall rose some 25 feet and extended the 40 foot width of the altar's platform. Its marble-chip brick glistened by its overlay of shimmering gold leaf. Narrow skylights, running the perimeter of the concrete walls of the outer sanctuary, subtly enhanced all these magnificent features, showcased the imprinted angels, and filled the entire sanctuary with abundant soft light.

Just the mere presence within my spiritual home fortified my shattered comfort. The drills from my Catechism School echoed in my head: *The Roman Catholic Church is the one, true, original church. All others, including Sheila's, are deserters. We have the truth, they don't.*

Mass consoled me even more. The priest, ornamented in his decorative, layered robes of white, purple, and gold; the two altar boys, adorned in white and black robes, meticulously assisted the priest in designated tasks; the pews packed to capacity by laity in their Sunday best; the formality; the splendor; the solemnity—all visions etched in my very being since childhood.

Yet, during communion, as the priest took both, the bread and the cup, while I and all others were permitted only the bread, the words of Jesus forced forth in my mind: "*Drink from it, ALL of you.*"

So straightforward, I insisted. *So easy to understand. If the simple "take, eat" means everybody, then even more so does "drink from it, ALL of you" mean everybody. Surely, something that simple isn't over my head. If Jesus Himself said it, just what can my priest say to get around it?*

Following Mass and after shaking several hundred hands at the only exit, the priest drifted toward his parish office and right to where I patiently waited. I sat upon one of the cement benches arranged along the rock-embedded walkway that meandered throughout the parish garden. I arose and mustered my courage. "Father, if you have a moment, there is something we do in worship that I need help in understanding."

His words flowed smoothly like a well-seasoned counselor. "Certainly my son. And what might that be?"

"In the communion, why does the laity not drink from the cup when Jesus said, 'drink from it, *all* of you'?"

"Oh, yes, that would be quite concerning. That is, unless you recall what you were taught in Catechism." He took a seat on the bench and patted a place next to him for me to sit.

"You remember, do you not, God gave the Church another source of authority, not just the Bible alone. God's Word was to be delivered to mankind in two ways. The first was in writing, which is called the Scriptures. They came to us as the Holy Spirit inspired a few Catholics in the first century to write down His Word. In this way, the Catholic Church gave the New Testament to the world. The other way God delivered His Will was accomplished orally, which is called the Tradition. This began with the apostles as they taught orally from either what they learned from Jesus' words, life, or works, or from what they learned at the prompting of the Holy Spirit. The usage of Tradition is taught in 2 Thessalonians 2:15, '*hold the traditions that you have learned, whether by word or by letter of ours.*' It is also taught in 1 Corinthians 11:2, '*keep the traditions, as I delivered them to you.*'" His words slowed and then paused as he noticed me pulling paper and pen from the pocket of my ironed white shirt.

"Please, go on," I begged after I scribbled the two verses on my paper.

"Of course, the apostles would one day die, so they left the bishops as their successors and gave them the oral teaching authority. This is told in 2 Timothy 2:2, '*the things that you have heard from me through many witnesses, commend to trustworthy men who shall be competent in turn to teach others.*' These bishops continue to succeed one another until the end of time. So, this continual, Holy Spirit-guided transmission of God's Word is called Tradition. And it is with the Tradition that we obtain the *entirety* of the Word of God, and not by the Scriptures alone."

His voice emitted no tone of chastisement. There should have been. How could I have overlooked Tradition? Mr. Babbitt used only the Scriptures, but we Catholics have *all* the Word God.

I prodded him on. "So, there's more of God's Word about the communion found in Tradition?"

"Yes, indeed. The Holy Spirit led the assembly of bishops in the Council of Constance in 1415 into issuing the decree that only the wafer, not the cup, was to be taken by the laity, and that the priest should drink from the cup on behalf of the people. This was God's Word by means of Tradition—the authority of God. That is why the laity does not drink from the cup, and that, I think, answers your questions."

"Yes!" My relieved outburst startled him.

We both rose smiling. He, for passing on to a young Catholic the Catholic beliefs; and me, for reassurance in the Catholic Church.

34

With renewed confidence and a touch of swagger, I headed for Ol' Blue. "Yes, Tradition! I'll set that Bible-thumping Mr. Babbitt straight!"

CHAPTER 8
THE NOTEBOOK PAPER

Randy Thomas darted three yards, cut to the center, snatched the pass in a leap, and, as usual, got smacked. Such characterized our fourth game of the season. Smacked! With our 3-0 record in which we ran up 62 points while holding our opponents to 6, including a shut-out of the state's 5th ranked team, we committed the familiar crime of overlooking the next game with an inferior team by looking to the following week's big showdown with Altus, the team ranked 2nd. We learned the lesson, but too late, and we paid for it with a bitter loss. As much as we wanted to replay that game and do it right, we couldn't. "That is just like life," I warned myself. "I have only one opportunity to live right religiously—there is no second chance to do it over again."

"The nerve of someone saying the Catholic Church is wrong!" The words sneered under my breath as I swerved into the parking lot of Sheila's church. Friday's loss still stung and it escalated my irritation at Mr. Babbitt. My eyes scanned the perimeter like a sniper searching for his target. I located him and maneuvered through the cars to intercept his slow approach to the building.

"Mr. Babbitt."

He stopped and turned toward me. "Why, hello Gary," he responded. His patent smile lifted his entire face.

"Mr. Babbitt," I continued, but without returning the congenial facial expression, "what you told me about the communion is not all God says about it."

"Oh?" he replied, offering to hear me out.

"No sir." I still spoke with respect to my elder even though I felt angry at him for disturbing me with his narrow minded denominational doctrine. "The Bible is only *part* of God's Word. The other part is given to us in Tradition—the oral teachings of the apostles which were given only to the true Church, the Catholic Church." I proceeded to quote, at least as best I could, the two verses my priest taught me. Then I nailed my conclusion, "So, when we want to learn what God requires of us, we cannot use *only* the Bible as you do. Otherwise, we will end up with a false belief and a false practice as you have done."

Without any evidence of alarm, Mr. Babbitt, in noticeable kindness and control, responded, "That will make for a good topic to discuss in class this morning. Shall we go on to our classroom?"

"No thank you." I was firm, but fought back any rudeness. "You would use only the Bible to try to tell me what I just told you is wrong. But, by leaving out Tradition, what *you* would say would be wrong. So there's no sense in me listening to you."

Mr. Babbitt, seeing my mind was made up, gently countered, "Do you Catholics believe the Bible is God's Word?"

"Definitely," I answered sharply, thinking that might have been an insult.

"Then," he said as he tore out a blank sheet of paper from his blue spiral notebook, "since there is no sense in listening to me, surely there is sense in listening to God." He positioned the paper on top of his notebook and wrote—as I tried to make it out from an upside down angle—a reference to a verse in the Bible. "Here." He extended the paper to me. "Since this is God's Word, you might want to see what He says in this verse."

In one motion I snatched the paper and turned to depart before he could extend his hand. Shaking hands manifests a level of acceptance, and expressing such to a false teacher who tried to lead me astray did not set well. "That will be the last I see of him," I congratulated myself.

I hopped into the car and fired up the engine. We—Ol' Blue and me—soon headed south on Rockwell Avenue. I estimated my driving time to St. Patrick's at fifteen minutes, max. Nothing like being plenty early for Catechism class.

As I drove along, assisting the Beatles in singing "Yesterday," an unconscious thought smacked me from out of nowhere. *When I mentioned the need of Tradition, which makes his belief wrong, he wasn't rattled at all. He didn't even blink.*

I turned off the radio.

Actually, he wasn't even at a loss to offer to respond in class without any preparation. What does he know that kept him so collected when his beliefs got stabbed in the heart? I wonder what he wanted to tell me in class.

"The verse!" I blurted. I swerved—a little too abrupt—into the Bank of the West's Sunday-vacant parking lot and glanced at Mr. Babbitt's paper lying on the passenger seat. "Second Timothy 3:16-17." I repeated it over and over as I flipped through the pages of Mom's Douay-Confraternity. "Here it is." I read carefully, determined to understand every phrase and every word.

"All Scripture is inspired by God."

Yes, the Catholic Church insists on that, and Mr. Babbitt does too. There's got to be something else he wants me to see. I returned to the verse.

"And is useful for teaching, for reproving, for correction, for instruction in righteousness."

I agreed again, the Bible is to be used for these things. *But the priest told me the Bible is not the only thing to be used. Tradition must be used too. Why would Mr. Babbitt think this verse teaches that only the Scriptures are to be used?* But then, I read on.

"That the man of God may be perfect, equipped for every good work."

The words stunned me. I read them again. *Man! This says the Scriptures are given so the Christian can be perfect. And if the Scriptures can make a Christian perfect, then nothing else is needed! And, since the Scriptures give us everything we need "for every good work," then there is nothing else God gave us for our teachings and instructions, including Tradition!*

Much like the daze of disbelief as the clock ticked out in our loss to El Reno, I sighed in empty helplessness. I cross-examined myself to try to find a mistake in my reasoning. "If this verse, which is indeed God's Word, teaches that the Scriptures are all we need to make us perfect and fully equipped for everything, then God is saying…." I did not finish. I didn't want to. I didn't like it.

Inside the yellowish brick, multi-classroom building, Mr. Clay, my Catechism teacher, turned his head toward me as I entered the room. His beaming face displayed his delight that one of the students in his all male class saw fit to arrive early. A nice-looking man in his 50's, dressed and conducted himself distinguishingly at all times. Whenever he gazed downward with his pipe in his mouth, he appeared as he was—a wise man in thought. I liked Mr. Clay and took pride in my teacher's name appearing in raised letters on the metal plaque embedded in the concrete bell tower for all to see when passing in or out the only door to the church.

"Mr. Clay," I took advantage of our solitude, "I was reading the Bible this morning, and I need your help in understanding something." I dared not tell him of my conversation with Mr. Babbitt, nor of my attendance in his class. The Catholic Church sternly frowned upon such mingling in the attempt to censor Catholics from anti-Catholic propaganda.

"Ask on." He laid down his pen and swiveled in my direction to give me his full attention.

I began. "God's Word is included in both, Scripture and Tradition. Right?"

"Right," he agreed without hesitation.

"That means, doesn't it, the Bible alone cannot make us perfect nor give us instructions for *everything* we do in religion?"

"Exactly," answered the proud teacher.

"Then how do we explain what God says in 2 Timothy 3:16-17?" I opened my Bible to the page marked with the attached black-ribbon bookmark, and handed it to him.

With forehead leaning upon his fingertips and elbow propped on the desk, he examined the Bible as it lay before him. I patiently waited a minute or more. The faint hum of the electric wall clock monopolized the only sound in the room. I didn't know the room could be so quiet.

He lifted his head. His face broadcasted concern and he spoke as though the outcome of World War II depended upon my precise following of his instructions. "You must understand, although these verses look like they teach that only the Scriptures are needed, they don't. Your faith in Tradition and the Catholic Church, as well as your salvation, depends upon you understanding that. Are you listening to me?"

"Yes sir" were the only two words I managed to squeak out. Was I listening to him?! I could not have been more attentive than at Judgment Day waiting to hear "to the right" or "to the left."

"There are two things about this passage you must never forget. First, the Scriptures of verse sixteen are identified in the previous verse which says, '*from thy infancy thou hast known the Sacred Writing,*' and since a good part of the books of the *New* Testament had not yet been written in Timothy's boyhood, then the Scriptures in verse sixteen refer only to the *Old* Testament Scriptures. You got that?"

"Yes sir," peeped the mouse.

"Second, never forget that verse sixteen's reference to the Scriptures is only *part* of what is being said. Look at verse fourteen. It reveals that Timothy was *also taught orally* by Paul, and that, young man, is Tradition. So, *both* are taught in this passage, Scripture *and* Tradition. Do you follow?"

This time I just nodded my head.

He concluded, "So you see, this verse is *not* teaching that the New Testament Scriptures are the only authority. And, the very context teaches that oral Tradition is *also* our authority—an authority which belongs only to the Catholic Church."

I thanked him, found a seat, and waited for the class to begin. In spite of his intimidation, Mr. Clay explained away what Mr. Babbitt intended with 2 Timothy 3:16-17.

Or did he?

CHAPTER 9
THE BIG GAME

riday night arrived, and so had the state's number two ranked team. Even though Altus rolled over us the previous year in a 45-0 thrashing, we knew we would beat them if we avoided mistakes.

On each play both teams strained every muscle to run, pass, block, and tackle to our limits, and then some. They, to keep their ranking; we, to take it.

In the first quarter, the Patriots and the Bulldogs each scored on hard fought drives that ended in one-yard runs. First quarter: 7-7.

The second quarter kept the spectators on their feet with three more touchdowns. We struck on a 34 yard pass, but they scored twice, one of which came on a lone 70 yard pass. Half-time: Altus lead, 21-14.

But then, as anticipated, our observant coaches made the perfect modifications in our stone-wall defense. In the second half, PCW shut down the state's second ranked team to sixteen yards rushing, seventeen yards passing, and a meager one first-down. Their offense could not move the ball against our fine-tuned defense.

At the end of the third quarter, the score remained 21-14. But the fourth quarter was something to behold. On a fine Altus punt plus a penalty, our offense lined up in our own end zone with the ball on the one yard-line. Our quarterback took the snap, waited two seconds, and tossed the ball for our end crossing the middle. As though he knew the exact play we called, the big Altus center lineman leaped up, snagged the ball, and stepped over the goal line. The extra-point attempt failed, and Altus lead, 27-14.

Aggravated by the cheap points we gave up, we still knew their offense could no longer score on us. Now needing two touchdowns, one came courtesy of our kicking game. I punted the ball from our 43 yard-line to near their goal line. Their receiver could not handle the squirming ball and we recovered it on their eleven yard-line. In two plays we scored. Our run for two extra points fell short. Now,

Altus led by only one touchdown, 27-20.

With less than four minutes remaining, we kicked off needing a stop and a score. Our defense got the stop. At fourth and seventeen on their 34 yard-line, Altus lined up to punt. With the rage of an angered bear, a Patriot tore through the would-be defenders and blocked the punt. The precious pig-skin ricocheted thirty feet up in the air and just beyond the line of scrimmage. As punts go, the ball would be dead at the 35 yard-line, and our offense would then steadily march the ball in for the score, run for the two extra points, and seize the victory. The Altus players stood in disbelief; the Patriots celebrated. Vainly, one of the Bulldogs caught the fizzling punt and ran 65 yards through all the standing players and crossed the goal line.

Then came the shock. The referees said the ball was live! Unbelievable to everyone, the touchdown counted! Our victory slipped through our very fingers on a freaky play.

We won the statistics, but lost in points. Years later, Randy became friends with the Altus head coach who admitted to Randy that he himself conceded we were going to win the game. But, we didn't. We were demoralized and deflated.

I learned from that game, anything put in the hands of humans is never certain. Whether football or religion. Give some men a Bible and let them be the interpreter and teacher, and there is no telling what kind of false doctrines they will come up with. Including Mr. Babbitt.

"Maybe I'll feel better on Sunday after I go set Mr. Babbitt straight on his saying that 2 Timothy 3:16-17 teaches our only religious authority to be the Scriptures."

CHAPTER 10
IT WAS IN MY OWN BIBLE

"So, Mr. Babbitt, that is why 2 Timothy 3:16-17 does not mean the Scriptures are our only religious authority. Rather we must use both, the Scriptures and Tradition," I concluded.

We sat across from each other in the student's gray, metal chairs of his Sunday morning classroom. I requested to meet with him forty-five minutes before class, strategically giving myself plenty of time to escape the building before anyone else arrived. Mr. Babbitt just got educated by a determined young whippersnapper—Mr. Clay's protégé. For the past eight to ten minutes, he intensively focused upon every word I uttered as though there would be a test after the lecture. His genuine respect for me demanded a return of my respect for him, even though he was wrong on that verse. His lamblike mildness made it easy to discuss such difficult differences with him. I began to feel like a heel for the way I walked away from him the previous Sunday.

He began slowly, lacking even a hint of combat, "So, a good part of the books of the New Testament had not yet been written in Timothy's childhood? And that means the verse is not referring to the New Testament when it says the Scriptures make us perfect, and thereby the verse does *not* mean the New Testament is our only religious authority?"

"That's right," I answered, glad to see he got my point.

"I see you have your Catholic Bible," he said, looking and nodding once toward it. "Does it have, at the beginning of each book, an introduction that includes the date of writing?"

I flipped through the pages until I found the beginning of one of the books. "Yes."

"Let's do this," he said as he moved to the chair next to mine, "you take my pen and notebook; I'll take your Bible and find in the introduction of each New Testament book the date it says it was written."

Again I detected his protection of my ego from embarrassment. In Catechism school we did not study the Bible very much, if at all. So I did not know where any of the New Testament books were located, and we did not have time for me to hunt page by page.

He quickly found the introduction of every one of the 27 books and told me the date each was written. After I rewrote the list chronologically, it laid before me.

No date given	John; 1 John; 3 John
42-50 A.D.	Matthew
51	1 Thessalonians
51	2 Thessalonians
54	Galatians
57	1 Corinthians
57	2 Corinthians
57-58	Romans
Pre—60	Mark
60-62	Jude
Pre—63	Luke
63	Acts
63	Hebrews
63	Ephesians
63	Philippians
63	Colossians
63	Philemon
63-64	1 Peter
65-66	Titus
65-66	1 Timothy
66-67	2 Timothy
66-67	2 Peter
90's	2 John
96	Apocalypse

"Let's see now," he investigated with me, "when was 2 Timothy 3:16-17 written?"

"There." I pointed the pen and tapped at its location "66 or 67 A.D."

"And, when was the Gospel of Matthew written?" he asked.

44

I saw Matthew at the very top. "It was the very first one written, dated somewhere between 42 and 50 A.D.," I answered, actually enjoying the research for myself.

"Gary, this is simple. You need neither me nor the Catholic clergy to tell you what the answer is. Now think, since Matthew was written somewhere between 42 and 50 A.D. and 2 Timothy 3:16-17 was written 66-67 A.D., then Matthew could have been written as much as twenty-five years before 2 Timothy was written. Now, since Timothy was a youth in 66-67 A.D. when Paul said Timothy knew the Scriptures, then would it be possible that Timothy, as a young boy, could have known the New Testament Scriptures of the Gospel of Matthew which had already been around for some 25 years?"

"No, I don't think so." Stupid answer, but I couldn't say "yes." If I did, it would destroy the first point Mr. Clay bound me never to forget: Timothy only had the Old Testament Scriptures.

"Why not?" Mr. Babbitt pushed me mentally like Coach Webb pushed me physically. Hard, but for my benefit.

After a few moments dragged by, it became apparent. He was waiting for me to break the silence. He was not going to answer it for me. There were no other students to answer it. Mr. Clay was not there to answer it. But even if any of them were there they all would have to answer "yes," if they were honest. Either I walked away without answering and thereby stopped being honest, or I answered him.

"Yes, Timothy as a young boy could have known the Scriptures of the Gospel of Matthew," I consented as I clutched onto Mr. Clay's second point.

He looked at me for a moment with eyes of sympathy, not moving so much as a lip. "Gary, I know that must have been difficult for you. And you are correct; he could have known the book of Matthew and even some of the other New Testament books. But, that which makes it *certain* he knew the New Testament Scriptures is found in the rest of that verse. Why don't you read it for yourself?"

The rest of the verse? Mr. Clay didn't say anything about the rest of the verse. I read with interest:

"For from thy infancy thou hast known the Sacred Writings, which are able to instruct thee into salvation by the faith which is in Christ Jesus."

"Is it the *Old* Testament Scriptures," Mr. Babbitt inquired, "that is able to instruct a person into salvation by faith which is in Jesus?"

"Certainly not. Only the Scriptures of the *New* Testament can do that," I replied with conviction. My thoughts began to click off in rapid succession. *How easy was that to see! This verse, without question, refers to the New Testament Scriptures because these Scriptures are identified as those that instruct a person into salvation through Jesus. So, Timothy did know the New Testament Scriptures. What Mr. Clay said about the Scriptures in 2 Timothy 3:15-16 being solely the Old Testament is not true!* Then, in a mix of worry and anger, I wondered, *Why did Mr. Clay distract my attention from this? Why did he ignore it? Why did he use only part of the verse and then twist it to make it say what it does not say? I saw his alarm when he read it, and by his prompt "remember-two-things-about-this-passage" lecture, it's evident he is very familiar with this part of the verse. Am I getting too close to the door of a serious Catholic glitch?*

"Gary," Mr. Babbitt caught my attention with his ever kindly voice as he slowly rose from his chair due to his aged joints. "I am sorry, but we are out of time. Class begins shortly. We did not get to your second point regarding Oral Tradition being included with the Scriptures as our religious authority. If you would like, we can look at that another time."

After what he just showed me about verse fifteen, I figured I ought to hear him out. "Sure."

He responded without hesitation, "I admire your pursuit to discover religious truth. In Acts 17:11, God says this about people like you, *'These* [Bereans] *were more noble than those in Thessalonica, in that they received the word with all readiness of mind, and searched the Scriptures daily, whether those things were so.'* So, keep investigating what you are taught with an honest mind, accepting only what can be proven by the Scriptures."

I had never heard such advice. In Catholicism, what I am to believe and do has always been drilled into me, and the admonition to search the Scriptures to see whether or not their indoctrination harmonized with the Bible was *never* offered. I didn't even know Acts 17:11 existed. No wonder. They, just as Mr. Clay did with me, declare that 2 Timothy 3:15 is referring to the Old Testament, and by keeping us from searching the Scriptures to determine "whether those things are so," we go on our merry way, duped!

The three Parker girls, Dee Dee, Terri, and Christie, with their talking and giggling, announced their approach.

"I suppose you will want to depart now," he offered.

"I tell you what," I bartered, "last Sunday in the parking lot, I turned down your invitation to class to hear you out regarding the use of only the Scriptures for our religious authority. If I stay today, would you go into that?"

With a beaming face and a slight nod of his head, "It's a deal."

CHAPTER 11
AN OLD GUIDE

The Parker girls switched to mute as they entered the classroom. The three enjoyed their sisterhood but knew when to shut it off—evidence of good parental training.

Within five or six minutes the room filled to nearly a dozen teenagers, each one being greeted with an inquiry of their week's activities by Mr. Babbitt's remarkable rapport.

Even though I deeply disagreed with him and his non-Catholic church, it was impossible not to respect him. An old man who, when others his age had long retired to warming a place in the pew, desirously pushed his limits to help young people discover the Word of God for themselves. He taught as a gentle and caring guide, not a dogmatic indoctrinator. Always taking us to the Bible so we could determine what it teaches and what it does not teach, his knowledge appeared unfathomable. God and His Word wholly occupied his heart, and to teach us about them delighted and drove him.

"My young friends," he addressed us as he truly considered us, "this morning we shall consider a question so fundamental, that virtually everything a person believes and practices in religion stands or falls because of it. It is this: 'Is the Bible the sole authority in religion?' Some think 'yes' and try to do only what the Bible teaches, but others think 'no' and appeal to additional sources of authority resulting in the addition of beliefs and practices not taught in the Bible. Can anyone name such a group?"

"The Mormons," a fellow named Marty quickly responded. "They use the Bible plus the Book of Mormon. They claim the Mormon book is inspired by God and is more important than the Bible."

Mr. Babbitt nodded, but said not a word, waiting for others to reply.

"The cults use the Bible but claim they got an additional revelation from God," added Marty's older brother, Kent, a senior in the other Putnam City high school. The two brothers, unbashful to speak up, must have fed off of each other's boldness. Intelligent fellows, but daring.

"The denominations have their own creed books, and, although they do not claim them to be inspired, they go by them for their authority anyway," added Dee Dee.

"And I've heard so many at school say God guides them through their feelings for some kind of illumination," a student named Teresa gave her observation.

Every time someone began to speak, I expected him to say "the Catholics." *Were they unaware that we, in addition to the Bible, use Tradition?*

Mr. Babbitt retook the floor, "Since all of these believe and begin with the Bible, so shall we as we answer the question, 'Is the Bible the sole authority in religion?'"

I listened with eager ears, ready to catch every word as would a courtroom recorder listening to a witness on the stand.

He began, "First, let us learn what Revelation 20:12 reveals. Richard, would you read it for us?"

As he read aloud, I followed with my Confraternity.

> *And I saw the dead, the great and the small, standing before the throne, and the scrolls [Richard's King James Version read, "books"] were opened. And another scroll was opened, which is the book of life, and the dead were judged out of those things that were written in the scrolls, according to their works.*

"Trena," Mr. Babbitt directed a question to Teresa's younger sister, "what is the event that is mentioned in this verse?"

"Let's see," she whispered to herself as she looked over the verse, "people were standing before God and were being judged." She raised her voice: "It's Judgment Day."

"That is correct. And Sheila, what does this verse say will judge us at Judgment Day?"

Scanning the verse, she replied, "That which is written in the books."

"Jackie," he directed a question to Sheila's younger sister, a sophomore at PCW, "does the verse say there is anything else that will judge us at Judgment Day other than what is written?"

"No, nothing else," she answered.

"And you are right," he said. "So, this verse informs us about Judgment Day at which time we will be judged by what is written in the books—nothing else."

I looked at the verse again. Surely they twisted it. But I could not find so much as a wrinkle. They were right.

"Gary," Mr. Babbitt said quite distinctly.

What?! I mentally yelped. *What is he doing? I'm a visitor! An observer! Man, this better be super easy!*

"Would it be fair of your history teacher to tell the class that the semester test would be over the entire textbook, but then only test you over the last half of the book?"

I replied to the obvious with a slight hint of a student's irritation, "Certainly not!"

"Why not?"

"Because half of all that agonizing study would have been for absolutely nothing. For her to put us through the ordeal of cramming names, dates, and events of a full textbook into our heads would be unfair. No, worse. She would be unjust. She would not be fit to be a teacher over students. Besides, she would have lied to us."

Still standing directly in front of me, Mr. Babbitt applied the analogy, "Gary, would God, Who is perfect in justice as Isaiah 45:21 states, tell us we will be judged by both, the Scriptures AND the Book of Mormon, or human creed books, or later revelations, or some type of illumination, or oral Tradition, but then, at Judgment Day, only judge us by what is written the Scriptures?"

I tried not to squirm in my chair. His reasoning was simple, and it was right. A perfectly just God Who does not lie would not tell us our authority is both, the Scriptures AND Tradition, and then at Judgment Day judge us by *only* the Scriptures. He would have told a lie, and God would be unjust. I replied, "No."

"And you are correct," his low-volume words came slowly and sensitively, as though he acknowledged my grueling struggle. "God, in that verse, tells us it is *only* the Scriptures that will judge us. That means the Scriptures are the sole authority in religion. God has not given us any additional authority to which we must listen, obey, and be judged by at Judgment Day."

After a long pause to let such a crucial truth set in, he broke the silence. "A second verse I want us to look at is 1 Corinthians 4:6. This also answers our question as to whether or not the Bible is the only authority we are to use. Read it for us, would you, Marty?"

Following in my Confraternity, the last part of the verse read,

> "... learn not to be puffed up one against the other over a third party, transgressing what is written."

"Richard, come up here next to me," the teacher instructed. "Now take this chalk and draw a circle around you."

Richard dropped to one knee on the tan-colored tile floor and encircled himself as told.

Extending his hand palm up to retrieve the chalk, Mr. Babbitt quipped, "Be sure to erase that before we leave."

He proceeded to make his point. "If I were to instruct Richard to stay in that circle, then, for him to step outside the circle would be to transgress what he was told. Now imagine this circle to represent all that is written in the Bible, and that God commands Richard, 'Do not transgress what is written.' If Richard goes outside the circle—the Scriptures—to get authority from an additional source, such as the Catholic's oral Tradition, in order to practice something not taught the Bible, he would be '*transgressing what is written.*' And this is the very thing God tells us in this verse not to do."

That is so simple. Maybe I need to start reading the Scriptures so I can learn some things. After all, the Bible is God's Word.

"There are other verses that teach that the Scriptures are our only source of authority, but we have time to observe only one more. Terri, please read for us, Romans 16:25-26."

My Confraternity read:

> Now to him who is able to strengthen you in accordance with my gospel, and the preaching of Jesus Christ, according to the revelation of the mystery which has been kept in silence from eternal ages, which is manifested now

through the writings [Terri's King James read, "Scriptures"] of the prophets according to the precept of the eternal God, and made known to all the Gentiles [King James: "nations"] to bring about obedience to faith.

Our guide directed our attention to the first part of verse twenty-six, "Something was made manifest to all people. What was it?"

Teresa answered. "Verse twenty-five tells us it is the gospel."

"That is correct." Mr. Babbitt confirmed, and then pressed on, "So, we learn that the gospel was made known to the entire world. Now, by what means was the gospel made known to the entire world?"

More than half of the class spoke in unison, "The Scriptures."

Mr. Babbitt then challenged the class. "But, couldn't God have also handed out oral teachings so that the gospel would be made known to us by the Scriptures *and* Oral Tradition?"

Sheila countered, "God can do anything He wants. But He explains right here what He *did* do: He now makes known the gospel to the world by means of the Scriptures, period."

"Okay, I give up," Mr. Babbitt conceded with gleaming eyes. "Sheila is right. When God tells us what He did, then that is how He did it. He is not going to deceive us. And notice, in verse twenty-five, He mentions preaching—the oral means. Yet, He noticeably *omits* the oral means when telling us how He now makes known the gospel to the entire world. It was not 'by the Scriptures AND the oral teachings of the prophets,' but, look at the verse again, 'by the *Scriptures* of the prophets.' And since we are not to go beyond what is written, we know it is by the Scriptures *only*."

During my fifteen minute commute to St. Patrick's, I rehearsed the morning's eye-openers. Second Timothy 3:15-17 did *not* mean the Old Testament, like Mr. Clay said it did; the Scriptures that can make us perfect for every good work is indeed the *New* Testament. And that means Oral Tradition ceased being part of God's continuing Word once the New Testament Scriptures were completed. Also, laid before my eyes were three verses of Scripture—God's very words—each distinctly teaching the sole authority in religion to be the Scriptures *only*. I had seen it for myself, and I was convinced. It is the Scriptures, without anything else, which can make us perfect and are provided for *every* good work. It is, at Judgment Day, the Scriptures and only the Scriptures that we will be held accountable to for how we had lived. It is the Scriptures that we are not to go beyond to get our religious authority. It is the Scriptures and only the Scriptures through which God makes the gospel known to the entire world.

I was not mad at the Catholic Church. The Roman Catholic Church was my church. It was my mother's church. It was the church of my ancestors to no telling how far into the past, perhaps nearly to the church's very beginning. But, the belief that the Scriptures are not the only authority was definitely wrong.

I would be early again. *I wonder what Mr. Clay will say about these three verses?*

CHAPTER 12
"BECAUSE I SAY SO!"

"Gary! What's HAP-ning?" The cheery call, with extra emphasis on "hap," came from my good friend Bruce.

"You are!" I completed the teen's stylish greeting. As I turned and waited, he jogged to catch up with me in the Church's near-empty parking lot.

Since moving four years earlier from Houston to Bethany—a northwest suburb of Oklahoma City—our lives naturally interwove. We attended the same school, the same Catholic Church, and lived within a quick quarter-mile bicycle ride of each other. Fishing at Lake Overholser, although we never caught much, always topped our list of things to do. Bruce, a dark-haired, nice-looking guy, persistently smiled. He must have smiled in his sleep.

"Hey, where is everybody?" His question matched his confused expression.

"Oh, Bruce, you didn't!" I set him up for the punch.

"Didn't what?" He hurried me on to tell him.

"Set your clock back! Last night was the daylight savings time change!" I rubbed it in.

I laughed. After frozen for a moment with a blank face, he cracked up too.

"Come on Bruce, let's go see Mr. Clay. I have something to talk to him about, and your being there will give me support." The somber thoughts of the approaching visit vaporized the humor.

Mr. Clay sat at his desk reviewing his class lesson, but turned his head to the unexpected entrance of the two early birds. "Fellows, don't tell me that you..."

"I don't know about Gary, but, no, I did not set my clock back," interrupted my shyless, outgoing friend as we each took a student desk at the front.

"With any luck, maybe our chronic late-comers did likewise," added Mr. Clay. He walked around to the front of his desk and leaned back on it with his arms crossed. "Gary, have you remembered what I told you about 2 Timothy 3:16-17?"

Well, at least he saved me the hard part of bringing it up. Recalling his intimidating lecture last Sunday, I nervously responded. I assured him his words were not forgotten, but, mustering the courage, I brought up Mr. Babbitt's point. Holding our Catholic Bible's introductions before him, I pointed out that Matthew was written between 42 and 50 A.D. while 2 Timothy was 66 or 67 A.D. Then I reasoned, since Matthew and other New Testament books were in circulation when Timothy was a youth, it was possible that the Scriptures referred to in 2 Timothy 3:15-17 were the *New* Testament Scriptures. I included the fact that, since these Scriptures led to faith in Jesus, then they must be the New Testament Scriptures, not the Old Testament as he had told me.

I halted my daring confrontation, desiring to hear his response. I kept in reserve the other verses Mr. Babbitt showed me. As it turned out, they were not needed. The always confident Mr. Clay stood expressionless without a rebuttal to offer. Noticeably baffled, he looked every part of a soon-to-retire employee arriving at work as normal, only to discover the corporation closed due to bankruptcy. Apparently, this had been suppressed from him too.

He collected himself and resorted to the fail-safe response we Catholics run to for *every* anti-Catholic interpretation *anyone* may offer to *any* Scripture. "It may *look* like 'the Scriptures' in this verse are the New Testament Scriptures, but only the Catholic Church has the authority to interpret the Scriptures, and only the Catholic Church has the authority to teach the Scriptures, and those teachings are infallible. And the Church tells us that these are the *Old* Testament Scriptures."

Still leaning on his desk, he turned slightly to retrieve a book from his black leather briefcase. As he searched the pages, I made out the cover's title through his fingers, *The Baltimore Catechism.* This standard—the Catholic school text in the United States since 1885—contains our doctrines. It sets forth what we are to believe and practice.

With relief restructuring his somber face, he regained his authoritative tone. "You know what this is, do you not?"

"It's our Catechism," I replied.

"It is the third volume of the Catechism—the advanced edition," he added. As he looked at the inside cover, apparently at some notes he had written down, he said, "Questions 156 and 157 tell us of our reliance upon the Church for the interpretation and understanding of the meaning of Scriptures. Listen to them."

> Q. 156. How shall we know the things which we are to believe?
> A. We shall know the things we are to believe from the Catholic Church, through which God speaks to us.
>
> Q. 157. What do we mean by the "Church, through which God speaks to us"?
> A. By the "Church, through which God speaks to us," we mean the "teaching Church"; that is, the Pope, Bishops, and priests, whose duty it is to instruct us in the truth and practices of our religion.

"This means," Mr. Clay explained, "the Church teaches us what the Scriptures mean by means of the pope, bishops, and priests. They are the only ones who have the authority to interpret and teach. So, if you, I, or anybody else has a different interpretation from that of the pope, bishops, and priests, our interpretation is wrong. An example is what you said about 'the Scriptures' in 2 Timothy 3:15-17 to mean the New Testament. Since the pope, bishops, and priests tell us those Scriptures are the *Old* Testament, then to interpret it to mean the *New* Testament, is wrong. Furthermore, we know that their teaching is always correct because, as the answer to Q. 526 informs us, 'By the infallibility of the Church I mean that the Church cannot err when it teaches a doctrine of faith or morals.'"

"So," I interjected, making sure I understood completely, "everything I am to believe and do in religion is solely dependent upon what the pope, bishops, and priests tell me to believe and do? And I don't have to try to interpret or understand the Bible myself?"

"Exactly. Actually, that is what the Catechism teaches." He

obtained another reference from inside the cover and turned in the book and read.

> Q. 561. Must we ourselves seek in the Scriptures and traditions for what we are to believe?
>
> A. We ourselves need not seek in the Scriptures and traditions for what we are to believe. God has appointed the Church to be our guide to salvation and we must accept its teachings as our infallible rule of faith.

"See how easy that is for us?" he commented. "All we have to do is accept what the pope, bishops, and priests say simply because they say so."

"This is what the Bible itself teaches in 2 Peter 1:20," he added after he glanced at his notes inside the cover.

Bruce found it first and read aloud.

> *This, then, you must understand first of all, that no prophecy of Scripture is made by private interpretation.*

"Which means," Mr. Clay explained, "the interpretation of the Scriptures is not for private individuals like you and me. Rather, the interpretation is for the Church, and the Church tells us what to believe. Now add to that, chapter three verse sixteen of this same book. Bruce, you're there. Read it for us."

As Bruce read, I followed in my Bible.

> *In these epistles there are certain things difficult to understand, which the unlearned and the unstable distort, just as they do the rest of the Scriptures also, to their own destruction.*

Mr. Clay interjected, "So, if anyone is not a pope, a bishop, or a priest, he cannot understand the Scriptures. And when he tries, he will most likely distort the true teaching and produce a false teaching. That is why there are such contradictions and divisions among the denominations."

As other students began to enter the room, Mr. Clay closed the tutoring session. "Remember, only the Catholic Church has the authority to interpret the Scriptures, and only the Catholic Church has the authority to teach the Scriptures—those teachings are infallible.

Your part is very easy, you don't need to try to understand the Bible, but just accept what the teaching Church tells you simply because they say so."

While we waited a few minutes for others to trickle into the classroom, I reviewed my notes on that bombardment of information. Compelled to admit it sounded good, especially with the statements in the Catechism and the supporting verses, recent experience taught me to hear the other side. Even our judicial courts recognize that. It would be unfair indeed if the judge or jury heard only one side, no matter how lopsided the case may seem. Thus, the defense attorney in my court case, Mr. Babbitt, would have his turn.

CHAPTER 13
THINKING IT THROUGH

S everal students clustered together throughout the high-school grounds on a crisp Tuesday morning awaiting the unlocking of the doors. I chose to wait in Ol' Blue as I again sorted through the Catholic Church's trump card: the authority to interpret and to teach the Bible infallibly belongs only to the Catholic Church, and the laity must heed what the Church says without question.

BAMM! A thunderous hand-slap just above my head on the car's white top got its intended result. I hoped no one else witnessed my spasmodic reaction.

"Bruce!" He could hear me even with the windows up. "Get in here, man!"

He pranced to the passenger side and slid in. "Just a little payback for rubbing in my daylight savings time goof. Hey, where did you get this?" he asked as he eyed the book he scooted across the seat when he hopped in.

"Sunday, after Mass, Mr. Clay gave it to me," I explained casually, not wanting to make Bruce jealous.

"It's just like his, but brand-new. *The Baltimore Catechism*, volume three." He was impressed.

"Yeah. He said I'm so inquisitive I need to read up on Church doctrine. I don't know; do you think he's getting tired of me asking him questions?"

We both laughed.

"Bruce," I asked, wanting his input on what I had been thinking, "how do you feel about all that info Mr. Clay unloaded on us before class?"

"Great," he replied with spunk. "What he said proves the Catholic Church to be the only true church because we're the only one who has the true, infallible interpreters and teachers. And all we got to do is just listen to what they tell us."

"Well," I began to spill out my concern, "I think I see a problem. Follow me as I draw this out on paper."

Bruce nodded.

"Suppose I ask Mr. Clay, 'How do Catholics know we must believe and practice those things that we do?' Mr. Clay would answer, 'The pope, bishops, and priests tell us what to believe and practice.'

"Then I would ask, 'How do we know we are supposed to believe and do what they tell us?' Mr. Clay would answer, 'Because God set them up as the authority to interpret the Scriptures and teach without error.'

"I then ask, 'How do we know God set them up like that?' Mr. Clay replies, 'Because they tell us God did.'

"And that puts me right back to asking what I asked the first time, 'How do we know we are supposed to believe and do what they tell us?'"

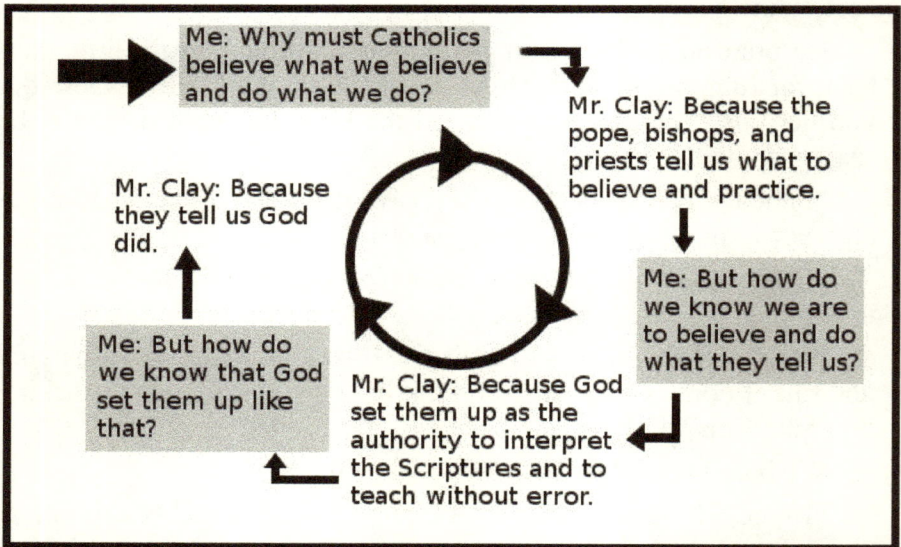

Me: Why must Catholics believe what we believe and do what we do?

Mr. Clay: Because the pope, bishops, and priests tell us what to believe and practice.

Me: But how do we know we are to believe and do what they tell us?

Mr. Clay: Because God set them up as the authority to interpret the Scriptures and to teach without error.

Me: But how do we know that God set them up like that?

Mr. Clay: Because they tell us God did.

"Bruce, do you see what has happened?"

"Yeah, you're right back where you began," he correctly observed.

"We made a big circle, and if Mr. Clay and I kept going, we would go on indefinitely. Nothing is ever proven."

I was not finished. "Yesterday, I talked with our school's debate team teacher about this. He said this method of reasoning has been known as a fault throughout the world for centuries. As a matter of fact, it is so well known that it has been given a name: 'reasoning in a circle.' He showed me in one of his books that circular reasoning is one of many fallacies and that such tricks and deceptions do not and cannot prove anything. So, Bruce, I can't see how any of what Mr. Clay told us proves that you, me, and others in the laity cannot interpret the Scriptures and understand it for ourselves."

Bruce, realizing it was time to go to class, but sensing my dismay, slapped my leg as he opened his door and said in an upbeat voice, "Hey. Don't sweat it, Gary. All of this is above our heads. We don't need to figure it out. Why, we can't even understand the Bible. But, to lead us through this maze, always lean on the fact that we got the pope!"

"But, Bruce...." It was too late. The door shut and he was gone. I knew he saw the erroneous circular reasoning in my example. Why couldn't he see that is exactly what he just did?

FRIDAY

Letting the Altus game slip through our fingers demoralized us even more than we realized. With our morale crushed, we showed up for our sixth game with Northeast High School only in body. When we finally pulled our heads out of the daze, we drove 90 yards for the game winning score, only to lose the ball on a fumble at the seven yard-line.

During our quiet bus ride home, Coach Webb rose, faced us, and spoke with words that speared our souls. "Three and three. This is not where we wanted to be, nor is it where we ought to be. But it is where we are at. We can either learn from our mistakes, make corrections and better ourselves, or just stay the way we are, give up, and keep losing. Where we stand at the end of the season, 3 and 7, or 7 and 3, is up to us right now."

We all knew our three inexcusable losses hung upon so little: we overlooked El Reno for Altus; lost to Altus on a freak play; and played Northeast in the 'Altus fog.'

So much can depend upon so little. Just like using the "little" error of circular reasoning to deceive ourselves into possibly a "big" error of thinking the laity cannot interpret the Scriptures and understand it for ourselves.

Sunday, I'll ask Mr. Babbitt and see what he says.

CHAPTER 14
WHAT'S GOOD FOR THE GOOSE IS GOOD FOR THE GANDER

I felt like a Ping-Pong ball getting whacked back and forth, but I was getting the best shots from both sides. Mr. Clay, a respected and knowledgeable teacher in the Church, presented our Catholic beliefs with clarity. Mr. Babbitt, deeply and comprehensively familiar with the Scriptures due to years of diligent study, methodically led me to understand the Scriptures for myself. But now the critical question loomed in the balance: Does anyone, including Mr. Babbitt, have the right to interpret and teach the Scriptures? Or, is that only for the pope, bishops, and priests? I anticipated learning the answer with the anxiety of a ten-year-old awaiting his birthday party.

We all heard the bell. The teenagers forced their energetic visiting into idle, and class began. Mr. Babbitt stepped to the front of the room after he finalized his usual mingling with his young friends. Turning to us, he wasted no time. "For the past few weeks, we have been honored by the presence of a visitor." He momentarily extended his hand towards me. "He is an example of one who is not afraid to examine his religious beliefs. He is one who wants the truth, no matter what that truth is. Whether he knows it or not, he is doing exactly what 1 Thessalonians 5:21 tells everyone to do, *'Prove all things; hold fast to that which is good.'*

I felt uneasy with the stage-light cast upon me. I lowered my eyes to the back of an empty chair.

"Gary gave me permission to let you know that he is in the Roman Catholic Church, and that he would like me to address a question of his. So, let's get right to it, shall we? Gary, would you please state your question for us?"

It no longer bothered me to let them know of my religious heritage. I had learned that the people here, teenagers included, extended consideration and respectfulness to others even though they may not agree with their beliefs. They viewed others as important souls created by God, and so, belittling those who differed was not in their makeup. They produced an unintimidating atmosphere favorable to open discussion and learning. These people, like me, wanted to know truth, for, as Jesus said, only the truth makes one free.[1]

All eyes and ears turned to me. "I want to know whether God allows the church members to interpret the Bible, or is that right limited to only the pope, bishops, and priests?'"

Mr. Babbitt proceeded in his usual teaching method, wanting us to think for ourselves instead of being forced with indoctrination. "Gary, please tell the class *why* the clergy says that only the pope, bishops, and priests—by the way this threesome group is called the Magisterium—why the Magisterium are the only ones who can correctly interpret the Bible?"

The pendulum swung from hero to heel. Now I felt uneasy for telling them something they did not believe in. "Because we are taught that God guided certain men to write the Scriptures, but we cannot understand them on our own because we are fallible, and we come up with faulty interpretations, so God guides the Magisterium—and them only—to interpret the Bible correctly."

"Class, you heard Gary's question. Does anyone have an answer?"

Outspoken Kent jumped right in with his characteristic animation of hands and face. "Well, nothing's been solved. If we cannot understand the Bible, then we won't be able to understand the Magisterium either! I mean, if God guided the writers of the Bible, and if God guided the teachings of the Magisterium, then we still have the same exact problem—trying to understand what God-guided men say. Like the old saying goes, 'What's good for the goose, is good for the gander.'"

"That's right," agreed Marty, using brother-like-brother gestures. "And to look at it another way, this has men doing what God cannot do! You see, it has men, the clergy, capable of explaining things in a way that other men, the laity, can understand because God cannot do it in the Scriptures!"

"Yeah," Kent could not hold it back. "And if the Magisterium can speak in a way that we can understand *them*, then certainly the perfect God can speak in a way that we can understand *Him*! Is the Magisterium smarter than God?! I mean, come on!"

Why had I not seen that before? That is so transparent. Had I been conditioned not to think? Had I become a mental slave who believed and did what others said just because they said so? But it is all so clear.

"I thought of something else," Sheila added. "If God is not capable of writing the Bible so we ourselves can accurately understand it, then God has a weakness and is imperfect."

"That is correct," Mr. Babbitt ended his silence. "If God wrote the Bible in a manner that we cannot understand, then either He is not smart enough, or He is not capable, or He does not want us to understand. Well, He is smart enough because He '*is perfect in knowledge*,' Job 36:4 informs us. He is also capable because He is all-powerful, as Revelation 19:6 says. And, He does want us to understand His Will as Ephesians 3:3-4 teaches. So, yes, to say that God is incapable of revealing His Will to the normal human mind is to say that God is imperfect. But it is false that God is imperfect; God is perfect in every aspect as Psalm 18:30 says. Which leaves us with precisely this: God wrote the Bible in such a manner so that our human minds *can* interpret and understand it."

With embarrassment rising, I regretted not privately discussing this question with Mr. Babbitt. Even those my age, and younger, could see through the error of what I had been taught. Were we, indoctrinated Catholics, the only ones who did not see this?

Raising and waving his hand like a desperate man signaling for help, Marty offered another observation. "But, if Catholics claim normal people can't understand what the Bible teaches, then why do they tell us to look at what the Bible teaches when they try to prove one of their beliefs? On one hand, if we *can't* understand the Bible, then it does no good to look at the verses. On the other hand, if we *can* understand those verses, then they cannot say that we can't. Either way, when the clergy claims that people can't understand the Bible, they teach something that exposes itself. And that's because it is false."

Good point. I was impressed. So was Mr. Babbitt. "What Marty just explained is quite revealing. When Catholics appeal to the Bible to see what it says, they are actually showing that the clergy's doctrine, 'we cannot understand the Bible,' is false. So, a Catholic cannot even go to the verses in the Bible to try to prove his point. Nevertheless, we will look at the verses they use anyway. After all, we have just learned that we *can* understand the Bible for ourselves. So, let's all turn to 2 Peter 3:16. Do we have a reader?"

Christie found it first.

> *As also in all his epistles, speaking in them of these things; in which are some things hard to be understood, which they that are unlearned and unstable wrest, unto their own destruction.*

"Gary," Mr. Babbitt asked in visual humility, "overlooking the self-contradiction your Catholic teacher committed by using the Bible to tell you that you cannot understand the Bible, what were you told about this verse?"

Shamed for falling for the self-contradiction, I shrugged my shoulders and said, "Well, I was told it means just that, the Bible is just too hard to understand."

Like a lawyer in court presenting his case-making point, Mr. Babbitt spoke while slowly pacing the floor. "Now, look at that verse again. Does it say there are 'some things *impossible* to understand,' or does it say, 'some things *hard* to understand'?"

I did not have to look. I noticed it the first time. "Hard."

"I understand you punt and kick for the Putnam City West football team. Is it hard or is it impossible for you to kick a fifty yard field-goal?"

"I have done it before, so it's not impossible, but it sure is hard to do," I admitted.

"Then, 'hard' does not mean impossible." The lawyer made his point, then applied it. "So, when 2 Peter 3:16 says 'some things *hard* to understand,' it does not mean they are *impossible* to understand. Unmistakably then, the verse does not teach that the Scriptures are impossible to understand."

Simple enough for a fifth-grader, his words were true. Yet, I had been intimidated into believing the verse meant the Scriptures are impossible to understand. This verse does not teach what the clergy says it teaches. It does not say "impossible," it says "hard," and things hard to do are not impossible to do.

After pausing to let that sink into our heads, Mr. Babbitt proceeded. "The second section to investigate is in this same book, chapter one, verses twenty and twenty-one."

The room fell quiet as we read it to ourselves.

> *This, then, you must understand first of all, that no prophecy of Scripture is made by private interpretation. For not by will of man was prophecy brought at any time; but holy men of God spoke as they were moved by the Holy Spirit.*

With hands clasped behind his back, and looking squarely at me, Mr. Babbitt kindly asked, "What were you told this means?"

I recalled Mr. Clay's words and replied, "The interpretation of the Scriptures is not for private individuals, but for the Magisterium."

"That is what you were *told* it means. Now, look at it for yourself with the reasoning ability God gave you. Go ahead," he encouraged me. "What do you observe in this verse?"

After rereading it, I raised my head. "Well, I am to first understand what the verse is teaching."

"You are to do what?" He asked to emphasize the point.

"Understand the teaching of the verse," I repeated, thinking over what I was saying. I knew he wanted me to see something. *This must be one of those "I'm overlooking the nose on my face" things.*

"Of course!" I blurted, too loud for the indoor classroom. "The verse itself tells us we '*must understand*' the verse! So God tells us we *can* understand the Scriptures!"

"Yes," Mr. Babbitt said, clapping his hands once with a pop. "Furthermore, if, as you were told, the phrase '*no prophecy of Scripture is of private interpretation*' means we cannot understand the verses, then, within this verse itself, God would be saying both, we *can* understand and we *cannot* understand. And that would make God contradict Himself. But God does not contradict Himself. So that means that phrase does *not* mean we cannot understand the Scriptures!"

"So, what the clergy tells us isn't true! But, Mr. Babbitt, what then does the verse mean?"

"The rest of the sentence, contained in verse twenty-one, explains what it means," he assured me. "So, take a look at it. Does everyone see the words, 'spoke as they were moved'? Okay, you English buffs, is that past, present, or future?"

"'Spoke' and 'were moved' are past tense," contributed the oldest Parker girl.

"Yes, past tense," confirmed Mr. Babbitt. "It happened in the past. They '*were* moved,' not '*are* moved today.' This verse, then, has to do with the *making* of the Bible in the past, not the *reading* of it today. It is informing us about the Holy Spirit inspiring the selected men in the past to *write* the Scriptures, not the certain few of the Magisterium to *interpret* them. It is revealing where the Scriptures came from, not what we do with them now that we have them. And they came from the inspiration of God, not from man's private, uninspired writing.

"In order for this verse to teach the clergy's doctrine of continuous, God-given interpretation to the Magisterium, the verse would have to read, 'holy men of God *speak* as they *are* moved by the Holy Spirit.' But it doesn't."

Mr. Babbitt paused, but remained standing and looking at me with tender eyes and lips curved up.

"Does that help you understand what this verse means, Gary?"

I was not one of those blind and deaf people Jesus talked about. I could see this verse does not teach what we Catholics are told. It is not about the Magisterium's authority and our lack of the right to interpret the Bible. Rather, it is all about the *writing* of the Bible by the inspiration of the Holy Spirit—all done and completed in the past. "Sure does," I answered.

"Good." He turned to his right, took a couple steps while looking downward as though in thought, and then faced us again. "Now, let us look at some verses where God teaches us that when the common man reads the Bible, he can understand it. The first few are in the Old Testament. Gary, would you read Nehemiah 8:8?"

"Okay, but I'll be reading from my Catholic Bible."

"That is fine."

I looked in the table of contents, located the page, and then read.

> *And they read in the book of the law of God distinctly and plainly to be understood: and they **understood** when it was read.*

Mr. Babbitt then pointed out the facts. "This 'law of God' was the Law of Moses, that is, the first five books of the Old Testament. The people listened to its reading for four long hours. And verses one and two reveal that *all* the people of Israel heard the reading. Then it tells us these common people understood! So, can common people understand God's Word? Yes, we can."

Mr. Babbitt continued to present similar verses I had never seen. In Daniel 9:2, Daniel read and **understood** the book of Jeremiah. In Psalm 119:130, the hearing of God's Word "*gives **understanding** to the simple.*" In Deuteronomy 31:11-12, God commanded all the people of Israel, including children, to gather together to hear the reading of the law of God so "*that they may **learn** (understand).*"

In the New Testament, he showed us more. "*He that received seed into the good ground is he that hears the word, and **understands** it,*" (Matthew 13: 23), and that "word" is the Word of God (Luke 8:11). Again, it was Jesus who said, "*whoso reads, let him **understand**''* (Matthew 24:15). Then, in Ephesians 3:3-4:

> *How that by revelation made known unto me the mystery; as I wrote afore in few words, whereby, when you read, you may **understand** my knowledge in the mystery of Christ.*

After reading all that, I analyzed it. *Moses the law-giver, Daniel the prophet, Nehemiah the leader, the psalmist, Paul the apostle, and Jesus the Lord, all say we can understand our reading of the Scriptures. But, Mr. Clay and the Catechism —which men wrote— say we can't. Hmmm, just who should I believe?!*

The unexpected buzzing of the bell abruptly halted the highlight of my week. Maybe my month. The class passed so quickly, it seemed. Like they say, time goes by fast when you are enjoying what you are doing, and I hung on every treasure of truth uncovered.

Whether providential or incidental, Mr. Babbitt's entrance into my life helped me understand God's Word. His vast knowledge of the Scriptures, his careful analysis of each phrase, and his talented ability to humbly guide me through the verses for myself, brought forth truths unknown to Catholics. *But, why are these truths not known to us?* I grew up accepting without question what Mom, my family, and my teachers told me. I respected them as I should, and to trust them to be right is natural in a child. But, had they been bred to believe what they believed just as I had? How far back does this "domino effect" go?

"Our time is up, but we did not finish answering Gary's questions," Mr. Babbitt apologized. "Gary, tell the class your other two questions."

"I also would like to know, 'Does the Catholic Church have the sole authority to teach the Scriptures?' And, 'When it does teach, is it infallible?'"

"Two critical questions," said Mr. Babbitt as he dismissed the class. "We'll look at them in next week's class."

CHAPTER 15
CROSS EXAMINATION

P oor Mrs. Stoltz! Whatever motivated such a gentle teacher to take on an experimental project—the first boy's cooking class in Oklahoma—I'll never know. We all liked her, and it is not that we terrorized the school, but, just for her class it seems, some of the guys possessed a disposition for pranks.

Recalling the antics of my friends made me chuckle as I consumed a bowl of Raisin Bran on Sunday morning. One occasion, while one of the girls in the first hour sewing class worked after class-time putting away her project, a couple of the guys stuffed her into the locker. Unable to open the door from within, the unfortunate captive banged on the narrow metal door while yelling to be let out. In unrehearsed unison as though we read each other's minds, we pounded the desks and sung a school chant.

But the purple ribbon of pranks goes to my track buddy, Clint Marcum. During class change, while Mrs. Stoltz stood in the hall, Clint climbed a stool he put on a work-table, removed one of the ceiling tiles, pulled himself into the attic, and, by counting the number of tiles to the front of the teacher's desk, positioned his feet upon the metal braces. When hearing his name in the role-call, during which Mrs. Stoltz always sat at her desk, Clint hopped off of the beams, crashed through the tile, and landed, debris and all, directly in front of her. As Mrs. Stoltz, still only partially recomposed, escorted Clint out the room to the office, he looked back at us wearing an ear-to-ear grin.

"Whoops! Time to go," I alerted myself as I jumped up from the breakfast table. I did not want to miss any of Mr. Babbitt's continuation of last week's class.

"Does anyone recall the questions we are going to consider today?" Mr. Babbitt stood before us in a navy-blue, pinstriped suit.

Several students raised their arms. Mr. Babbitt pointed to Richard with his hand topping all others. "We are going to study two questions. First, 'Is the Catholic Church the only ones who have God's authority to teach the Scriptures?' And second, 'is their teaching infallible?'"

"These are important questions to the Catholic, and, actually, to us too," Mr. Babbitt explained as he looked intently at us. Kent, what would it mean if the answers are 'yes'?"

"Then all non-Catholics are in error and need to become Catholics," Kent, never caught off guard, correctly replied.

"And what does it mean if the answers are 'no'?" Mr. Babbitt directed his question to Sheila.

She timidly glanced at me, then at the floor in front of her. "Then the good people in the Catholic Church are being misled," she said, almost in a whisper. Being so tenderhearted toward the feelings of others, I knew it hurt her to say that. But, if the answers are 'no,' what she said was true.

Mr. Babbitt then asked for my assistance, "In order to make sure we are being fair in answering exactly what the clergy of the Catholic Church says, Gary, please tell us what was explained to you regarding the pope, bishops, and priests being the only ones who are allowed by God to teach the Scriptures, thereby making them the only ones we are to listen to."

Still unaccustomed to all eyes staring at me, I sensed their sincere desire to hear me and that made it easier to begin. "I was shown in our Catechism that it is the God-given duty of the pope, bishops, and priests—the Magisterium—to teach the Scriptures, and that right belongs only to them. I was shown that the Scriptures teach this in Matthew 18:17-18."

The anxious students, even before Mr. Babbitt spoke, fingered through the pages of their Bibles to see what the verse said. "Gary, would you read it from your Catholic Bible while we follow along in the King James Version?"

After everyone's flipping of pages settled down, I began.

> *But if thy brother sin against thee, go and show him his fault, between thee and him alone. If he listens to thee, thou hast won by brother. But if he does not listen to thee, take with thee one or two more so that on the word of two*

or three witnesses every word may be confirmed. And if he refuse to hear them, appeal to the Church, but if he refuse to hear even the Church, let him be to thee as the heathen and the publican. Amen. I say to you, whatever you bind on earth shall be bound also in heaven; and whatever you loose on earth shall be loosed also in heaven.

Mr. Babbitt launched the analysis. "Can anyone tell me what this is talking about?"

It was simple. My head would have to be in neutral to not see it. This is instruction on what to do when a fellow Christian sins against another Christian. Even my Catholic Bible, at the beginning of these four verses, printed the heading, "Fraternal Correction." This passage is not even discussing the topic of the Church teaching doctrine!

Mr. Babbitt, after endorsing the answer of one of the students, which echoed mine, elaborated. "Since this passage is dealing with church discipline, then to use the verse in reference to the church's sole teaching authority is to take the passage out of context. When you do that, you will not get its true teaching. Rather, you will only get what men *want* it to say. It's like an atheist quoting Psalms 14:1, '*There is no God*,' and then says, 'See there! The Bible itself says there is no God!' However, he did not quote the first part of the verse which adds, '*The fool has said in his heart, there is no God.*' The atheist took the passage out of context. It isn't the Bible itself saying there is no God, but rather, the Bible is saying it is the fool who says that. The atheist took the verse out of context, claiming it to teach what it does not teach in order to make it teach what he wants." He paused, looked at me, and then spoke slowly. "Gary, I am sorry, but I am sure you see that is exactly what the clergy did with Matthew 18:17-18. It is not teaching about a Magisterium's sole authority to teach the Scriptures."

Why sure! That's a no-brainer! I furthered that thought in an unfocused stare. *Why did I not see that before?* I knew why. It was because I had never read it for myself. Rather, I believed and did what I was told merely because somebody said so. I am just one domino in a long chain of dominoes, taking my turn to do what the ones before me did, as did the one before him, and the one before him, until going all the way back to the one who started it all—the initial miss-user of Matthew 18.

"Although this was the only verse presented to Gary," Mr. Babbitt resumed, snapping my vision back into focus at him, "there are other verses the people in the Catholic Church are told teach the idea that only the Magisterium is authorized by God to teach the meaning of the Scriptures. Luke 10:16 is the first of two others that are most commonly used. Gary, would you again read for us?"

"Luke 10:16? Sure."

He who hears you, hears me; and he who rejects you, rejects me; and he who rejects me, rejects him who sent me.

"The Catholic clergy claims this is spoken to the apostles," Mr. Babbitt correctly informed the others, "and explains it to mean that Jesus gave only the apostles, including their successors, the authority to teach. However, what the Catholic laity is not told, and for good reason, is the ruinous information in verse one."

I quickly read it. We all did. He was right, again. I was getting accustomed to the disappointments. Verse one does indeed prove wrong the claim that Luke 10:16 teaches what we Catholics are told.

*Now after this the Lord appointed **seventy-two others**, and sent them forth two by two before him into every town and place where he himself was about to come.*

Luke 10:16 was not *spoken to the apostles at all!* I realized that Jesus said this to seventy-two *others* who were different from the apostles whom Jesus also sent out. The words, 'He who hears you, hears me,' were *not* said to the apostles as we Catholics are told. Rather, it was said to seventy-two men who were *not* apostles. If the words, 'he who hears you hears me,' establishes the Church's teaching authority, then it is not the apostles and their successors who have that authority, but some unknown seventy-two others. *Imagine that! God giving the Church a teaching authority and we do not know who it is! No, God did not blunder. Rather, some ancient domino began an erroneous chain—a chain which is still active today.*

Although Mr. Babbitt was meek about it, his words shredded the blinders fixed around my eyes. Like a flashlight wherever pointed enlightens objects one by one, Mr. Babbitt cast a brilliant beam on verse after verse. I grew upset with myself for never attentively reading the Bible. I had been trained to leave my thinking to others, and just believe and do what they tell me. How gullible!

Mr. Babbitt resumed. "John 21:15-17 is also claimed to teach the Magisterium's teaching authority." This time, he only winked at me. Taking my cue, I began.

> *When, therefore, they had breakfasted, Jesus said to Simon Peter, "Simon, son of John, dost thou love me more than these do?" He said to him, "Yes, Lord, thou knowest that I love thee." He said to him, "Feed my lambs."*

Mr. Babbitt raised his hand to stop me. "That will do. The rest of the passage reads about the same as Jesus and Peter twice repeat this question and answer. The Catholic clergy tell their people that, since Peter was told to feed the lambs and sheep, then Jesus placed him as the head of the teaching Magisterium. However, what you are about to see falsifies that claim. Actually, it falsifies the entire claim that only the Magisterium—the pope, bishops, and priests—have the sole God-given right to interpret and teach God's Word to all others who then must believe and do what they are told."

Feeling a little tense, I watched him turn to the chalkboard, select a stick of chalk, and begin writing. We sat in total silence, except for the clacking of the chalk and the overhead hum of florescent lighting.

Finished, he stepped to the left and allowed us time to read what he wrote.

> If the Scriptures teach that God allows **any** knowledgeable Christian to become a teacher of doctrine and practices in religion, then it is false to claim that **only** the Magisterium is to be the teacher of doctrine and practices in religion.

"You see," he explained, "if only the Magisterium is to be the teachers of doctrines and practices in the church, then the Scriptures will never have even one verse telling us that God expects *all* Christians to be such teachers."

Mr. Babbitt paused. I waited. I waited some more. Finally, without raising my hand, I spoke out. "Well, sir, is there such a verse?"

"Yes, indeed," he replied, pleased at my curiosity. "Everyone turn to Hebrews 5:12 through chapter 6:2."

Without waiting for the teacher's recognition, impetuous Kent, arriving at the verses, read aloud.

> *For when the time ye ought to be teachers, ye have need that one teach you again which are the first principles of the oracles of God; and are become such as have need of milk, and not of strong meat. For everyone that uses milk is unskillful in the word of righteousness: for he is a babe. But strong meat belongeth to them that are of full age, even those who by reason of use have their senses exercised to discern both good and evil. Therefore, leaving the principles of the doctrine of Christ, let us go on unto perfection; not laying again the foundation of repentance from dead works, and of faith toward God, of the doctrine of baptisms, and of laying on of hands, and of resurrection of the dead, and of eternal judgment.*

Step-by-step, Mr. Babbitt walked us through. "In verse 12, what were those Christians expected to be?"

"Teachers," answered Dee Dee.

"And, what were those first principles they were supposed to be able to teach?" asked Mr. Babbitt.

Jackie cited the list, "repentance, faith, doctrines of baptisms, laying on of hands, the resurrection, and Judgment."

He then asked, "When somebody teaches those things, is he teaching those 'doctrines and practices in religion' that only the Magisterium is to teach?"

"Of course," I answered.

To which Mr. Babbitt replied, "Then, the only thing left to do is to find out who is the 'you' in 'you ought to be teachers.' If they were members of the Magisterium, then the Catholic doctrine about the Magisterium having the sole authority to be God's teachers of doctrines and practices in religion is right. But, if they were common Christians, then that very important Catholic doctrine is false."

As he began another moment of silence, Kent begged, "Please don't leave us hanging in suspense again. Go ahead and tell us where to look for the answer."

Slightly leaning toward us, he spoke softly, "It is right there in the very first verse you read." He waited while we looked and reasoned it through. "Do you see it?"

I did. I already knew that a man who is in the Magisterium is automatically a teacher in the Church. But, since this was written to those who *ought* to be teachers, then they were not teachers. If they were not teachers, then they were not members of the Magisterium—the Church's teaching body of the pope, bishops, and priests. If they were not members of the Magisterium, then they were the *common* Christians who were to be teaching!

Mr. Babbitt settled the question even more firmly when he also pointed out that the book of Hebrews, which, of course, included 5:12 to 6:2, was written to the "brethren" (Hebrews 3:1, 12) which is a word that unmistakably refers to "the whole church"(Acts 15:22-23). Truly then, these verses teach that even common Christians— the laity—can learn and grow in their knowledge of the Scriptures to the point where they can be teachers of doctrine and practices!

Looking at the chalkboard, I read again the words Mr. Babbitt had written.

> If the Scriptures teach that God allows **any** knowledgeable Christian to become a teacher of doctrine and practices in religion, then it is false to claim that **only** the Magisterium is to be the teacher of doctrine and practices in religion.

I could not deny it. Hebrews 5:12 through 6:2 do indeed teach that God allows *any* knowledgeable Christian to be a teacher of doctrines and practices in religion. The conclusion, then, was inescapable: It is *false* to claim that *only* the Magisterium is to be the *sole* teacher of doctrines and practices in religion! And, Jesus telling Peter to feed His sheep and lambs *cannot* mean that Jesus is setting up a teaching Magisterium!

The Scriptures just exploded one of, if not *the*, most important Catholic doctrines. I suffered a ten-point earthquake in my religious heritage and my teenage comfort collapsed. No way though, was I quitting the Catholic Church. It is THE Church of Christ. But, I learned a biblical truth, and, sometimes, the truth hurts.

"Now then," Mr. Babbitt advanced on, "we have answered two of Gary's questions, which leaves us with his third." Looking at me and extending his hand, he asked, "Gary, would you repeat that question?"

I complied, "Is the Magisterium's teaching infallible?"

"And the answer, now, is quite simple," he assured us as he casually moved to a position in front of the students to his right. "Since it is the Magisterium itself that teaches the doctrine that they are the sole, God-authorized teachers, and since that doctrine itself, as we have just seen, is false, then..."

"...then their teachings are *not* infallible!" Kent blared out.

"Thank you," replied the slightly startled Mr. Babbitt. "Yes, since the Magisterium teaches a false doctrine, and such a prominent one at that, then they prove themselves not to be infallible. And actually, that, in and of itself, answers your question, Gary. But, to be fair, let's look at the verse you told us was shown to you, claiming to teach their infallibility. It is John 14:25-26."

> *These things have I spoken unto you, being yet present with you. But the Comforter, which is the Holy Ghost, whom the Father will send in my name, he shall teach you all things, and bring all things to your remembrance, whatsoever I have said unto you.*

Giving us a moment to read it for ourselves, I recalled having been told this to mean that the Holy Spirit would be with the Church forever as He infallibly taught through the apostles and their successors in the Catholic Church.

However, Mr. Babbitt pointed out that the promise of the Holy Spirit was only for the apostles, not any successors. This is made plain when verse 25 mentions the teachings Jesus had spoken to them *while He was present with them.* And, verse 26 says the Holy Spirit would "bring all things to your remembrance, whatsoever *I have said unto you.*" This means, in order for a person to receive this promise of the Holy Spirit, he had to have lived when Jesus lived, been in Jesus' presence, and heard Jesus speak all His teachings.

Since no one after fifty or sixty years of Jesus' death can have those qualifications, then no one fifty to sixty years after Jesus' death has been given this promise of the Holy Spirit. This means that Jesus' promise of the Holy Spirit was *only* for the apostles, *not* the Magisterium. Which means the Holy Spirit is *not* speaking through the Magisterium. And that means, at no time does the Magisterium teach with infallibility. Rather, they speak as mere men, capable of errors, in both their interpretations and their teachings.

It was so easy to see, not only this verse, but *all* the verses Mr. Clay gave me—the verses the Catholic clergy gives the Catholic laity—fail to teach our beliefs and practices regarding the Magisterium's sole teaching authority. I scanned my notes and I pooled the information: Matthew 18:15-18 are instructions about church discipline, *not* the teaching of the Magisterium; "he who hears you, hears me" is spoken to seventy-two men *other than* the apostles; "feed/teach my sheep" includes *common* Christians teaching doctrines and practices; and, "the Holy Spirit shall teach you all things, and bring to your remembrance, whatsoever I have said to you" applies *only* to the apostles who lived in the presence of Jesus and heard Him teach. And then to top it off, since the Magisterium teaches wrong on this, then they prove themselves *not* infallible! This doctrine of the Magisterium as the sole teacher, and infallibly so, is just not in the Bible. It is merely a false concept erroneously forced into a few verses by some ancient interpreters, resulting in its Church acceptance, and we are told to believe it simply because the Magisterium tells us to believe it. What a perfect monopoly!

Deep in disturbed thought, Mr. Babbitt's dismissal of class passed by me unnoticed. Just the two of us remained in the room. His sorrow-filled, bloodhound-like eyes broadcasted his concern for my feelings.

"It is a little shattering," I answered his unspoken question, "but I'm okay. I still know God established the offices of the pope, bishops, and priests as leaders of the Church. So I'm satisfied with that."

"Gary, having answered your three questions, I realize I might not see you again. So, I want to ask you, what is the name of the pope's wife?"

"Aw, Mr. Babbitt," I frowned. "You know the popes are not

allowed to be married."

With a sparkle in his eyes, he placed in my hand a twice-folded sheet of paper. As he walked by me through the door into the auditorium for worship, he lightly placed his elderly hand on my shoulder, and gave it a grandfather-like squeeze.

I opened the paper. There was nothing on it except the words, "Matthew 8:14."

CHAPTER 16
NO PLACE LIKE HOME

"**H**IS WHAT?!**"** Having returned to Ol' Blue, I had just read Matthew 8:14. I read it again, "*and when Jesus had come into Peter's house, he saw Peter's MOTH-ER-IN-LAW lying in bed, sick with a fever.*" If Peter had a mother-in-law, then Peter had a wife! But, if popes do not have wives, then Peter never was a pope! I don't know which word described it best: disbelief; traumatized; or sick. All three fit perfectly.

"There must be an answer," I tried to calm my alarm. I looked at the footnote to that verse. It referenced Mark 1:29-34 and Luke 4:38-41. "Maybe these verses will explain that she really wasn't his mother-in-law," I hopefully assured myself as I feverishly fanned through the pages. I found the verse in Mark. It was the same event, and the same words, "mother-in-law"! "Then Luke must have the answer, surely!" I found Luke's. "Nope. 'Mother-in-law.'" Instead of explaining it, they enforced it. No mistake about it, Peter was married. And since he was married, he could not have been the pope!

"I'll ask Mom about this," I resolved as I turned the car's ignition. "She has probably already dealt with this and can easily explain it."

Pulling into our driveway, I arrived home. Located in a northwest suburb of Oklahoma City near 27th and Council, it relaxed upon one of the highest spots in the metropolis. Only five years old, the housing addition gleamed with newness and modernization. Our street boasted full-grown Blackjack Oaks that stretched their robust limbs over the road and formed a drive-through tree-tunnel.

Our house, with smooth reddish brick and white mortar, four A-frames, and a white shingled roof, distinguished itself by several homey features. The porch, resting under an extending A-frame, transformed the house into a home, welcoming any who approached. Many times we relaxed under its cool canopy for shade, or hunkered beneath its large umbrella from rain. Dad hung a wooden bench-swing—a favorite of young and old. Running the length of the land-scaping-brick walkway beamed a semi-oval flower bed bordered by a hedge of two-foot shrubs. One end of the walkway merged into the double-garage driveway which was actually poured around our huge oak tree that shaded the cars and half of the lawn. Of course, Mom kept all flower-beds and window flower-boxes full of colorful flowers. It was always nice to come home, but the nicest part of this house was the people inside.

As I entered the house onto the marble-floor hallway, I saw Dad in the living room reading the paper. Dad was a nice-looking, healthy guy. I still couldn't beat him in arm wrestling. "Hi, Dad. Lunch ready?"

"Almost. But you'll need to race me to the table; I'm starving," he challenged me.

"I'll give you a three-second head start," I shot back.

WHAM! The swinging saloon-styled doors that separated the hallway from the kitchen burst open, and Danny, my four-year old brother, slammed into my lap. Chuck, our seven-year old brother who trailed in hot pursuit by two steps, hit with even a harder collision.

"Hey you two! You hit pretty good. Maybe I'll talk to Coach Webb about letting you play linebackers." I then bent down and whispered, "What are you doing running through these doors? You want Dad to give you a spanking?"

"Danny knocked over my domino train and the white one didn't fall down," Chuck growled.

My brothers got a juvenile ecstasy by standing dominoes on end one behind the other with a one-inch space between each. If set up correctly, a slight push on the first toppled the next which toppled the next, and the next, until all had fallen. They always put an ivory domino at the end of the black domino train, which, if knocked over—gauging by their reactions—signified a win equivalent to saving the world from utter annihilation.

"They're *my* dominoes!" reasoned the four-year old.

"Go back to your room; ask permission to use the other's toys; and don't knock over the other's domino train." *Oh, boy, do I really want to have kids?*

Expecting Mom to be in the kitchen, I entered through the swinging doors. Instead, I saw my ninth-grade sister, Kandy, setting the table with plates, glasses, and silverware. As much as a brother might not want to admit it, my sister was pretty. She was also quite an athlete. In a school softball game, I saw her smack a hit beyond the outfielders, and then run the bases like a cheetah, scoring an in-the-park homerun.

"Hey junior high upperclassman, don't let the cat get on the table," I joked.

"Hey high school upperclassman, I think I'll put a drop of milk on your plate and let her lick it," Kandy teased back.

"I just lost my appetite," I conceded, letting her win the jousting. "Mom out in the backyard?"

"Yes, and let her know there's ten more minutes on the casserole," she said, trying to look threatening while shaking a large serving spoon at me.

"Yes ma'am!" I answered, holding up my palms as though frightened.

She gave in and laughed first. Then I joined in.

Sitting on a black, steel-framed lawn-chair, Mom surveyed the backyard. She dreamed of building an in-ground swimming pool, which she did *after* I moved out for college. Tough luck for me!

"Hey Mom, your cook said the casserole will be done in ten minutes," I informed her.

"My cook?!" she quipped back with fake indignation, catching my joke.

"Okay, your apprentice," I granted.

"Mom, I'm completely puzzled about something. I thought you may know the answer," I began as I reclined in one of the matching chairs next to her.

"I'll be glad to help if I can," she offered.

I went on. "A man who is a pope isn't married, is he?"

"Of course not. Actually, none of the clergy are to be married. Is that what's bothering you? You want to get married, but you also want to be the pope?" She spoke with light humor, trying to lighten my spirits. She detected her son to be deeply troubled.

"Mom, listen to this," I beckoned as I located Matthew 8:14. *'And when Jesus had come into Peter's house, he saw Peter's mother-in-law lying in bed, sick with a fever.'* Mom, what are we to make of that? Peter had a wife."

"So that's what you are troubled about. And a perplexing thing it is indeed," she agreed.

So she does know about this problem. Good. Then she also knows the Church's explanation. Let me have it, Mom.

She spoke with all the tenderness a mother could possibly muster, "Gary, that is one of the mysteries of the Bible which we leave to the clergy, trusting them that there is an answer and that we are doing everything correct."

"But Mom," I submissively objected. "There's no way to misinterpret *'Peter's mother-in-law.'* That can only mean that Peter had a wife. And since popes don't have wives, then Peter could not have been a pope. Something is seriously wrong here, Mom."

"See," she tenderly responded, "that's why we have the pope and the rest of the clergy, to figure out these confusing problems. All we need to do is just listen to what they tell us and put our trust in them."

I pressed her no further. Satisfied with the patent Catholic response, "just trust what the clergy tells you," she was completely unaccustomed to thinking and reasoning for herself about the Bible and religious doctrine. Her response to this contradiction between the teaching of the Bible and our fundamental Catholic teaching matched Bruce's response with precision: "Hey. Don't sweat it. All this is above our heads. We don't need to figure it out. Why, we can't even understand the Bible. But, to lead us through this maze, always lean on the fact that we got the pope!" This seems to be our way of thinking: "Just let the pope and the clergy tell us what to believe and practice." Has this mindset been methodically drilled into us? Can't we think for ourselves to see this is "reasoning in a circle" which does not prove anything? To say, "We must believe and obey the pope because the Bible says so, and we know the Bible says so because the pope tells us the Bible says we must believe and obey the pope," is to put us right back where we began without ever having proven a thing. And, whether or not we realize it, that is exactly what we are doing! Furthermore, I saw for myself with Mr. Babbitt's guidance that the verses in the Bible the clergy use to try to show that the pope and the clergy are the sole teaching authority to whom we must blindly heed do not even come close to teaching such a doctrine.

Yes, Mom, we're in the one true apostolic Church all right, but something indeed is wrong, seriously wrong. And I am going to find out what it is.

CHAPTER 17
BETWEEN A ROCK
AND A HARD PLACE

"Hello Mr. Babbitt. This is Gary Henson. That verse…I'm doing fine, thank you for asking. How about yourself? …That's good. That verse you wrote on that paper says Peter had a wife. I never knew that was in the Bible. I would like to talk with you about it sometime this week if I could….Did you say today? …At your house? …Seven o'clock? …How do I get to your house? …Okay. Thanks a lot. I'll see you then."

Turning north off of 39th Expressway onto Beaver Street just past Rockwell Avenue, his house nestled in the trees two miles south of his church building. He must have been watching for me, for he opened the door and stood at the threshold as I walked to his porch. With a big smile highlighting a brightened face, he looked like my granddad delightfully welcoming me for a visit. Holding open the spring-tensioned glass door with his back, he extended one arm with palm up into his home as he said, "Come on in." As I entered, he laid his other arm across my shoulders. It was no facade, he really was glad I came.

"Agnes, Gary is here," He raised his voice to announce me to his wife in the kitchen.

Scurrying around the corner, she wore a full-length apron and held a bowl in one hand while waving a dish-towel in the other to greet me. "Hello, Gary. It is soooo nice to have you in our home. May I get you a glass of tea or water?"

"Thank you, but I'm fine," I replied, trying to speak in her same cheerful tone of voice.

"Well, you and Loral have a good visit. But let me know if you need anything. Okay?"

"Okay," I said, thinking what a pleasant woman she was.

"How about you and me go into my den?" He said as he again

extended his arm to direct the way.

As I entered the room, I saw a large hardwood desk resting in the middle of the room. Upon the spacious but uncluttered desk-top sat, one on each side, two highly decorative bronze antique lamps crowned with wavy, cream-colored glass shades. Between the lamps stood several thick books held upright by marble bookends carved in the shape of praying hands. Directly behind his desk against the wall stood a black, four-drawered filing cabinet. When I scanned the rest of the room, I saw several full bookshelves standing against all four walls. It was a library in a house.

Noticing my surveillance of his room, Mr. Babbitt explained, "Being right before God is the most important thing a person can do. Ecclesiastes 12:13-14 tells us so. By living according to God's commandments, as Mark 10:30 teaches, a person will not only have the best life on earth he can possibly have, he will also live forever in heaven. Gary, I want that more than anything. I do not want to go to eternal punishment in hell. So, I have spent my life diligently studying the Bible, making sure I know exactly what the Bible teaches. Especially since false teachers exist in abundance, as God warns in 1 John 4:1.

"Also, for many, many years, I have taught Bible classes, and God lays a most serious charge upon teachers. He commands us in 1 Peter 4:11 to teach precisely what *He* says and '*to teach no other doctrine*' (1 Timothy 1:3). Then, in Galatians 1:6-9 and 5:1-4, those who *did* teach a misinterpretation were cursed. That, Gary, is why I study as thoroughly as I do.

"So, for these two reasons, I carefully study the Bible extensively in great depth. With all the different, even contradicting doctrines out there, a person must distinguish between God's teaching and the erroneous misinterpretations of man, because, as Matthew 15:9 warns, '*in vain they do worship me, teaching for doctrines the commandments of men.*' So, as a result of many years of such studying, that filing cabinet is nearly filled up with my studies and class lessons.

"Now, I did not invite you here to talk about me. So, let's look at that verse, shall we?"

As he motioned me to take the chair in front of his desk, he walked around to his old, wooden, swivel chair behind the desk. Pushing his well-worn Bible across the desk, he tested me, "Do you remember where that verse is located?"

"I know it like the location of my school locker," I replied, turning through the pages.

"Well then, let us also see if you can still read," he humored me.

I audibly read Matthew 8:14 from his King James Version.

> *"And when Jesus was come into Peter's house, he saw Peter's wife's mother laid, and sick of a fever."*

"You read, 'Peter's wife's mother,' whereas your Catholic version reads, 'Peter's mother-in-law.' Same thing, right?"

"Of course," I said, shrugging my shoulders.

"Which means what?" he followed up.

"Peter had a wife," I answered the obvious.

"So, what's your question?" he asked. But I knew he knew what was bothering me.

"If Peter had a wife, and since popes cannot be married, then Peter could not have been a pope," I explained.

Considerate of my feelings, he spoke kindly, "Gary, you have reasoned correctly."

Then I countered with the Scripture that every Catholic heard of, although hardly any of us had any idea where it was. "But Mr. Babbitt, Jesus made Peter the pope. Jesus said that Peter was the rock upon which the church was built."

"That would be Matthew 16:18-19," he responded without hesitation. "Let's look at it. And if you would feel more comfortable using the Catholic version, a copy of the Douay-Confraternity is on the second shelf of the bookcase next to the window."

I retrieved the book, laid it upon his desk and begin to locate the verse.

"When you find it," he interjected, "go ahead and read verses thirteen through twenty. That way we will observe everything that happened.

> *Now Jesus, having come into the district of Caesarea*

Philippi, began to ask his disciples, saying, 'Who do men say the Son of Man is?' But they said, 'some say, John the Baptist; and others, Elias; and others, Jeremias, or one of the prophets.' He said to them, 'But who do you say that I am?' Simon Peter answered and said, 'Thou art the Christ, the Son of the living God.' Then Jesus answered and said, 'Blessed art thou, Simon Bar-Jona, for flesh and blood has not revealed this to thee, but my Father in heaven. And I say to thee, thou art Peter, and upon this rock I will build my Church, and the gates of hell shall not prevail against. And I will give thee the keys of the kingdom of heaven; and whatever thou shalt bind on earth shall be bound in heaven, and whatever thou shalt loose on earth shall be loosed in heaven.' Then he strictly charged his disciples to tell no one that he was Jesus the Christ.

"Gary, have you ever noticed when Jesus spoke to Peter He said, 'thou,' that is, 'you,' but when He spoke about the rock He said, 'this'?"

"No. What about it?"

"If he was still speaking about Peter when He referred to the rock, wouldn't He have said 'upon *you* the rock'? 'You' would refer to Peter, but 'upon *this*' refers to something other than Peter. For example, Bob says to Jim, 'Jim *you* are a smart person and *this* report card of straight A's proves it.' '*You*, Bob' and '*this* card' are two different things. Likewise, '*you*, Peter' and '*this* rock' are two different things."

Like getting hit by an All-State linebacker at a dead-run, I was stunned. Mr. Babbitt was right. I just assumed Peter and the rock were the same thing. But this shows they are different.

"I want you to see something else." He reached for one of the well-worn books on his desk between the marble praying hands. "The New Testament was not written in English, but in Greek. This book is a Bible interlinear—a Bible printed in the original Greek with the translated English word below each Greek word."

At his suggestion, I moved my chair around the desk, positioning it next to his so I could follow along in the book as he pointed to certain words. There they were. The actual words God inspired men to write.

συ   ει   Πετρος   και   επι   ταυτη   τη   πετρα

Thou   art   Peter   and   on   this   -   rock

οικοδομησω   μου   την   εκκλησιαν

I will build   of me   the   church[1]

"Now, haven't you been taught that Peter's name meant 'rock,' and therefore Jesus was saying Peter was the rock upon whom He would build His church?" he asked.

"That's right"

"Let's see if that is so," he said as he launched the investigation. "Do you see the Greek word for 'Peter'?"

"Yes, but I don't know how to say it," I confessed. "Now I know what people mean when they say, 'It's Greek to me.'"

"Don't worry. You don't have to know Greek in order to understand what you are about to see," he assured me. "Now look at the word for 'rock.' Is that word, and the word for Peter, the same?"

I looked back and forth letter by letter. "No, they are not the same. The first letter in each word looks the same, but Peter's letter is larger. Would that be because, since it's Peter's name, it is the capitalization of the same letter in the word for 'rock'?"

"Yes. The letters are the same. But keep looking. Do you see any differences?"

"I do. In both words, the first four letters are exactly the same, but after that 'p' looking letter, they are different. The word for 'Peter' has two letters that look like 'o' and 's' but the word for 'rock' has but one letter that looks like 'a'."

"So, they are different words, aren't they?" he asked, emphasizing the point.

"Can't miss it. I may not read Greek, but anyone can compare letters. They are definitely not the same words."

"Gary, there are two important facts about these two different words. Either one of them will show you whether or not Peter is the rock upon whom Jesus built His church. By these two facts, you will know whether or not Jesus was making him pope."

He reached for another book, about three inches thick, from between the marble bookends. *These books must be the ones he always uses in studying the Bible.*

He explained, "This is a highly respected dictionary of Greek words of the New Testament."[2] He randomly opened it. "As you can see, it is written in English and alphabetized according to the English words. It is very easy to use, just like using a dictionary in English."

Giving me a moment to familiarize myself with its format, he resumed, "Go ahead. Look up 'rock.'"

As easy as searching for a word in Webster's, I quickly located it. Upon reading the very first sentence, an entire team of linebackers clobbered me.

> ROCK: *petra* (πετρα) denotes "a mass of rock," as distinct from *petros*, "a detached stone or boulder," or a stone that might be thrown or easily moved.[3]

The two words did *not* mean the same thing. "Rock" was a large mass of rock, something like the Rock of Gibraltar, but "Peter" was a *petros*, a stone small enough to be thrown or easily moved! And that Greek dictionary said the two words are "distinct from" each other. No, Jesus was not saying that Peter, a small stone, was the large mass of rock upon which He would build His church. Quite the opposite. By the use of those two words, Jesus was explaining that Peter was *not* the massive foundation of His church!

Mr. Babbitt continued. "If you tell a Catholic priest what you just saw about these two different words, this is what he would say: 'But, the Gospel of Matthew was originally written in Aramaic, not Greek. And, in the Aramaic, these two words are identical, not different. So, Jesus really identified Peter as the rock.' Gary, that is the Catholic's 'knot at the end of the rope'– a desperate attempt to hang onto Matthew 16:18 before it slips away from their hands and from their ability to use it to keep people believing that Jesus made Peter a pope."

"But, how are we to know whether it was written in Greek or

Aramaic?" I asked.

He explained. "God tucked inside the Bible an easy rebuttal to this false assumption. Let me illustrate what I am about to show you. Suppose you wrote someone a letter which included the sentence, 'Jim is a man, which is translated, the human male.' Is there anything wrong with that?"

I wished my English teacher would ask such easy questions. "Certainly. Since it is written in English, an English reader already knows what 'man' means and it does not need an English translation by adding: 'that is to say, the human male.'"

"Exactly. Now observe a couple of verses in Matthew." Mr. Babbitt turned to them and I read the passages.

> *And when they were come unto a place called Golgotha, that is to say, place of a skull. (Matthew 27:33).*

> *And about the ninth hour Jesus cried with a loud voice, saying, "Eli, Eli, lama sabachthani?" that is, "My God, my God, why hast thou forsaken me?" (Matthew 27:46).*

He reached for another book from those on his desk. "See those strange words, 'Golgotha 'and 'sabachthani'? Find those words in this Bible dictionary to see of what language they are."

Locating each word, I read:

> Golgotha. This name represents in Greek the Aramaic word Gulgaltha.[4]

> Sabachthani. One of the Aramaic words uttered by our Lord on the cross.[5]

"They are Aramaic words," I reported my findings.

"Gary, what do those two Aramaic words, which are translated within the verse, tell you?"

"My mother didn't raise a dummy," I said. "It tells me, if Matthew was written in Aramaic, he wouldn't translate an Aramaic word into Aramaic! It's just like that English sentence, 'Jim is a man.' It would not translate the English word 'man,' into English because it was *already* written in English. God left no doubt about it. Since those words were Aramaic words that were translated into Greek, then Matthew was *not* written in Aramaic, but in Greek."

"Which means?" he prodded me on.

"Which means that Matthew 16:18 was written in Greek, and that 'Peter' and 'rock' are indeed *different* words," I answered.

"And the different words mean what?" he asked.

"It means they cannot be referring to the same thing. 'Peter' is a small stone, but 'rock' is a large foundational mass of rock. And that dictionary of Greek words tells us the two words are distinct from each other, and that means, Peter, the small stone, is *not* the large foundational mass of rock upon which Jesus was building his church. It means Jesus was *not* setting up Peter as pope with a line of successors. Mr. Babbitt, Matthew 16:18 does not mean what we are being told," I grumbled as I tried to control my anger. But I was not doing a very good job. I was fuming.

That bomb rattled my world to shambles. He sat in quietness for a few moments. So did I.

Breaking the prolonged silence, he said, "I said there are two crucial facts revealed by these two words. Are you up to the other one?"

"Mr. Babbitt, I got to know the truth about this verse. Go ahead." I spoke with a far deeper deflated spirit than I had following our third, excuseless loss to the Northeast football team.

He sustained his guidance in such a way so that I could see it for myself. He showed me in one of his books that the two Greek words *te petra*, which are the words for "the rock," are feminine. It read, "The article *e* [which includes *te*] indicates that the nouns are feminine."[6] Yet, *petros*, the name for Peter, being a male, is masculine. The conclusion was inescapable: just as it would be grammatically erroneous for someone to call me a female, so it would be erroneous for Jesus to describe Peter with a female noun. And Jesus never made errors. No. Jesus was *not* identifying Peter as the rock upon which He would build his church! He was *not* setting up some papacy! We have *not* been told the *truth*!

Mr. Babbitt went on to explain that the "rock" upon which Jesus built his church referred to the truth Peter had just confessed—Jesus is *"the Christ, the Son of the living God."* Jesus would build His church on the foundation of *Who He was.* The fact that Jesus is the Christ, the Son of the living God, is the very truth Peter preached the day the church began when 3000 people became convinced of that truth and were baptized into the church (Acts 2:22-41).

Mr. Babbitt also clarified the meaning of *"the keys to the kingdom of heaven"* which were given to Peter. "Keys" open doors that are closed (Revelation 3:7; 9:1). The kingdom's doors remained closed on the very day Jesus left Earth to return to heaven (Acts 1:6-9). Yet, just before ascending, Jesus told the apostles to wait in Jerusalem for the power the Holy Spirit would give them—the very sign of the beginning of the kingdom (Mark 9:1). When, in Acts 2, the apostles received miraculous power from the Holy Spirit, Peter, at that very moment, used those keys to burst open the door to the kingdom of heaven by preaching the very first Gospel sermon. That door to the kingdom, now opened by Peter, saw 3000 people pass through (Acts 2:36-41, 47). It all made sense now. Jesus gave Peter the keys to be the one who opened the door to the kingdom of God by preaching the Gospel sermon to thousands of people. And once the door swung open, Jesus promised it would never be closed again (Matthew 16:18). This means the keys were to be used only once— by Peter, and on that day. The keys were never to be used by a succession of popes throughout the following 2000 plus years.

Then, regarding the part of Matthew 16:19 that says "...and whatsoever thou shalt bind on earth shall be bound in heaven: and whatsoever thou shalt loose on earth shall be loosed in heaven," Mr. Babbitt referred me to chapter 18:18 where I read Jesus saying the exact same thing to all the apostles. It took no effort at all to see that Jesus was not giving Peter some kind of isolated and special pope-privilege. Rather, all the apostles obtained the privilege to tell the world what was allowed and disallowed in the Law of Jesus as the Holy Spirit inspired their speaking and writing. Then, once the apostles died and the New Testament was completed, that binding and loosing—that revealing of the New Testament—stopped. The binding and loosing was never something for a succession of popes.

With all these undeniable facts in Matthew 16:18-19, unless I wanted to join the ranks of those stiff-necked Pharisees who denied the flawless evidence of Jesus' miracles in order to keep believing what they wanted to believe, I discovered that never could a doctrine be more false than that of Jesus setting up Peter as a pope. *"This rock"* indicates something other than Peter. The original Greek words verify that difference: *petra* is a massive, immovable rock foundation, but *Petros* is a small and movable stone. Furthermore, *petra* is feminine, but *Petros* is masculine. So, it is *impossible* for Peter to be the rock. And, in the very verse itself, Jesus gives us all the information we need so we can know that. But that information is held back from us. It is suppressed. Censored! Why? Because it would not take any Catholic two minutes to see that Jesus did not set up Peter as a pope. So why are there popes? Only one other possibility remains: somewhere along the way, mere human beings invented the papacy in spite of the Scriptures' condemnation of men changing Jesus' church:

> *In vain they do worship me, teaching for doctrines the commandments of men. (Mat. 15:9).*

> *If any man shall add unto these things, God shall add unto him the plagues that are written in this book. (Rev 22:18).*

> *But though we, or an angel from heaven, preach any other gospel unto you than that which we have preached unto you, let him be accursed. (Gal 1:8).*

Only utter disappointment surpassed the numbness I felt. My life-long, unquestioned conviction and my pillar in my religious stability fell irreparably shattered into the bottomless pit forever. Yet, my belief in the Catholic Church as the one, true, original church remained untouched. But somehow, at some ancient time, mere men pulled off the greatest religious hoax in history. And I had fallen prey.

However, I had no idea there was more to learn about the pope. Much more.

CHAPTER 18
"PROVE ALL THINGS"

The morning sun lit my bedroom of solitude and the golden glow gently pulled me out of slumber. I lazily lifted one resisting eyelid just enough to make sure the outside world was still there, and then slowly focused on the clock.

"Yeow!" Both eyes shot wide open. "I gotta get!" In a single action, one arm threw off the covers while my other arm and both legs ejected me from the bed. I was off and running. Mr. Babbitt promised me his class would examine the Bible for more of the Catholic-censored contents about the papacy, and this I wanted to see. The truth about Peter and the papacy stands at the very top of the most important doctrines of Catholicism, and nothing else held more interest to me.

Throwing on clothes faster than a stage actor changing costumes between scenes, I scampered down the hall and pushed open the double-swinging doors to the kitchen filled with the aroma of sweet warm bread. Mom, with her back to me as she stood at the stove, blocked my vision of the breakfast she was cooking.

"Good morning, Gary," she cheerfully greeted me without looking to see who entered. She could decode who passed through the swinging doors by the way each of us swung them open in our own unique way.

"Morning, Mom. What'cha making?"

"Can you not tell?" she asked. Her tone hinted at a surprise.

Looking at the table she set, I saw the spread of blueberries, diced strawberries, and pecans, and a large bottle of Log Cabin syrup. *It could be French-toast. And it could be...* I snuck up, peeked over her shoulder, "...pancakes!"

Mom's pancake breakfast thrilled me like Christmas morning.

"You're going to make me late, Mom," I sung as I gave her a bear-hug.

"Are you going to early Mass?" she asked as she slid two large steaming hotcakes of perfection onto my plate.

"I'm going to late Mass," I said with conviction. I knew she knew about my visits to Mr. Babbitt's class. Yet, as long as I persistently attended Mass and held firm to the Catholic Church, she did not fuss.

Noticing my arrival at the church's parking lot, Sheila and Richard waived at me and then waited for me to catch up.

"You guys sure stomped Star Spencer," Richard said with admiration. He played football for Western Oaks Junior High School and would be on the high school team next year.

"Maybe so, but we couldn't have done it without your sister leading the crowd in the cheers," I responded.

"Yeah, right," countered the sarcastic little brother. Little? He was already as big as me.

"All right you two. Let's get to class," interrupted Sheila, evading a brother-sister clash.

I now looked forward to hearing what Mr. Babbitt said. He earnestly lived a life deeply devoted to God, and he studied the Bible and religious doctrines comprehensively. He unbiasedly craved the truth on every verse and Bible topic, and then helped others to see it too. How wrong I was, when I first met him, to view him as an antagonist.

"This morning," Mr. Babbitt began the class, "we will examine some verses that will answer a specific and crucial question. That question is, 'Does the Bible prove or disprove the position of the pope?' And you will notice, it is one or the other. It cannot be both, and it cannot be neither. But, one or the other *must* be true. So, which is it? Let's begin by looking at Ephesians 4:11-13. Teresa, would you read it please?"

She raised her Bible to read; I followed in my Catholic Bible.

> *And he himself gave some men as apostles, and some as prophets, others again as evangelists, and others as pastors and teachers, in order to perfect the saints for a work of ministry, for building up the body of Christ, until we all attain the unity of the faith and of the deep knowledge of the Son of God, to perfect manhood, to the mature*

measure of the fullness of Christ.

Our guide directed a question for the entire class "Is the position of the pope in this list?"

All the class, including me, shook our heads no.

"Rather significant, is it not, that in such a list God did not include the office of a pope?"

Mr. Babbitt made a valid point. If Jesus had established the all-important papacy with Peter, it is unthinkable that the most important position would have been omitted from the list of church officers.

"Furthermore," Mr. Babbitt carried on, "God, without including an office for a pope, ordained this list of positions in the church for what reasons?"

Trena spoke up. "The verse tells us those positions will make the church perfect in its work, and to make it grow."

Richard turned his head back around from looking at Trena and added, "Also, so that the church can attain unity and deep knowledge of Jesus. And the last verse includes two more reasons for those positions: our growth to perfection, and our fullness in Christ."

Mr. Babbitt then asked a question to make us think. "Now, if these offices are sufficient by themselves to enable the church to achieve perfection, growth, unity, deep knowledge, and fullness in Christ, what other office is needed?"

"None," popped Dee Dee. "All the needs are met. And besides, anything that is perfect cannot be improved."

The Parker girls' visiting cousin, Sheila Gamble, spoke with noticeable modesty, "It's like the perfect sacrifice of Jesus for the forgiveness of sins. Since it was enough by itself to forgive sins, God did not have to also send the Holy Spirit to be born, live as a man, and then be sacrificed for forgiveness of sins. Jesus' sacrifice was perfect. His did the job. It fulfilled the need. For God to have then sent the Holy Spirit to be sacrificed would have been totally unnecessary. But God, who is perfect, does not do unnecessary things. Likewise, since those offices were enough to make the church full and perfect, then a pope is totally unnecessary, and God, who is perfect, does not do unnecessary things."

"Excellent point," Mr. Babbitt consented. "And you are so right, all of God's ways are perfect, as Psalm 18:30 so informs. So, God does not sin, make mistakes, or do that which is unnecessary. This verse, by itself, reveals there is neither position nor place for a pope."

"Uh, Mr. Babbitt," I interrupted, "aren't there other verses that mention the word 'pope'?"

Pointing to a small bookshelf at the back of the room, Mr. Babbitt requested, "Marty, would you hand Gary that big, dark-blue book?"

As Marty stretched for the book, Mr. Babbitt explained, "This is *Strong's Exhaustive Concordance to the Bible.* It lists, in alphabetical order, every word in the Bible. Under each word, it lists every verse in which that word occurs. If the word, 'pope,' is in the Bible, this book will have it."

Arriving at the page with the heading "POM-POR," I would soon know the answer. The only movement in the room came from me sliding my index finger down the page. "POOL," "POOR," "POPULAR." "Pope" was not there. In all of Peter's own writings, he never referred to himself as "pope." In all of the words of Jesus, He never uttered "pope." None of the New Testament mentions "pope." No prophecy in the Old Testament contains "pope." In the *entire* Bible, there is *not even one occurrence* of the word "pope"!

My lips, robbed of shouting "there it is," laid sealed shut. My silence, as I closed the book, broadcasted my finding.

"That tells you something, doesn't it?" Mr. Babbitt meekly asked while looking directly at me. "If the church in its beginning had a pope as their celebrated, central figure who held prominence in virtually every aspect of their religion as the pope does today, why the complete emptiness in the Bible of the pope?"

No, it did not make sense. There was nothing at all written about popes. And that means there wasn't one. Evidently, sometime later, men invented the pope and set up that position in the church.

"In addition," Mr. Babbitt went on, "while God gave, in 1 Timothy 3, a list of qualifications men must meet in order to become bishops and deacons, no such list exists for a pope. If God exerted such care and concern for the church to select only God-qualified leaders of lesser positions, then how could He be so careless to fail to list such qualifications for the ultimate single controlling leader in the church? The answer should be evident to anyone: God did not give a list of qualifications for a pope because He did not give us a pope."

After a moment of silence to let that sink in, Mr. Babbitt then proceeded from where I had interrupted. "Terri, would you read a second verse for our study, Luke 22:24-26?"

I followed in the Douay-Confraternity.

> *Now there arose also a dispute among them, which of them was reputed to be the greatest. But he [Jesus] said to them, "The kings of the Gentiles lord it over them, and they who exercise authority over them are called Benefactors. But not so with you."*

"Does anyone see how this falsifies the idea of a pope?" asked Mr. Babbitt with arms extended toward us.

Jackie raised her hand. "I do. The apostles were contending for the position of highest authority in the church. But Jesus set them straight. There would be no one-man 'king' exercising authority over the church. He distinctly said, '*But not so with you.*'"

"Correct," Mr. Babbitt agreed. "If there was supposed to be a pope with the highest honor and authority among even the other apostles, then that was the opportune time for Jesus to say so. But He did not. Actually, He denied it."

Wow! God made that so effortless to see. It's right there! But I just hadn't read the Bible for myself. I merely accepted what I was told. What a big mistake!

Mr. Babbitt took a small step closer to us. "Let's look at another one. Everyone turn to Acts 10, and Richard, when you get there would you read it for us?"

> *As Peter was coming in, Cornelius met him and fell down at his feet, and worshiped him. But Peter took him up, saying, stand up; I myself am also a man.*

100

Not waiting for our teacher to ask his usual follow-up question, I quickly interjected, "Being Catholic, I can tell you popes today don't do that. I mean, with all the bowing before him and the kissing of his feet. He does not tell *anybody* to get up and quit kissing him."

"And here's the reason why," Mr. Babbitt explained. "I read in your Catechism, somewhere around question number 500, the pope is believed to be the Holy Father the Pope, the Vicar of Christ and the Head of the Church on earth. I agree, if Peter was all that, then he *should* have received Cornelius' bows and adoration. But he did *not*. Instead, he stopped Cornelius. Why? It is certainly not because he was, as Catholics are taught, mistakenly superstitious. And we know that because he was already a believer in the true God and had received instructions from Him to send for Peter. Rather, Peter refused the godly adoration of Cornelius because he was *not* the pope."

As Mr. Babbitt helped me discover all these things tucked in the Bible, I kept asking myself, *Why didn't I know that was there?* The answers were always the same: I didn't read the Bible; the Catechism schools didn't teach the Bible; and, the Church trained me to believe and do whatever they told me.

"Turn with me now to Acts 15." Mr. Babbitt advanced onward.

Once again, the flipping pages of a dozen Bibles clattered the air. The teacher respectfully waited for the last page to settle, and then began.

"The bulk of this chapter deals with what Catholics regard as the first general counsel of the church. Those gathered included the apostles, the elders (bishops) of Jerusalem, Barnabas and those with him, and the church at Jerusalem. Concerning the doctrine discussed, Peter spoke, then Paul, and then it was James, not Peter, who gave his judgment on the doctrine to which all agreed.[1] Now, the unavoidable question is, does this look like Peter is functioning as the pope, the head of the church?"

"Not at all!" Kent shot out. "This is the big meeting of the church to discuss a critical doctrine that troubled the whole church. If Peter was pope, that was the time to act like it. That's certainly what the pope today would have done. But Peter did *not* decide what should be done and then give orders to all the others. Quite the contrary. It was James who made the decision, and then all the church agreed. No, Peter wasn't a pope. He knew it, and so did the church."

Mr. Babbitt then challenged us. "What if you were told that Peter was letting James chair the meeting because they met at Jerusalem and James was the bishop of the Jerusalem church?"

"That would not be correct," I admitted, shaking my head. "Everyone knows the head of the universal Church is the head of the Church *wherever* he is. Furthermore, as Kent mentioned, this doctrine troubled not just the Church in Jerusalem, but the whole Church and that called for the decision of the pope." Then I said to myself, *No, Peter did not function as a pope because he wasn't a pope.*

"See," Mr. Babbitt said, "with a little guidance and a little thinking, anyone can easily understand what these verses reveal. We have time for a couple more. Go to Galatians 2:7-8, and Marty, read it for us please."

The Douay-Confraternity read:

> *When they saw that to me [Paul] was committed the gospel for the uncircumcision [Gentiles], as to Peter that for the circumcised [Jews], for he who worked in Peter for the apostleship of the circumcised [Jews] work also in me among the Gentiles.*

"The entire world is made up of either those who are Jews or those who are not Jews, that is, Gentiles," Mr. Babbitt explained. "Was Peter given the apostleship of the entire world, or only a part of it?"

"Only part of it. A very small part of it. Only the Jews," spoke out Christie.

"So," he asked, "does this teach for or against the universal pope-hood of Peter?"

Everyone seemed to be waiting for me to answer. So I did. "Against. It's so visible; Peter did not have sole authority over the entire church. So he could not have been pope. Actually, he didn't even have the sole authority of the Jewish portion of the church, because, in verse nine it was Peter *and* James and John who went to the Jews. And of the three, Peter wasn't even mentioned first—the place of prominence."

"Gary, you are absolutely right," Mr. Babbitt consented as he briefly pointed to me. He then summed up the investigation to that point. "These verses present seven reasons that prove Jesus did not set up Peter, nor any other man, as a pope. But, before class is over, I want to be sure we look at John 21:15-17. This is another verse, like Matthew 16:18-19, the Catholic clergy uses to get the laity to believe that Jesus was setting up Peter as pope. Richard, read it please."

I followed in Mom's Bible.

> *When, therefore, they had breakfasted, Jesus said to Simon Peter, "Simon, son of John, dost thou love me more than these do?" He said to him, "Yes, Lord, thou knowest that I love thee." He said to him, "Feed my lambs." He said to him a second time, "Simon, son of John, dost thou love me?" He said to him, "Yes, Lord, thou knowest that I love thee." He said to him, "Feed my lambs." A third time he said to him, "Simon, son of John, dost thou love me?" Peter was grieved because he said to him for the third time, "Dost thou love me?" And he said to him, Lord, thou knowest all things, thou knowest that I love thee." He said to him, "Feed my sheep."*

"Gary, do you remember what you were told this passage means?" asked Mr. Babbitt, wanting an authentic Catholic explanation.

"We're told that the lambs are the laity and the sheep are the clergy, and that Peter is to feed both—the whole Church—by his teaching the doctrines of faith and morals."

"Now, let us see if what you were told holds up," Mr. Babbitt challenged. "Have you considered this? If the lambs are the laity and the sheep are the clergy, then just as *all* young and immature lambs mature into sheep, this would mean that *all* the laity are to mature into the clergy!"

Wow! I had never considered that! I must have, like usual, just accepted what they told me and put my own thinking in neutral.

"Mr. Babbitt," I said, "that makes it so clear-cut. Jesus was *not* dividing the church into clergy and laity of which Peter was to feed."

As he slowly stepped to another position before the students, he continued. "Also, no doubt, you were not told about Acts 20:28, which says:

> *Take heed therefore unto yourselves, and to all the flock, over the which the Holy Ghost hath made you overseers, to feed the church of God, which he hath purchased with his own blood.*

Mr. Babbitt explained, "The word 'overseers' are the bishops. Actually, your Catholic version translates it 'bishops.' Now notice, these bishops were *also* 'to feed the church' which is the very same thing Jesus was telling Peter to do."

"So," I interrupted, "since others were to do the very same thing Peter was to do, then many others were given the same job as Peter. And that means Jesus was not making Peter a one-man overseer and feeder, or shepherd, of the Church."

"That is it!" Mr. Babbitt concurred, slapping one palm down onto another.

How easy he had made this to understand. And the verses he showed me were not vague, nor did they leave me with the uncertain thought, "maybe that's what it means; but maybe it doesn't." Instead, the verses presented the certainty of the Scriptures' denunciation of the doctrine and position of a pope in the church. The Bible genuinely makes plain: the office of a pope is not in the church's list of positions—positions God uses to make the church perfect; the word "pope" does not even occur in the entire Bible; although there are lists of qualifications for lesser officers, there is no such list for a pope; Jesus emphatically declared there would *not* be one man as the head in His church; Peter himself disclaimed the papacy by refusing man's adoration; Peter's subordinate role in the crucial meeting of the church shows Peter not to be the pope; even if Peter was a pope, he was pope of only the Jewish Christians—a *very small* segment— and *not* the universal church; and Jesus did *not* refer to Peter as pope of the lambs/laity and sheep/clergy, but rather gave him and many others the exact same responsibility of feeding the church.

In addition, I recalled how I earlier learned at Mr. Babbitt's home: Peter was married—but popes aren't; the Catholic fail-safe verse, Matthew 16:18-19, got cracked wide open displaying its emptiness; and when he proved to me that Peter (*Petros*) is a masculine noun and means a small stone, but rock (*petra*) is a feminine noun and means a massive foundational rock, I knew then the verse cannot teach what we've been told. Jesus was *not* setting up the papacy with Peter being the first pope. And the information Mr. Babbitt presented in class firmly confirmed it. The rock upon which Jesus built the church was *not* Peter. The Bible is not only completely blank of one single verse teaching in favor of a pope, it instead contains numerous teachings to prove the papacy to be: absent from the Word of God; a position made up by people; and, a doctrine and practice condemned by God.

Earlier, I biasedly rejected Mr. Babbitt's claim that the Scriptures do not teach the position of a pope. But the facts do not lie. Yet, I'm a Catholic, and a Catholic I will stay. Anyway, everything else is the great falling away. *But,* I thought with a chuckle as I tried to lighten my spirits, *Mom may be disappointed that I don't want to be the pope.*

As class concluded and everyone made their way to the door, Mr. Babbitt motioned me over to him. "Gary, I am, as I'm sure all the students are, impressed that you returned to examine such a touchy topic."

He had more to say, but I interrupted. "There is nothing to fear from careful study of the Scriptures. The Bible itself commands us to "prove all things,"[2] and Jesus says to believe and follow only the truth."[3] I had been doing a lot of reading in the Bible.

He took up again with what he wanted to say. "Since you have been listening to me so much, and since I am not a Catholic, and even though we have looked only in the Bible, I think it would be good for you to read about the pope in some of your own Catholic books. I visited the library of the Bethany Nazarene College[4]....I'm sure you know where that is."

"Downtown Bethany, three or four blocks east of your house."

"A set of the original, multi-volume *Catholic Encyclopedia,* from 1907, located in the reference section, contains a great amount of information on the popes. I encourage you to go investigate what your official Catholic publication reveals."

We have a Catholic Encyclopedia?! I marveled. *And Mr. Babbitt wants me to explore it?!* Which surprised me even more. *Doesn't he know this will give me more information to support Catholicism?*

Or, did he know something I had yet to find out?

CHAPTER 19
STRAIGHT FROM
THE HORSE'S MOUTH

MONDAY

"Excuse me. Could you tell me where the library is?" By his *are-you-kidding-me?* reaction, I sensed I goofed. Eleven weeks on college campus and a student—well, I passed for one—did not know which building was the library? Boy howdy!

After Mr. Babbitt told me the previous day that the Bethany Nazarene College library contained a set of our *Catholic Encyclopedia*, excited butterflies swarmed around in my stomach just as they always did before a football game. *Just think,* I repetitiously told myself, *an official record of the Catholic Church presenting the facts of what happened in the Church throughout the centuries.* My quest to read up on the popes drove me this far, and that college guy's belittling reaction was not about to bother me.

Shaking his head in disbelief, he pointed to a three-storied building. Strategically positioned in the middle of the peaceful campus of enormous trees, several sidewalks angled from different directions that led to and converged at its door.

As I entered and passed through the broad, L-shaped foyer, I thought, *Surely, no one at the desk will stare at me with a weird, twisted face if I ask for the location of the Catholic Encyclopedia.*[1] I was right. They were kind and helpful. My distress of going to college next year subsided.

Following their directions to the reference shelves, I soon stood right before them—our *Catholic Encyclopedia*. The fifteen large, light-brown volumes of fancy decorated, ancient looking books made me feel as though I should take off my shoes. Pulling out of my spellbound gaze, I reached forth and touched one. A moment later it rested in my hands. As I opened it I almost expected a breeze to gust out. I observed the small print in the double columns of the

800-paged set of books. *Our encyclopedia is loaded with information!* I bragged to myself. There I stood before an official and prestigious work of the Catholic Church that could tell me anything I wanted to know about the Church's past: its people, doctrines, practices, events, and, yes, the popes.

I shelved the volume I held and retrieved volume XII, "PHI - REVA." Thumb-fanning the pages, I located the article: "Pope." There, on pages 273 to 274, the list of popes laid before my eyes. Two hundred, fifty-nine of them—that is, up until 1907 when the encyclopedia was printed. *Certainly are a lot of them, but surely I don't need to read about every pope. Besides, if I want to return, now that I know the library's location, I won't need to vex another college student with a face-distorting, nauseous fit.*

I took a seat at an unoccupied table and began to read the articles on various popes. Some were quite brief; others were much lengthier. The first two or three confirmed what I expected: good fellows doing their job. *Yep, what the Catholic Church is today, it has always been—always the prime example to all mankind of godliness as led by a righteous, godly, morally upright pope.* I took pride in the Church, even though I now knew, as proven by the Scriptures, the papacy was a man-made office. I was just going to have to live with it.

At that point, I should have closed the book, shelved it, and walked away. What I then discovered caused me to have *my* turn with nauseous fits. But my cause was legitimate. My eyes raced over sentence after sentence in utter disbelief. If I had read a secret document that revealed Mom and Dad not to be my true parents, it could not have stunned me more.

As I grew up, the picture painted over my eyes by the clergy presented a marvelous array of rich colors depicting the Catholic Church as led into righteousness and godliness by those chosen by God to stand in the place of God—the popes. But I had just tripped into a basin of paint-thinner, and that picture began to dissolve, uncovering the true painting the clergy concealed.

I read on and on. Article after article. Pope after pope. I fought back the tears, but often to no avail. My shattered emotions deteriorated to the point it became too much for me. I left the library. But, after mustering some stability, I returned the next day. I returned all that week. I needed to see the *real* picture.

Surely, this isn't true! I thought, experiencing denial. *But it is*, I countered myself. *It is an official publication of the Catholic Church.* On the title page it says, "Under the auspices of the Knights of Columbus Catholic Truth Committee." Furthermore, printed on the next page, it has '*Imprimatur*'— 'let it be printed,' as ordered by an examining bishop. I conceded, *These are true historical records. They happened. I can't deny them, and neither Mr. Clay nor any priest can explain them away.*

The article on **Pope John XII** devastatingly read:

> Before his [that is, Alberic, the political ruler of Rome] death he administered an oath to the Roman nobles in St. Peter's, that on the next vacancy of the papal chair his only son, Octavius, should be elected pope. After the death of the reigning pontiff, Agapetus II, Octavius, then eighteen years of age, was actually chosen his successor and took the name of John.[2]

But, I objected with disbelief, *that's not how we get a pope! The king, one mere man—not the college of the Cardinals—used his political power to get who he wanted on the throne of the Church. It was nothing more than a human power-play! And, an 18 year old leading the church?! That's the age I, and those in my Catechism class, are just now turning. There's no way we have the knowledge, wisdom, and maturity to be pope. It would be a disaster!* As I read on, my speculation proved correct.

> The temporal [political] and spiritual [Church] authority in Rome were thus again united in one person—a coarse, immoral man, whose life was such that the Lateran [center of Christian living and residence of the pope] was spoken of as a brothel, and the moral corruption in Rome became the subject of general odium.[2]

The mental anguish ripped my mind. *A pope so immoral that he made the Lateran a place of prostitution; so much so it even made the laity sickened and repulsed! This is the Vicar of Christ?!*

War and the chase were more congenial to this pope than

church government. John began secret negotiations with Adalbert, son of Berengarius, [King of Italy] and sent envoys with letters to Hungary and to Constantinople for the purpose of inciting a war against Otto [King of Germany].[2]

"Unbelievable!" I spoke out, earning the stare of others sitting nearby. *A pope provoked a war between nations that would cause multitudes a horrible death, loss of limbs, and mutilation, and the heart-aches of wives, children, and parents, and the severe economic upheavals! And to top it off, Catholics inflicted these atrocities against Catholics! Contrary to the ways of this "Vicar of Christ," the words of Christ came to mind, "My kingdom is not of this world: if my kingdom were of this world, then my servants would fight."[3]*

The article had more to say.

On 6 November a synod composed of fifty Italian and German bishops was convened in St. Peter's; John was accused of sacrilege, simony, perjury, murder, adultery, and incest, and was summoned in writing to defend himself.[2]

I discovered more details about the synod's demand for a confrontation with him. The *Catholic Encyclopedia* spoke highly of Philip Schaff's work, *History of the Christian Church.*[4] I searched for that book on the library's reference shelves, and that book turned out to be a massive eight volumes of material that bulged with references to the actual ancient documents he used to obtain his information. Schaff wrote:

John XII disgraced the tiara [diadem] for eight years (955-963). He was one of the most immoral and wicked popes, ranking with Benedict IX., John XXIII., and Alexander VI. He was charged by a Roman Synod, no one contradicting, with almost every crime of which depraved human nature is capable, and deposed as a monster of iniquity.* ([The footnote read:] Among the charges of the Synod against him were...that he never signed himself with the sign of the cross,...that he had made a boy of ten years a bishop,...that he had mutilated a priest, that he had set houses on fire like Nero, that he had committed homicide and adultery, had violated virgins and widows high and low, lived with his father's mistress, converted the pontifical palace into a brothel, drank to the health of the devil, and invoked at the gambling-table the help of Jupiter and Venus and other heathen demons! The emperor Otho would not believe these enormities until they were proven, but the bishops replied, that they were matters of public notoriety requiring no proof. Before the Synod convened, John XII had made his escape from Rome, carrying with him the portable part of the treasury of St. Peter. But after the departure of the emperor he was readmitted to the city, restored for a short time, and killed in an act of adultery by the enraged husband.[5])

I just sat there, trying to collect myself. I looked around the large room. The walls still stood. The shelves of books hadn't toppled over. Students remained undisturbed at the tables in study. How could everything go on as before while my world rattled like an earthquake? *Surely,* I fought to console myself, *that pope was the only wicked one among all the good popes.* But, remembering how Schaff mentioned **Benedict IX**, I returned to the *Catholic Encyclopedia.*

He was a disgrace to the Chair of Peter. Regarding it as a sort of heirloom, his father Alberic [the political ruler in Rome] placed him upon it when a mere youth of about twenty.[6]

"Not again!" I groaned. I learned from the Scriptures that God did not establish the office of a pope, and this confirms it. If I still believed God created the papacy and has a sovereign hand in selecting them, it would be impossible to explain how God did not learn from His mistake with the previous pope!

I read even more in Schaff.

His election was a mere money bargain between the Tusculan family and the venal clergy and populace of Rome…This boy-pope fully equaled and even surpassed John XII in precocious wickedness. He combined the childishness of Caligula and the viciousness of Heliogabalus. He grew worse as he advanced in years. He ruled like a captain of banditti, committed murders and adulteries in open day-light, robbed pilgrims on the graves of martyrs, and turned Rome into a den of thieves. These crimes went unpunished; for who could judge a pope?

Desiderius, who himself afterwards became pope (Victor III), shrinks from describing the detestable life of this Benedict, who, he says, followed in the footsteps of Simon Magus rather than of Simon Peter, and proceeded in a career of rapine, murder, and every species of felony, until even the people of Rome became weary of his iniquities, and expelled him from the city. Sylvester III was elected antipope, but Benedict soon resumed the papacy with all his vices, then sold it for one or two thousand pounds of silver to an archpresbyter John Gratian of the same house, after he had emptied the treasury of every article of value, and, rueing the bargain, he claimed the dignity again, till he was finally expelled from Rome.[7]

Indeed, as the *Catholic Encyclopedia* says, "He was a disgrace to the Chair of Peter." Meaning, he defamed the Church in the eyes of the world, both, then, and in the following generations, including, now, me. The Scriptures put it this way:

> *And art confident that thou thyself art a guide of the blind, a light of them which are in darkness, an instructor of the foolish, a teacher of babes, which hast the form of knowledge and of the truth in the law. Thou therefore which teachest another, teachest thou not thyself? Thou that preachest a man should not steal, dost thou steal? Thou that sayest a man should not commit adultery, dost thou commit adultery? thou that abhorrest idols, dost thou commit sacrilege? Thou that makest thy boast of the law, through breaking the law dishonourest thou God? For the name of God is blasphemed among the Gentiles through you. Romans 2:19-24.*

112

But that was not all. I also read in sheer disbelief about **Pope Boniface VII**, who:

> …was intruded into the chair of St. Peter…the Romans threw Pope Benedict VI into the Castle of Sant' Angelo, and elevated as his successor the Cardinal-Deacon Franco, who took the name of Boniface VII. The imprisoned pontiff was speedily put to death by the intruder.[8]

You mean to tell me that the Church took the pope by force, locked him up, claimed another pope who then killed the real pope so he himself could be the real pope?! A rebellion? Yes. An intruder? Yes. A murderer? Yes. A pope? So says the Catholic Encyclopedia!

Unbelievably, the Boniface saga kept going.

> But in little more than a month the imperial representative, Count Sicco, had taken possession of the city, and Boniface, not being able to maintain himself, robbed the treasury of the Vatican Basilica and fled to Constantinople. After an exile of nine years at Byzantium, Franco [Pope Boniface VII], on the death of [King] Otto II, quickly returned to Rome, overpowered [Pope] John XIV, thrust him into the dungeons of Sant' Angelo, where the wretched man died four months later, and again assumed the government of the Church…. For more than a year Rome endured this monster steeped in the blood of his predecessors. But the vengeance was terrible. After his sudden death, due in all probability to violence, the body of Boniface was exposed to the insults of the populace, dragged through the streets of the city, and finally, naked and covered with wounds, flung under the statue of Marcus Aurelius, which at that time stood in the Lateran Palace.[8]

Stunned, I lifted the large book directly in front of my face. I read it again. No, I had not misread it. This pope robbed the Church and ran away; overpowered and imprisoned another pope (the condition of which evidently caused his death); and reigned as a monster steeped in blood. No wonder the people hated him with a vengeance.

As the clergy's faultless painting of the Church dissolved before my eyes, the authentic picture in all its ugliness was emerging. Not only the loathsome wickedness of many popes stood out, but so did the manner of the pope's appointments and terminations which were nothing more than mere political and physical power-plays of the desires of men. Of course, that stands to reason since the Scriptures teach us that God has nothing to do with the papacy—an office created by men.

As I kept reading our *Catholic Encyclopedia* that week, I wondered how the Church could ever have printed it because it provides the chance for Catholics to read these condemning facts about the office of the pope. Maybe they thought the laity would never read them, but rather just take the clergy's word for what they tell them. If that is what they thought, they were right.

The wickedness of John XII, Benedict IX, and Boniface VII were not isolated cases. Far from it. **Pope John XXIII** "was utterly worldly-minded, ambitious, crafty, unscrupulous, and immoral, a good soldier but no churchman."[9] "He was destitute of every moral virtue, and capable of every vice."[10] Schaff's diligent research further reports:

> Having affirmed its superiority over the pope, the council proceeded to try John XXIII on seventy charges, which included almost every crime known to man. He had been unchaste from his youth, had been given to lying, was disobedient to his parents. He was guilty of simony, bought his way to the cardinalate, sold the same benefices over and over again, sold them to children, disposed of the head of John the Baptist belonging to the nuns of St. Sylvester, Rome, to Florence, for 50,000 ducats, made merchandise of spurious bulls [papal decrees], committed adultery with his brother's wife, violated nuns and other virgins, was guilty of sodomy and other nameless vices. As for doctrine, he had often denied the future life.[11]

These sad facts could not but convince me: the making and selecting of popes is the work of man, not God. In His all-powerful and sovereign control, God would not allow such continual wickedness in the lead of His blessed Church. Continual wickedness? Yes, it continued.

Pope innocent VIII "had two illegitimate children," "resorted to the objectionable expedient of creating new offices and granting them to the highest bidders,"[12] and "completely subordinated the interests of the papacy to the advancement of [his] own pleasure and the enrichment and promotion of [his] kindred."[13]

Pope Honorius I "was condemned as a heretic by the sixth general counsel."[14] I just shook my head. *The supposed "feeder of the lambs and sheep" found out to be a heretic?! Well, either God cannot protect His Church, or popes are not of God. And it does not take a theologian to figure that one out.*

Pope Pius IV presented a unique angle against the clergy's claim on popes. Our encyclopedia reads:

> His first official act was to grant an amnesty to those who had outraged the memory of his predecessor, Paul IV....The enmity of Spain and the popular detestation of the Caraffas caused him to open a process against the relatives of Paul IV, as a result of which Cardinal Carlo Caraffa and his brother, to whom Paul had given the Duchy of Paliano, were condemned and executed. The sentence was afterwards declared unjust by St. Pius V [next pope after Pius IV] and the memory of the victims vindicated and their estates restored. Cardinal Morone and other dignitaries whom Paul had imprisoned for suspicion of heresy were released.[15]

How see-through is that! I thought, flabbergasted at what I just read. If popes were of God, then they certainly would not rule against each other's decisions. But here is one pope who made a judgment; the second pope reversed that ruling; and, lo and behold, the third pope reversed what the second pope did! *If popes are the Vicar's of Christ, which one are we to believe? How are we Catholics today to know whether or not what our current pope says will not be reversed by a future pope? If God's plan is to lead the Church by the popes, He sure set up a faulty and confusing system. But, God's Word tells us, "God is not the author of confusion."[16] No doubt about it, God did not establish the papacy.*

Informing us of **Pope Alexander VI**, the encyclopedia admitted:

> In his twenty-ninth year he drew a scathing letter of reproof from Pope Pius II for misconduct in Sienna which had been so notorious as to shock the whole town and court. Even after his ordination to the priesthood, he continued his evil ways.[17] Alexander VI had eight children.[18]

Schaff described him potently, "Alexander VI was a monster of iniquity"[19] and was "guilty of the darkest crimes of depraved human nature."[20]

Reporting his findings on **Pope Sergius III**,[19] Schaff relays to us, "Under the protection of a force of Tuscan soldiers he appeared in Rome, deposed [Pope] Christopher who had just deposed [Pope] Leo V, took possession of the papal throne, and soiled it with every vice."[21] The *Catholic Encyclopedia* adds that he had a son.[22]

The disappointments persisted. **Pope John XI** took the Chair of Peter by means of his mother's (the political ruler in Rome) swindling schemes.[23] **Pope Benedict VIII** bought the office by open bribery, as did **Pope John XIX**, a layman, and passed through all the clerical degrees in a single day![24] **Pope Leo X**, our encyclopedia declared, created a scandal by "creating thirty-one new Cardinals thereby obtaining an entirely submissive college" to his demands. Also, many of these Cardinals were chosen, not because of spiritual qualifications, but "on account of the large sums [of money] they advanced."[25] Schaff adds, "Leo X took far more interest in the revival of heathen literature and art than in religion, and is said to have even doubted the truth of the gospel history."[26] **Pope Alexander VI** had an illegitimate daughter.[27] **Pope John XVII** "had been married and had three sons."[28] **Pope Julius II's** "early private life was far from stainless" and "was the father of three daughters."[29] **Pope Paul III** had a son.[30]

I kept on reading, expecting these horrible articles to end, like eventually driving out of a thunderstorm. But they kept pounding me one after another, seemingly endless, like waves of the sea. I came across twelve more cases in which a pope reversed, condemned, or nullified a decision made by a previous pope. In addition to seven of the popes I already encountered, another six had also been married and/or were familiar with women by whom they had children. Nine more popes, of all things, were declared heretics! Four popes held to the erroneous belief of astrology[31], and one believed in the fraud of magic. Six popes were killed, four of whom died at the hands of their intruding successor! Distressed Cardinals unsuccessfully attempted to poison a seventh. Six other popes were removed from office. The Church pursued the dead bodies of two other popes with cursing and stoning. At least three more popes were installed by force. Two popes were humanists. Two popes were described as simple-minded and a third as "hardly even a theologian."[32] At least eight popes made use of forgeries—phony documents.

I did not read all the articles on the popes. I didn't need to. Enough was enough. And I read far more than enough. What Mr. Babbitt wanted me to see for myself from our own Catholic books had been seen. The *Catholic Encyclopedia* exposed the highly heralded chain of successive popes as if it were a metal chain wrapped around a large stick of dynamite, which, upon explosion, left only a remnant of scattered links.

Vicars of Christ, my foot! I thought loathingly. *Vicars of Christ? The ones who are said to be set up by Jesus to guard the entire Church in Jesus' place?! The ones who are claimed to have supreme honor and jurisdiction?! The great religious leaders for the example of the Church and the image of Christ for the world?!*

"Yeah, sure!" I muttered with sarcasm drenching each word. Rather, these men—for my own sanity I stopped reading after disgustingly observing more than 60 of them—comprise a collection of adulterers, murderers, fathers of illegitimate children, robbers, bribers, non-celibates, heretics, astrologers, humanists, users of forgeries, intruders to the Chair, buyers of the Chair, instigators of scandals, reversers of previous pope's decrees, youths, dim-minded, and a sodomite—many of whom were rejected and removed.

My thoughts swirled with anger. *I'm supposed to believe that the all-powerful, perfect-in-foresight God put, or at least allowed, all these ungodly, morally corrupt men to be the Vicars of Christ with full, supreme, universal power over His magnificent Church?! Yeah, right!* I knew that God possessed the power to keep them off the throne.[33] So why did He not?! God knew ahead of time exactly what these men would do.[34] So why did He even permit them to become popes?! The only answer is, God never established the papacy. Instead, it was totally the doings of MEN! Men misunderstood what Jesus said to Peter about the "rock." Men, sometime later, created the "throne of Peter." Men put men on that imaginary throne—and did a disastrous job of selecting them.

Are we to think that God accepted these men as Vicars of Christ, who caused enormous and irreparable damage to His precious Church? Not to mention the multitude of individual Catholics therein, and to the Church's holy prestige in the minds of the world?! No wonder so many people left the Church in the Protestant Movement! If God really had established the papacy, then none of that wickedness would have happened! But all that the Catholic Encyclopedia recorded did happen! No, certainly not! It was not God Who set up the papacy, and, since man is to conform to God's Will—not God to man's will—then neither has God ever accepted man's invention of the pope nor guided the Church through them.

Consoling myself, I thought, *Well, at least my traumatic heartbreak reached its end. Nothing else can be worse than this.*

But then, I came upon something else about the popes in the *Catholic Encyclopedia's* article: "Inquisition."

CHAPTER 20
PHARAOH REINCARNATED

"**B**ruce, you ask him," I begged.

"Not on your life!" He responded sharply with eyes wide open.

I dropped by Bruce's home in the attempt to persuade him to take my place in the Saturday appointment I made with the priest to ask him about all those wicked popes. Bruce didn't seem to like the idea.

"But, if I keep asking Mr. Clay and the priest these taboo questions, they might excommunicate me or something," I replied jokingly.

"Yeah, but if I ask him, he will think I am in this with you." He held his hands up with palms toward me and waved them back and forth. "Gary, you ought to leave this alone. I mean, everybody else is satisfied with the pope."

"Yeah…perhaps. But apparently, everybody else hasn't read those things I told you about." Bruce's uncharacteristic lack of response and his unfocused, downward glare off to my side told me that it might be beginning to make sense to him.

I left it at that. Actually, I felt a little embarrassed. I shouldn't have asked him to do my dirty-work. "Hey, Bruce, I'm sorry I asked this of you. Maybe I'm just chicken."

"Hold on!" he stopped me. "Any guy who will slam into fullbacks and blockers is no chicken! Besides, what you're going to do is really nervy."

"Thanks, Bruce. You're a good friend. Well, I need to get it over with." As I opened the door to Ol' Blue, I turned and said with a grin, "If I don't make it back alive, you can have my fishing pole."

"Aw, go on, get outta here," he said with a laugh and a grin twice as big as mine. "And," his frivolity changed to seriousness, "good luck."

A bit early, I wandered around the church's buildings. Near the entrance of the sanctuary I heard a voice that seemed distant. Unable to make out the words, I slowly and quietly peeked around the door. To my left, in the corner of the roomy space between the angel-imprinted concrete walls and the enormous glass walls of the inner sanctuary, stood the three gallon baptistery with the priest, four young adults, and an infant. "A baptism!" I excitingly announced to myself. The god-parents stood near the baptistery and held the infant's head over the basin while the priest performed the ceremony and poured water out of a vase onto the child's head. The proud parents glowed with joy—their precious baby was getting his sins forgiven.

When the ceremony concluded and the family left, the priest noticed me, cast a pleasant look, and beckoned me with his hand to follow him. We entered the glass sanctuary and took a seat on the last row of the long oak pews. He angled himself toward me and laid his arm over the back of the pew which caused the long white silk robe to drape like a gathered curtain.

The setting worked against my already frail composure. *Here I am, sitting alone, one-on-one with the clergy of the Catholic Church robed in his priestly apparel in the place of worship, and I'm going to question him about the popes? Why didn't Bruce do this?!*

"You mentioned over the phone," he began with a soft, but authoritative tone, "you read some disturbing articles in our *Catholic Encyclopedia.*"

My heart pounded, but I couldn't back out now. "Yes sir, Father. I read where some of our popes lived...well, I hate to say it, but...some lived wickedly."

He broke eye-contact and slightly gazed downward. "True, and it causes us no little shame." He regained eye-contact and added, "But, the number of them were so very, very few. Rare, actually."

I thought my ears went bad. Astounded, I asked, "Have you read many articles in our encyclopedia on the popes?"

"Well, no," he answered, "but those I trust—my teachers—informed me of and answered this problem for me."

I dared not tell him what I was thinking—that he fell right into the "domino-effect," blindly accepting what those he trusted told him. "Perhaps, Father, you may want to read them for yourself, because," I pulled from my pocket the paper on which I listed the popes and their notorious deeds, "I came upon more than sixty."

Taking a moment to survey the list, he was visibly stunned. "Well, uh, you know that popes are men, and as men they can do wrong. Peter himself is an example. In Galatians chapter two, he committed the sin of hypocrisy."

The pathetic and probably standard "domino" reply irritated me. I felt an unexpected boldness shove aside my nervousness. Yet, without raising my voice or speaking degradingly, I asked, "Did Peter *persist* in that act of hypocrisy?"

"No, he did it once and then quit the practice when Paul confronted him," he explained.

Next I asked, "Did Peter do a lot of other sinful acts?"

"No," he replied.

"Then," pressing the obvious, "how can Peter, who *once*, in a moment of peer-pressure, acted with mere hypocrisy but then quit, be compared with popes who *lived* in adultery and with the gain they got from their murders, briberies, heresies, reversals of papal decrees, and more?!"

With his first reply falling flat, he attempted another, "But, just because the pope, at times, is infallible in his teaching, that does not mean his conduct is flawless. He can still act wrong."

"Father," I maintained my respectful conversation as I shifted to face him more squarely, "infallibility has nothing to do with it. Rather, the problem is this: how could the all-powerful, perfect-in-foresight God place, or allow, all these ungodly and corrupt men to be His leader of His holy Church? Pope after pope, for long periods of time, did major, wide-spread, unfixable damage to His kingdom, His glory, and the salvation of man. It would have been as easy as snapping a toothpick for God to have kept them off of the throne. So why didn't He?"

He did not answer. He was thinking. But there was no reply.

"My son, this is the second question you have asked me in the last few weeks that concerns me. Has somebody been putting strange ideas in your head that is making you weak in the faith?"

That tiny amount of nervousness still harboring within me abruptly inflated to the max. *Now I'm in for it! I'll have to tell him about Mr. Babbitt.* I answered, "No, I'm not getting weak in the faith, Father. The Roman Catholic Church is the one, original, true, apostolic Church. Everybody else fell away. There is no other true church to go to. I attend Mass every Sunday. But, I'll admit, I have sometimes been going to the church of a high-school friend."

Upon telling him the name of the church, the priest replied, "Oh, that church. It was with them, I recall, that one of our bishops, I think Purcell was his name, debated one of their well-known preachers. It took place sometime in the mid-1800s. Bishop Purcell, I am told, soundly won the debate, magnificently upholding the truth about the Church. I advise you to stay away from them."

Gently taking hold of my forearm, he rose from the pew and gave my arm a slight upward lift to initiate my own arising. "My son," he began as we made our way out of that row of the pews and walked up the center aisle to the exit doors, "I know these bad popes must be confusing to you because it is indeed a complicated matter. However, think about this: If there was really a problem, how could the more recent popes have been silent and undisturbed about it all this time?"

Leaving it at that, he bid me farewell.

As I walked toward Ol' Blue I noticed she sat all alone in the parking lot. That is how I felt. Alone. "He couldn't answer my question," I muttered. "He gave up on every reply he offered after he realized it wouldn't stand. 'Rare wickedness'; 'believe what others tell me'; 'those wicked men were like the saintly Peter'; and, 'let's divert the issue to infallibility.' And then, after failing with those worthless dodges, he ended our meeting, without allowing me to respond, with another feeble sidestep: 'Today's popes would have told us if there was a problem.' But, since the office of the pope is an early invention of mere men that has been deeply woven into the Church, then the men recently serving as popes would not know there really was a problem. So, of course they would be silent and undisturbed." The priest acted like Pharaoh when confronted with the evidence God worked through Moses. Time after time, both,

Pharaoh and the priest ignored the evidence and held on to what they wanted.

I had dreaded that meeting and then suffered through it in order to get an answer as to why God, if He established the papacy, would allow those sixty-plus wicked men to serve as popes who caused such enormous damage. I got my answer, but it was not what I hoped for. The alarming truth is, WE DO NOT HAVE AN AN-SWER!

Halfway home as I drove down 23rd street, I remembered the priest mentioning our bishop's debate. I veered into a parking lot to write down his name before I forgot it. Not having any paper, I wrote on my palm, "Find Purcell debate."

However, that would come later. First, I had a date at the library with the Inquisition.

CHAPTER 21
A DATE WITH VACANDARD

"Gargoyles!" I whispered. Protruding from the top of a pair of castle-like, octagon shaped, notch topped towers, and looming high above the European styled building that housed the library of the University of Oklahoma, perched at least a dozen stone-frozen gargoyles. The 1929 building looked like a picture in a history book of medieval times.

The article I read in the *Catholic Encyclopedia* on the Inquisition that Monday at the Bethany Nazarene College led me 10 miles east on Interstate 40, then 16 miles south on Interstate 35 to OU's Bizzell library. Our encyclopedia's article not only approved of the voluminous work by Schaff, from which I also collected information on the Inquisition at the Nazarene college, it also kept alluding to the book, *The Inquisition*, by our Catholic historian, Vacandard. With help from the BNC librarian, I located that rare book in only three libraries within Oklahoma. Not wanting to make the long drive to either Tulsa or Altus, I found myself on the campus of OU.

I walked through the massive, cavern-like and highly decorative entrance and stepped into the building through a fifteen-foot tall door that curved up and inward on both sides to form a point at the top. The building's interior, extensively arrayed in decoratively carved hardwood, made me feel as though I had entered into a place of royalty.

Following the directions I obtained at the information desk, I meandered through several hallways as though on a treasure hunt. But the treasure on this hunt would be more precious than jewels. Entering the specified room and locating the correct aisle, I found where "X marked the spot." Opening the green, well-worn book to its title page, it read, *THE INQUISITION: a Critical and Historical Study of the Coercive Power of the Church,* by E. Vacandard. And there, on the facing page, appeared the important stamp of Catholic approval: '*Imprimatur*'—'let it be printed,' as ordered by an examining bishop. I had found our authoritative book on the Inquisition.

Although the book contained 257 pages, with its broad margins, large print, small pages, and numerous footnotes, it read quickly. Within four hours, it laid closed on the table. I finished it. All its factual information from the Catholic historian on the Inquisition swirled in my head along with the historical records I learned from the *Catholic Encyclopedia* and Schaff's *History of the Christian Church.* Last week, after reading about the wickedness of so many popes, I thought the worst had been discovered. I was wrong. Very wrong.

The first sentence of our *Catholic Encyclopedia* read, "By this term [Inquisition] it usually meant a special ecclesiastical institution for combating or suppressing heresy."[1] After devouring the historical records of those three world-reputable resources, I now knew that statement translated into: The popes, during the centuries of the Middle Ages and beyond, led the Church and civil authorities throughout Europe to inhumanely torture and punish thousands upon thousands of helpless victims, even condemning thousands to be tied to a stake and burnt alive, in order to force Catholicism upon others.

When Vacandard, warned in his preface—

> Granting that the history of the Inquisition will reveal things we never dreamt of, our prejudices must not prevent an honest facing of the facts. We ought to dread nothing more than the reproach that we are afraid of the truth.[2]

—I braced myself for a wild, white-knuckle roller-coaster ride. I just didn't know it screamed only downward at a heart-in-your-throat speed and would crash at the bottom.

The ride began with an abrupt jolt:

> "Under the direction and protection of the Church, an institution was being prosecuted which has scarcely been equaled in the history of human cruelty, the Inquisition...."[3]

"The Church was responsible for horrible cruelty?" I asked, fearing the book's answer.

The roller-coaster carriage picked up speed.

> The horrible massacre of St. Bartholomew (Aug. 24,

1572) was sanctioned by Pope Gregory XIII, who celebrated it by public thanksgivings, and with a medal bearing his image…. (*footnote*: The number of victims of that massacre in Paris and throughout France, is variously stated from 10,000 to 100,000.)[4]

Pope after pope issued orders not to spare those who were in league with the devil, but to put them to torture and cast them into the flames.[5]

The Inquisition of Spain is one of the bywords of history. The horrors it perpetrated have cast a dark shadow over the pages of Spanish annals. Organized to rid the Spanish kingdoms of the infection of heresy, it extended its methods to the Spanish dependencies in Europe, Sicily and Holland and to the Spanish colonies of the new world. After the marriage of Philip II with Mary Tudor it secured a temporary recognition in England. In its bloody sacrifice, Jews, Moors, Protestants and the practitioners of the dark arts were included.[6]

"And the Church, led by a multi-succession of popes, did this?!" I groaned in agony. "Heathen barbarians, I could understand. But all these popes? Those who claimed to stand in the place of Christ?!"

No mistake about it. It was the popes themselves who led the Church into the centuries of this widespread, unequaled human cruelty that terrorized the world with torture and death by burning.

He [**Gregory IX**] will ever be remembered as the Pope who established the Inquisition as a permanent tribunal, and did his utmost to enforce everywhere the death penalty for heresy.[7]

The aforesaid Bull [a papal letter of **Innocent IV**] "*Ad exstirpanda*" remained thenceforth a fundamental document of the Inquisition, renewed or reinforced by several popes, **Alexander IV** (1254-61), **Clement IV** (1265-68), **Nicholas IV** (1288-02), **Boniface VIII** (1294-1303), and **others**. The civil authorities, therefore, were enjoined by the popes, under pain of excommunication to execute the legal sentences that condemned impenitent heretics to the stake.[8]

The prosecution and the punishment of heretics in every diocese was one of the chief duties of the **bishops**, the natural defenders of orthodoxy.[9]

It is therefore proved beyond question that the Church, in the person of the **Popes**, used every means at her disposal, especially excommunication, to compel the State to enforce the infliction of the death penalty upon heretics.[10]

Pope after pope issued orders not to spare those who were in league with the devil, but to put them to torture and cast them into the flames.[11]

Even several of the popes fell to the false belief that the make-believe power and ability of witchcraft actually existed![12] No uncertainty about it, the popes themselves brought the horrible Inquisition upon humanity. As I read those words and others like them, which included multiplied statements regarding the cruel orders of pope after pope, my heart sank to a depth it never before experienced. *No wonder we're not told about the Inquisition, at least not everything. Not the facts. Not the truth. Otherwise, it wouldn't take a sixth grader five minutes to figure out that something was very, very wrong.*

I read about the cover-ups that have been attempted, but the feeble dodge that the civil authorities did the torturing and torching—not the popes and the Church—fizzles when that claim is shot to pieces by official documents of those days.

The Inquisition was a thoroughly papal institution, wrought out in all its details by the popes of the thirteenth century, beginning with Innocent III and not ending with Boniface VIII. In his famous manual for the treatment of heresy, *the Inquisitor*, Bernard Guy, a man who in spite of his office elicits our respect, declares that the "office of the Inquisition has its dignity from its origin for it is derived, commissioned, and known to have been instituted by the Apostolic see [papacy] itself."[13]

Our Catholic historian himself, Vacandard, in no uncertain words, falsifies such a pathetic, modern cover-up of the popes' guilt.

> Modern apologists [Catholic defenders] have clearly recognized this [i.e., the Church's responsibility for the tortures and killings]. For that reason they have tried their best to show that the execution of heretics was solely the work of the civil power, and that the Church was in no way responsible. It is altogether a modern perversion of history to assume, as apologists do, that the request for mercy was sincere, and that the secular magistrate [the civil power] and not the Inquisition [the Church] was responsible for the death of the heretic.[14]

He went on to call that cover-up story as "simply a legal fiction."[15]

The fact stands. History speaks. Truth emerges. The popes instigated, enforced, and led the Church into the barbaric Inquisition. And today's whitewashing can't do a thing to change it.

Furthermore, the various means used to find, try, and torture the hapless victims staggered my mind. And to think that the "ultimate Christians" —the popes, bishops, and others—ordered and enforced such brutal cruelties! My "tough-as-nails" self-concept took a downsize beating as I read about those methods of torture.

To find the so-called heretics, the Church depended upon the neighborhood to report them. Rewards offered to spies prodded the arrests,[16] and, "if two witnesses...agreed in accusing the prisoner, his fate was at once settled; whether he confessed or not, he was declared a heretic."[17] Then, forced into a trial already decided against him, the victim stood helplessly alone—personally and legally.[18]

> There was no personal confrontation of witnesses, neither was there any cross-examination. Witnesses for the defense hardly ever appeared...for in 1205 Innocent III, by the Bull "Si adversus vos" forbade any legal help for heretics: "We strictly prohibit you, lawyers and notaries, from assisting in any way, by council or support, all heretics and such as believe in them, adhere to them, render them

any assistance or defend them in any way."[19]

In its procedure, the Inquisition went on the presumption that a person accused was guilty until he had made out his innocence.[20]

In our modern sense, there was no protection of law for the accused. The suspicion of an ecclesiastical or civil court was sufficient to create an almost insurmountable presumption of guilt. Made frantic by the torture, the victims were willing to confess to anything, however untrue and repulsive it might be.[21]

"And we're supposed to think that God, Who is *perfect in justice*,[22] led all those popes who claimed to 'stand in His place' to carry on such ghastly injustice?! Yeah, sure," I cringed through my teeth with disgust.

The vicious tortures thrashed upon the "guilty" in order to get them to confess to their "heresy" manifests the Inquisition to be, not from God, but from men acting *without* God. First, their methods were ungodly. "In the beginning, torture was held to be so odious that clerics were forbidden to be present under pain of irregularity."[23] Physically and emotionally sickening? Yes, because the Inquisitors "used without mercy the most cruel tortures."[24] Imagining these tortures inflicted upon myself disturbed me more intensely than the worst of horror movies.

The rack was a triangular frame, on which the prisoner was stretched and bound, so that he could not move. Cords were attached to his arms and legs, and then connected with a windlass, which when turned dislocated the joints of the wrists and ankles.[25]

The *strappado* or vertical rack was no less painful. The prisoner with his hands tied behind his back was raised by a rope attached to a pulley and windlass to the top of a gallows, or to the ceiling of the torture chamber; he was then let fall with a jerk to within a few inches of the ground. This was repeated several times. The cruel torturers sometimes tied weights to the victim's feet to increase the shock of the fall.[26]

The punishment of burning.... First a good fire was started; then the victim was stretched out on the ground, his feet manacled, and turned toward the flame. Grease, fat, or some other combustible substance was rubbed upon them, so that they were horribly burned. From time to time a screen was placed between the victim's feet and the brazier, that the Inquisitor might have an opportunity to resume his interrogatory.[27]

In these wretched prisons the diet was most meager...bread and water.[28]

In the water-cure, the victim, tightly bound, was stretched upon a rack or bed, and with the body in an inclined position, the head downward. The jaws were distended, a linen cloth was thrust down the victim's throat and water from a quart jar allowed to trickle through it into his inward parts. On occasion, seven or eight such jars were slowly emptied.[29]

The thumbscrew, an oft used means of torture,[30] consisted of a vice into which the merciless Inquisitors forced the thumbs of the "guilty-until-proven-innocent" victim. The excruciating pain tormented the sensitive hand throughout extended lengths of time as the pope's men slowly turned the vice, crushing the thumbs and inflicting permanent damage. In some instances, sharp metal points lined the crushing bars so as to puncture the thumbs in order to create intense pain in the thumb-nail beds.

Barbaric; ungodly; repulsive; heathenish! Such words repeatedly pounded my mind while I read those atrocities. Even my three sources—two of them Catholic, and the third endorsed by our encyclopedia—expressed similar feelings.[31]

Indeed, the tortures were ungodly, but secondly, they were also foolish, for if the accused suffered torture until he confessed to being a heretic which resulted in execution, then the innocent either underwent unbearable torture for the rest of his life, or he lied about his guilt so he could die and end his horrific nightmare. What a choice!

Our *Catholic Encyclopedia* itself acknowledged that problem.[32] Actually, Pope Nicholas the 1st denounced torture for that very reason.

> "Such proceedings," he says, "are contrary to the law of God and of man, for a confession ought to be spontaneous, not forced; it ought to be free and not the result of violence. A prisoner may endure all the torments you inflict upon him without confessing anything. Is not that a disgrace to the judge, and an evident proof of his inhumanity! If, on the contrary, a prisoner, under stress of torture, acknowledges himself guilty of a crime he never committed, is not the one who forced him to lie, guilty of a heinous crime?"[33]

At least Pope Nicholas the 1st had some sense, but what was wrong with the rest of the popes?! Those tests of applying such horrible torture upon all those who were merely accused of heresy, which put the innocent into such a terrible dilemma, was completely senseless, even dumb.

I also realized, if God never leaves the popes, as we are told 'I am with you always'[34] is supposed to mean, then, either God broke His word and left the popes for centuries, or, God's intelligence is very deficient, or, God never established the papacy nor does He work through them to guide the Church. Well, a child could figure that out. I knew that God does *not* break His word,[35] and I knew that God is *not* stupid.[36] So, the Inquisition proves that God did *not* establish the papacy *nor* does He work through popes to guide the Church, just as, with Mr. Babbitt's guidance, I had seen for myself from the words of God in the Bible.

Why didn't I see that before? Don't we Catholics check up on what we're told? Can't we think for ourselves? Or, have previous dominoes trained us to likewise be dominoes—blindly accepting what we've been told to believe! My answer disturbed me.

While the methods of torture made use of cruelty beyond my

belief, the punishment inflicted upon the poor victims who confessed heresy even superseded the tortures. As I read, the impossi-
bility of believing that God had anything whatsoever to do with
those popes' and bishops' Inquisition grew firm.

> The civil authorities, therefore, were enjoined by the
> popes, under pain of excommunication to execute the le-
> gal sentences that condemned impenitent heretics to the
> stake.[37]

I shuddered at even the thought. I feared cremation *after* death,
but tied *alive* to a stake with wood heaped around me and set ablaze
mimics hell! Recalling a time I held my hands too close to a campfire helped me imagine the horrible pain. However, those helpless
people could not pull their hands back. And it was not just their
hands, but their entire bodies. The intense, engulfing heat and lick-
ing flames caused the skin of their bodies to bubble, turn dark, and
burst into flames. Their muscles literally cooked, then ignited in
blaze. In the end, the entire body burned in flames like a log, leaving
a shriveled, black figure of ashes. All the while the beguiled, "this-
is-what-God-wants," pope-led team of Inquisitors looked on.

Yes, to avoid millions of unanswerable questions and unwanted
consequences from the Catholic laity, I admit, it's a wise move on
the part of the clergy to keep the full truth of the Inquisition hush-
hush.

Other so-called heretics received the sentence of imprisonment,
even imprisonment for life, which may have been worse than a
quick death.

> …the prison cells…true condition was sometimes deplor-
> able…. In some cells the unfortunates were bound in
> stocks or chains, unable to move about, and forced to
> sleep on the ground…. There was little regard for cleanli-
> ness. In some cases there was no light or ventilation, and
> the food was meagre and very poor.[38]

> The prisons to which the condemned were consigned were
> wretched places, the abode of filth, vermin [rats; mice],
> and snakes.[39]

> The dungeon or cell …was, indeed, the tomb of a man buried alive.[40]

Including burning at the stake and life imprisonment, I collected a list of other punishments. Inquisitors cut out tongues,[41] killed by drownings,[42] excommunicated,[43] banished,[44] confiscated properties,[45] destroyed houses,[46] killed by hangings,[47] and "scourging [whipping] was executed in public on the bodies of victims, bared to the waist, by the public executioner…women of 86 to girls of 13 were subjected to such treatment."[48] Often, one or more of the non-physical punishments (excommunication, banishment, confiscation, house destruction) were in addition to the physical punishments.

Even the conservative figures of the number of tortured and/or killed boggled my mind. "Louis of Paramo triumphantly declared that in a century and a half the Holy Office sent to the stake over thirty thousand."[49] I wondered, *If 30,000 were burnt at the stake in a century and a half, just how many were burned in the Inquisition's six centuries?!* I also read:

> "The victims of the Spanish Inquisition also are said to outnumber those of the Roman emperors.[51] [Schaff's footnote read: The number of Dutch martyrs under the Duke of Alva amounted, according to Grotius, to over 100,000; according to P. Sarpi, the R. Cath. historian, to 50,000.]….During the eighteen years of Torquemada, the Spanish Inquisition punished, according to the lowest estimate, 105,000 persons, among whom 8,800 were burnt. In Andalusia 2000 Jews were executed, and 17,000 punished in a single year."[50]

> In September, 1609, a law was passed decreeing the banishment, under penalty of death, of all Moriscos, men, women, and children. Five hundred thousand persons, about one sixteenth of the population, were thus banished from Spain, and forced to seek refuge on the coasts of Barbary.[51]

Numerous readings such as these hacked away my Catholic innocence like a lumberjack chopping wood chips from a tree trunk. A letter written by one of the victims from his prison cell proved too much for me. He, a town's chief magistrate in 1628, after confronted by false witnesses, confessed under torture to the practice he was accused. He wrote this letter to his daughter.

> "Many hundred good nights, dearly beloved daughter, Veronica. Innocent have I come into prison, innocent must I die. For whoever comes into a witch-prison must become a witch or be tortured till he invents something out of his head and—God pity him—bethinks himself of something. I will tell you how it has gone with me....Then came the executioner and put the thumbscrews on me, both hands bound together, so that the blood ran out at the nails and everywhere, so that for four weeks I could not use my hands, as you can see from the writing....Then they stripped me, bound my hands behind my back and drew me up. I thought heaven and earth were at an end. Eight times did they do this and let me drop again so that I suffered terrible agony....[Here follows a rehearsal of the confessions he was induced to make.]...Now, dear child, you have all my confessions for which I must die. They are sheer lies made up. All this I was forced to say through fear of the rack, for they never leave off the torture till one confesses something....Dear child, keep this letter secret so that people may not find it or else I shall be tortured most piteously and the jailers be beheaded....I have taken several days to write this for my hands are both lame. Good night, for your father Johannes Junius will never see you more."[52]

With tears streaming down my cheeks, my quivering breath coarsely whispered in agony, "My God, my God, centuries of hundreds of thousands of situations like this one never would have happened if You really do lead the Church through popes and bishops. With Your infinite power and love for man, You never would have led the Church through popes to do this to people. We Catholics have been deceived! The papacy is *not* an office established nor led by You."

Emotionally disturbed, I needed help. But neither Mom, nor my priest, nor my Catholic friends would do. Like a talking parrot repeating the only sentence it knew, they kept saying: "Trust the pope; he would tell us if there was a problem." But six centuries of untrustable popes demolished that advice.

I wanted to talk to Mr. Babbitt.

CHAPTER 22
GOD GETS A WORD IN

In a daze, I somehow found my way out of the library's maze of hallways. Spotting a pay-phone booth on campus, and relieved to find the attached phonebook not yet stolen, I looked up the number and fed the slot a dime.

"Hello?" Mr. Babbitt answered with a question. (There was no caller-ID in those days.)

"Mr. Babbitt, this is Gary. Your suggestion to read up on the popes made me sick." Immediately, I realized what I said sounded like I meant his suggestion itself was sick. I attempted to correct myself. "No…, uh…, what I mean is, I've followed your advice and what I've learned really disturbs me."

Quick to read me, he replied, "Why don't you come over so you can tell me about it?"

"Well, actually, that's what I called for," I said with a sigh of relief.

"Hold on just a moment." I could hear him and his wife talking, but I could not make out what they were saying.

"Gary, it's almost suppertime, so why don't you eat with us?"

"Uh, that's okay. I don't want to barge in on you. I can pick up something at McDonald's drive-through and eat on the way." The truth is, I did not savor the thought of eating an old people's meal of turnips, squash, and something mushy that was supposedly meatloaf.

"Too late. Mrs. Babbitt already put three plates on the table," he insisted hospitably.

Trapped, I faked a cheerful tone of voice. "Okay. But I'm at OU. It'll be about an hour and a half."

"Mrs. Babbitt says that's perfect. See you then."

Arriving at his home, once again he watched for me as he stood at the entryway and held open the door as I approached. "Welcome! Right on time too. Agnes' cooking is just now done. What do you say we go on to the kitchen table?"

The growling and knotting of my stomach gave me hope that the intensity of my hunger would empower me to eat the food of old people.

As I entered the kitchen, Mrs. Babbitt turned from the oven, joyfully greeted me, then grabbed a pot-holder in each hand and turned back to the oven. I sat at the table visualizing the various possible prison meals she might set before me. She stood, turned, and I saw it.

"Pizza!" Surprised and relieved, the word just popped out. She laid on the table a thick, homemade, super-supreme pizza that put any fast-food pizza to shame. This couple possessed a magical knack in dealing with teenagers and in lifting the spirit of one desperately hurting inside.

While I exerted strenuous, but weakening, control over eating too fast and too much, I rehearsed my findings about the popes' horrible Inquisitions. I felt so much better just talking about it, yet, the king and queen of kindness helped even more.

"You know," Mr. Babbitt began, "you are experiencing a distressing discovery much like a certain fellow in the Bible did. He was an extremely devout Jew who persecuted the church and believed that the Jewish high priest was still the leader of God's people. He was the most dedicated Jew of his time. However, one day he learned that God had replaced Judaism with Christianity. Of course, that meant the Jewish high priest was no longer "God's man" on earth. True, the high priest was still recognized by the people, but not by God. That man was so disturbed, he did not even eat or drink for three days.[2]

I looked at my empty plate and glass, and then embarrassingly said, "He must have been totally devastated."

"Yes," he agreed. "He knew being right before God was the single most important thing on earth. Although he had Jewish parents, had grown up in the Jewish religion that had existed for 1400 years, had dedicated his life to Judaism, and held the high priest as God's ultimate leader of his people, yet, when it was proven to him that the one whom the Jews claimed to be God's acting high priest was *not* so, then, being true to himself and to God, he painfully accepted it."

Feeling the impact of what that admirable man did, I commented, "He must have been so dedicated to God that he went wherever the truth led."

"That is one of the prominent lessons of this account," he said, "and that is what you've done with the office of the pope. You have learned the facts, you have discovered the truth, and you have accepted that truth in spite of the emotional and mental pain it is bringing."

"It does hurt," I said. "I don't think you know how much. My mother, my sister and brothers, and my relatives are Catholic. I've been raised in the Church and attended Mass since birth; taught by nuns in Catechism school; and held the popes in highest esteem as God's Vicars of Christ. Indeed, I am a pure-blooded and whole-hearted Catholic. And, no offense Mr. Babbitt, but I know my church is the one, true, original church. Yet, somehow a major and far-reaching error arose within the church, and it's tearing me up."

"You are right, I do not know how you feel," he tenderly said. "But God does. And so does that man I told you about, as well as many, many others who have learned the same thing as you have. So, you are certainly not alone. By the way, that man I told you about became the great apostle Paul."

His words consoled me. And how I needed it!

"Gary, if we linger any longer at the table Mrs. Babbitt will have us washing dishes. I propose we move on to my study room."

"For such an incredible pizza, I'd be glad to help with the clean-up," I sincerely replied as I looked at Mrs. Babbitt.

"And have Mr. Babbitt break my dishes?" she humorously quipped. She picked up the pizza spatula, and, with several short swishes at us, said insistently, "Shew, shew, shew. You two scoot out of here."

As we walked through the living room and into his study, he explained to me, "I think you would want to see what the Bible says regarding what the church is to do with heretics and apostates, and I would feel guilty if I did not show it to you."

"Mr. Babbitt, just what exactly are heretics and apostates?"

He explained. "A heretic is one who differs from an established church doctrine. And an apostate is one who falls away from his church by either quitting the church or by becoming a heretic."

"And since some people do get that way," I reasoned, "then God will tell us what the church is to do with them?"

"Yes," he said as we both settled into chairs at his desk. "And it is crucial to remember that it is *God* who tells *us* what to do. It is not our place to tell God what we want and then insist upon Him to bend to our changes in His laws. He is God; we are but His creation. He is the Master; we are His servants. It is His church to direct, not ours."

"Of course," I whole-heartedly agreed as I remembered the last warning of the Bible.[3]

Pushing his Bible to me across his large wooden desk, he said, "Then, find for us Titus 3:10."

My frequent reading in the Bible enabled me to know the order of the 27 books of the New Testament. Quickly locating the verse, I read aloud.

> *A man that is a heretic after the first and second admonition reject.*

"So, what does God charge the church to do with a heretic?" Mr. Babbitt asked.

"He tells the church to *reject* them," I answered. "And that's all? Only reject them?"

"Yes. That is the maximum punishment allowed by God."

"Just a second Mr. Babbitt, I seem to remember...." My voice faded as I reached in the back pocket of my blue-jeans for a folded up sheet of notebook paper of the notes I took while reading those books on the Inquisition. "Well, how about that!"

"How about what?" Mr. Babbitt asked, leaning toward his desk.

Without lifting my head from the paper, I answered, "The *Catholic Encyclopedia* quotes Peter Canter, described as 'the most learned men of his time (12th century)' saying, 'although the Apostle said, a man that is a heretic after the third admonition, avoid, he certainly did not say, kill him.'"[4]

"So, the most learned Catholic of the 12th century agrees with your conclusion," Mr. Babbitt observed. "And why not? What God writes in Titus 3:10 is so easy to understand. Did you write down any other similar quotations?"

"Let's see." I quickly scanned my notes. "At the beginning of the article, it mentioned a lot of fellows—and they sure had strange names—that were against force and killing. Do you want me to read it?"

"Indeed." He leaned further over his desk and set both forearms upon it.

"Okay. The encyclopedia says Paul 'deemed exclusion from the communion of the Church sufficient (1 Timothy 1:20; Titus 3:10).'"[5]

Mr. Babbitt interrupted, "That's rather significant. The *Catholic Encyclopedia* itself acknowledges that God, through the apostle, taught that all that was needed was for the church to excommunicate heretics."

He motioned with his hand for me to continue.

"Now here comes the weird names. Tert...ul...lian," I stammered.

"That's Ter-**tul**-li-an," he interjected in a helpful, but non-belittling manner.

I resumed, "'Tertullian lays down the rule...the acceptance of religion was a matter of free will, not of compulsion.'[6] Here's another: Origen explained that, in contrast to the Old Testament, Christians 'were no longer at liberty to kill their enemies or to burn and stone violators of the Christian Law.'[7] Also, St. Cyprian added, 'excommunication replaces the death of the body' [as practiced in the Old Testament].[8] Lactantius wrote, 'Religion, being a matter of the will, it cannot be forced on anyone; in this matter it is better to employ words than blows. Of what use is cruelty? What has the rack to do with piety?....It is true that it (religion) must be protected, but by dying for it, not by killing others; by long-suffering, not by violence; by faith, not by crime.'[9] St. Augustine, 'almost in the name of the Western Church, says: "we wish them corrected, not put to death; we desire the triumph of (ecclesiastical) discipline, not the death penalties that they deserve."'[10] 'St. John Chrysostom says substantially the same in the name of the Eastern Church: "To consign a heretic to death is to commit an offense beyond atonement"; and in the next chapter he says that God forbids their execution.'[11] And here's one from Vacandard, 'Most of the early Fathers, St. John Chrysostom, St. Martin, St. Ambrose, St. Augustine, and many others, protested strongly in the name of Christian charity against the infliction of the death penalty upon heretics.'"[12]

When I finished, Mr. Babbitt, without breaking eye-contact, gradually leaned back in his chair and spoke slowly. "So, all the early Church Fathers taught what the Bible teaches: exclusion from the fellowship is the extent of punishment."

"Yeah. They even *opposed* force and killings. The Inquisition was wrong according these men."

"Gary, I see something else. In addition to all the other evidences you have already learned that shows the papacy to be a man-made invention, you just unearthed another one."

"I have?" This time, it was I who fell to the back of my chair. "Okay, give me a hint. What did I discover?"

He explained. "Those men with those 'strange names' are what the Catholic Church, and others, call Church Fathers—stand-out leaders, scholars, and writers in the early centuries of the church. Even that last quote you read identified them as the Fathers. These men make up a major portion of the Catholic's Tradition."

"Yeah, I remember," I abruptly cut in as I again leaned forward on the desk. "Mr. Clay, my Catholic teacher, told me that Catholics use *all* of God's Word which consists of the Bible AND Tradition, whereas Protestants use only the Bible. He said that is why there are so many denominations. They do not have the pope to correctly interpret both, the Scriptures *and* the Oral Tradition."

"That's what you are *told*," he said as he jabbed the top of the desk with his index finger. "But look at what you discovered! All those popes during the centuries of the Inquisition taught and led Catholicism *CONTRARY to the Church Fathers, that is, Church Tradition, AND contrary to the Scriptures*! In other words, for centuries, a long succession of popes led the Catholic Church *away from* God into the most horrible Holocaust in human history!"

He went on. "If God really did lead the popes, then it might be understandable if one renegade pope began to lead the church into an inquisition if God quickly corrected him with the next pope and put a stop to it. But it is *not* understandable how God would lead the church through numerous popes and never correct them to stop the centuries of torturing, the burning of live people tried to stakes, and the horrific heart-ache of children, wives, husbands, and parents. No, the popes are not led by God; the popes are not led by Tradition; and the popes are not led by Scripture."

"Mr. Babbitt, that reminds me of something I read today in our Church historian's *Imprimatur* book." I looked at my notepaper. "Let's see...here it is. 'It is evident therefore, that neither reason, Christian tradition, nor the New Testament call for the infliction of the death penalty upon heretics.'"[13]

"Checkmate!" he said as he slapped his palm on the desk. "That's just what you heard me say. The popes were not led by God's Word at all. Neither Tradition nor Scriptures."

After a pause, he continued. "Taking this one step further, think about this. Since a heretic is one who differs from an established church doctrine, and since the established church doctrine, according to the Scriptures *and* Catholic Tradition, is *not* to torture and kill, then what does that make all these popes when they departed from the Church doctrine and issued decrees to torture and kill?"

"Wow!" I exclaimed, nearly shouting. "That makes all those popes heretics!"

Mr. Babbitt possessed tremendous reasoning ability, and some of it was rubbing off on me. He swept away the cobwebs of my mind from lack of use due to merely being told by the clergy what to believe, and replaced it with facts and the challenge to think for myself what those facts meant. And the facts are: (1) the Scriptures allow *only* excommunication, NOT torture and killing; (2) Tradition teaches *only* excommunication, and CONDEMNS torture and killing; and (3) popes, for several centuries, tortured and/or killed hundreds of thousands. Therefore, those facts mean: (1) God does *not* lead the popes; (2) God does *not* lead the church through the popes; (3) that long succession of popes were heretics; and, (4) for centuries, the church fell far away from God into deep religious and moral error of rebellion against God and barbaric torture and murder of men.

The true picture of the office of the pope focused sharper. Unestablished by God, mere men invented the papacy. *But*, I wondered, *when and how? Are there historical records about it?* So I asked. "Mr. Babbitt, since God did not create the papacy, do you know where I could read about when and how it began?"

"Well, you certainly would never find that in a Catholic book. And if you read about it in a non-Catholic book, the clergy would merely say, 'That's just a non-Catholic presenting false information.' However, in the top row of that bookshelf," he pointed to the one at my left by the window, "is the printed debate of a non-Catholic with a bishop of the Catholic Church. Actually, sometime after the debate, the esteemed bishop became an archbishop. One of the many things that non-Catholic presented answers your question. Now, the priceless thing about that debate is the opportunity to see how the highly qualified bishop responded. That is, did he refute the non-Catholic's information as faulty, or, did he struggle with weak dodges that did *not* refute the information? So, the response of the bishop would indicate which position is correct."

"Mr. Babbitt, could I…."

"Yes, you may borrow it," he cut me off as he stretched a big smile.

We arose, retrieved the book, and exchanged parting words.

After I hopped into Ol' Blue, I found the title page and read, *A Debate on the Roman Catholic Religion between Alexander Campbell and the RT. Rev. John B. Purcell.* "Look at this! This is the debate my priest mentioned! And he told me Bishop Purcell thoroughly defeated Mr. Campbell. But, why would Mr. Babbitt, big smile and all, be glad for me to read it?"

I would soon find out.

CHAPTER 23
FOOTBALL FINALE

The countryside scrolled across the window of our chartered bus as we patiently traveled the 140 miles to northwest Oklahoma for our final football game. My excitement soared, yet, during the past four weeks football slipped to second place in favor of something else much more important—the pursuit of religious truth.

An unusual quietness among close friends permeated the bus. Coach Webb ordered it so. "Think about the game. Think about your plays. Think about what got you here." Whispers mixed with the soft hum of large tires whisking over pavement created a soothing mood for meditation a yogic would crave.

After wishing we could replay the fluked games with El Reno, Altus, and Northeast, I reflected upon the following three games. Classen came ranked 9th in state and with a loaded backfield, one of whom went on to play in the NFL. Even though they gained 68 yards on one run, our stalwart defense allowed only 58 additional rushing yards for the game. Jim Nance's two interceptions in the fourth quarter and our 33 points proved more than enough to earn the newspaper article's headline: "West Ices Classen."[1] The victory, however, included an infamous play which we laughed at only *after* the victory. Cole always served as the lone, backfield blocker for my punts. During the game, Coach Webb tried another at that position. An opponent broke through, and my new, untrained, inexperienced blocker back-peddled—the position's taboo—and backed his seat right into the burst of my foot with the ball still intact! No one ever replaced Cole again.

My thoughts moved on to the following week when we faced the state's 10th ranked team on their home field. Star Spencer, in the first half, fought every bit like their school mascot—a Bobcat. Even our defense had a costly slip. After booting the punt of my life from our side of the field to their two, in their second play, their running-back broke loose for a 90 yard touchdown. My ticker-tape hero status of a whole two minutes abruptly ended in naught. In the second half, the fans in the stands beheld a coach-incited attack of war. Our offense added three touchdowns to the two of the first half, and our smothering defense shut them down—allowing only thirteen plays, and a mere thirteen yards. Like they say, "Offense wins games, but defense wins championships." Across the top of *The Daily Oklahoman*, the large, bold letters read: "West Charges to Capital [Conference] Crown."[2]

The newsreel in my mind rolled on to last week's game—Chickasha. Known as a bull of a rushing offense, in this game, it was our quarterback who lit up the scoreboard. In the first quarter, Jason, on a screen-pass to his left at our 43 yard line, hit Bill Chaney, who, led by the blocking of Nance, punched his way to open field. The two dashed toward the end-zone, where, at the five yard line, crouched two Chickasha tacklers. Chaney positioned himself behind Nance. The defenders converged. Nance split them like a bowling ball between two pins. Chaney scored. Chickasha then scored next, but that was all they got. PCW notched the last four touchdowns, three by Jason's passes in his 210 yard aerial attack. The newspaper announced: "Patriots Ramble By Chicks, 34-7."[3]

Like Coach Webb said, "Think about what got you here." Our first three and last three games established how good we were; the middle three hammered the old adage into our heads that even the best of teams get beat if not focused. And, to keep our final ranking in the top ten, we needed both reminders for the game that night. Woodward, a strong team themselves, emotionally dedicated the game to one of their teammates who had died. Fighting bears in their own den after we were wearied by travel rated somewhere in the top five things not to do.

The game measured up to its hype as Woodward seemed to put their entire season into this final game. After the dust settled and the torn up turf lay still, the newspaper writer, in part, wrote:

Putnam City West Edges Woodward
Putnam City West staved off never-say-die Woodward in the last minutes Friday night to preserve a 35-29 triumph over the Boomers.[4]

The ride home was sweet. Inside the close confines of the bus, heart-knit friends rocked and rolled as we gloried in our hard-fought victory, and, in spite of our costly miscues, our successful season. Even the press and other coaches acknowledged our remarkable accomplishment against so many ranked teams by awarding Coach Webb as the state's Coach of the Year.

"Cole," I raised my voice and turned my head toward him from the pair of bucket seats we shared so he could hear me above our teammates' celebrating chatter, "just think, we are the Capital Conference Champions."

"And," he added, "we played four teams of the state's top ten. We defeated three, and lost to the number two team on a quirky play."

"Yeah, if we would have kept our heads on for that play and focused on the games before and after Altus, instead of on Altus, we would be first or second in state."

"But, seventh isn't too shabby."

"Not at all."

Somewhere on that long, dark, deserted highway, Coach Webb rose, flipped on the passenger lights, and addressed his team. "Fellows, after our third loss, I told you that 3 and 3 is not where we ought to be. I left it up to you to make the decision of either learning from our mistakes, make the corrections, and better ourselves, or, just stay the way we were, give up, and keep losing. Men, you made the right decision, and I, the coaching staff, your parents, your school's students, teachers, and administration, and your community admire you for it.

"Now, listen up. In your life you will encounter similar challenges that will likewise test who you are and will force you to make the same decision of either making corrections or keep losing. The final four games have taught you what the human will can do. So stick with what you have learned, champions!"

After the deafening cheers finally tapered off and the lights dimmed, I turned to the window and stared into the blackness of the night. *Coach, I'm already facing a monster challenge—no doubt the*

146

most important one of my entire life. I sighed. *My previous belief in the God-created office of the pope has been rattled by the Scriptures and by the life-style of centuries of popes. I know that somehow the earlier Church made a big mistake, but I can't change the Roman Catholic Church, and I'm certainly not going to quit the one, true, Church. Yet, I can't just ignore it. I gotta do* **something***.*

CHAPTER 24
"ONWARD CHRISTIAN SOLDIERS"?

"**O**UCH!**" As I quickly raised my hand from my lap to answer the question Mrs. Stowels posed to her psychology class, the back of my hand whacked—loud bang included—the underside of one of the room-length tables of the multilevel, theater-shaped classroom. Barry, my good friend (and future college roommate for a year) sat at my left struggling to suppress his laughter. I didn't get to answer the question to impress the teacher, but I did get the attention of the class—attention I'd rather not had.

In a few minutes the bell rang, third hour class ended, and lunch began. Adjacent to the cafeteria, our room boasted the honor of "best room" of that hour as it positioned us first in line. Yet, for the next four weeks, that privilege meant very little. Trying to shed some weight for track season, bypassing all that hot, steamy food—yes, even school food—on a harsh eating restriction proved most difficult. Since I would be eating so very little, I justified myself by thinking that what I *did* eat had better taste good. So, I took what became the norm for my diet's duration: a half-pint of chocolate milk and a huge freshly made cinnamon roll. It's a wonder I didn't die.

Taking a seat at one of the tables, I eyed my precious delicacies as a vulture descending upon its prize. I ate slowly. That way it tricked me into thinking I ate a lot. Other students arrived with trays full of food. I didn't look. My table filled up with other athletes who joked as always and verbally jabbed one another. As Nance and Thomas (we called each other by last names) joined us, I noticed their discussion centered upon their class on World History.

"For once, class kept me awake. Those Crusades amaze me!" Nance said as he squeezed a puddle of mustard onto his hamburger.

Thomas responded, "Yeah. So much of Europe going to battle with swords, shields, and archery to regain the Holy Lands."

Nance, just before pushing his mustard-messy hamburger into his face, added, "And to fight in a Christian cause, too."

"But," Thomas confessed, as he handed Nance a much needed napkin "the Church fighting a physical, blood-shedding war sounds strange, though."

My interest topped-out. "Hey you two scholars, what's this crusade thing you're jabbering about?"

Thomas answered (Nance's mouth still bulged), "Beginning in the 11th century, the pope directed the Church in Europe into war against the Turks in order to regain possession of Jerusalem and the Holy Land."

"Wow! Sounds like the real original World War," I replied, watching Nance force a big swallow. "Hey, your food is not going to run away. Don't take such big bites!"

"Yes, momma," Nance said with a big grin, and then took a bite bigger than the first.

"Sorry guys. The side-show is too much for me. Gotta go." Before Nance could do anything—and he couldn't *say* anything—I set my empty dish and milk carton on his tray, lobbed him a wink, and departed in haste.

Crusades, I thought as I walked down the hall to my locker. *The pope had the Church go into a military war? Sounds like something I ought to look up in the Catholic Encyclopedia.*

After school, I bee-lined straight to the Bethany Nazarene College less than four miles away. As I walked among the college students, I strolled through campus like I belonged there. In the library, I retrieved volume four, found a table, and located the article "Crusades." Wanting to also read what Schaff reported, I hoped for a short article. No such luck. Ninety-six pages.

With this much history to tell, I reasoned, *the Crusades must have been quite a lengthy and massive war.* My assumption was correct. However, I never could have pre-assumed what I was about to discover.

The first sentence of the article echoed what Randy told me. "The Crusades were expeditions undertaken, in fulfillment of a solemn vow, to deliver the Holy Places from Mohammedan tyranny."[1]

The article's introduction continued.

> The idea of the crusade corresponds to a political conception which was realized in Christendom only from the eleventh to the fifteenth century; this supposes a union of all peoples and sovereigns under the direction of the popes. All crusades were announced by preaching. After pronouncing a solemn vow, each warrior received a cross from the hands of the pope or his legates, and was thenceforth considered a soldier of the Church. Crusaders were also granted indulgences and temporal privileges, such as exemption from civil jurisdiction, inviolability of persons or lands, etc. Of all these wars undertaken in the name of Christendom, the most important were the Eastern Crusades, which are the only ones treated in this article.[2]

Just as Nance and Thomas said, I thought, shaking my head, *the popes sent the Church into physical, blood-shedding, life-taking wars.* And there were even more Crusades in addition to those against the Mohammedans, including Crusades against pagans, heretics, the excommunicated, the Moors of Spain, Prussia, Lithuania, the Albigenses of southern France, and John Lackland of England.[3]

The Crusades were certainly no small spat! They involved numerous battles throughout Europe and to its east. And its duration is unbelievable! Five-hundred, seventy-four years![4] I'm glad World War II wasn't that long.

I kept on reading, finding further confirmation of the bloody Crusades to be the creation of the popes.

> The idea of the crusade is chiefly attributed to Pope Urban II (1095)...[5]

> Urban II convoked a council at Clermont-Ferrand, in Auvergne. It was attended by fourteen archbishops, 250 bishops, and 400 abbots; moreover a great number of knights and men of all conditions came and encamped on

the plain of Chantoin, to the east of Clermont, 18-28 November, 1095. On 27 November, the pope himself addressed the assembled multitudes, exhorting them to go forth and rescue the Holy Sepulchre. Amid wonderful enthusiasm and cries of "God wills it!" all rushed towards the pontiff to pledge themselves by vow to depart for the Holy Land and receive the cross of red material to be worn on the shoulder. At the same time the pope sent letters to all Christian nations, and the movement made rapid headway throughout Europe.[6]

The history of the Crusades is therefore intimately connected with that of the popes and the Church. These Holy Wars were essentially a papal enterprise.[7]

"Why am I not surprised?" I closed my eyes and rested my forehead in my hands as I leaned on the table and thought it through. *These men in this man-made office embarrassed the Church and God again! The Scripture is clear and simple:* **God does not use the Church for physical war!** *Peter used his sword to strike at the men who came to harm Jesus, but Jesus stopped Peter's physical attack and told him,* "**Put up again thy sword into his place.**"*[8] But, did those popes do that? No. They did the exact opposite, and that, to an enormous scale for almost 600 years. Did they obey Jesus? No. Was Jesus leading them? No. Were they the Vicars of Christ? Certainly not! Also, when Jesus stood on trial before Pilate, He firmly declared,* "My kingdom is not of this world: if my kingdom were of this world, then would my servants fight, that I should not be delivered to the Jews."*[9] Anybody can understand that. Jesus' kingdom is not a physical kingdom, it's a* **spiritual** *kingdom. While physical kingdoms fight physically, His spiritual kingdom does* **not**. *Even if it was for the purpose of delivering Jesus from the Jews, or, for any lesser purpose, like, delivering the Jews' Holy Land from the Turks. Once again, these popes in this man-made office are their own worst enemy. Their anti-God activities prove themselves and that office void of the work and approval of God.*

As I returned to the article, the more I read, the more glaring the evidence for the man-made, without-God papacy. Paragraph after paragraph, page after page, the picture of the Crusades was painted before me with brushstrokes of: "plundered as they went along and murdered the Jews";[10] "bloody conflicts";[11] "took Antioch by storm";[12] "Christians entered Jerusalem from all sides and slew its inhabitants regardless of age or sex";[13] "a fleet of five galleys traversed the Red Sea for a whole year, ravaging the coasts";[14] "took the Balkan passes by assault";[15] "missile-hurling machines, worked by powerful machinery, were used by the crusaders to demolish the walls";[16] "had the Mohammedans hostages put to death";[17] and conducted numerous sieges of cities.

As if my battered head had not had enough, Schaff's *History of the Christian Church* presented vivid summaries of various Crusades.

> The culmination of the First Crusade was the fall of Jerusalem, July 15, 1099....The scenes of carnage which followed belong to the many dark pages of Jerusalem's history and showed how, in the quality of mercy, the crusading knight was far below the ideal of Christian perfection. The streets were choked with the bodies of the slain. The Jews were burnt with their synagogues. The greatest slaughter was in the temple enclosure. With an exaggeration which can hardly be credited, but without a twinge of regret or a syllable of excuse, it is related that the blood of the massacred in the temple area reached to the very knees and bridles of the horses. "Such a slaughter of the pagans had never been seen or heard of. The number none but God knew."...The religion of the Middle Ages combined self-denying asceticism with heartless cruelty to infidels, Jews, and heretics. "They cut down with the sword," said William of Tyre, "every one whom they found in Jerusalem, and spared no one. The victors were covered with blood from head to foot."[18]

> One of his [Becket, who occupied the chancellorship for seven years (1155-1162)] eulogists, Edward Grim, reports to his credit: "Who can recount the carnage, the desolation, which he made at the head of a strong body of

soldiers? He attacked castles, razed towns and cities to the ground, burned down houses and farms without a touch of pity, and never showed the slightest mercy to any one who rose in insurrection against his master's authority." Such cruelty was quite compatible with mediaeval conceptions of piety and charity, as the history of the crusades shows.[19]

And regarding one of the many Crusades launched upon people other than the Turks, the Crusade against the Albigenses served as a sickening sample.

>...the papal legate, Arnold of Citeaux, refused to check its march. Béziers was stormed and horrible scenes followed. The wild soldiery heeded well the legate's command, "Fell all to the ground. The Lord knows His own." Neither age nor sex was spared. Church walls interposed no protection and seven thousand were put to death in St. Magdalen's church alone. Nearly twenty thousand were put to the sword. According to the reports of the papal legates, Milo and Arnold, the "divine vengeance raged wonderfully against the city...Ours spared neither sex nor condition. The whole city was sacked, and the slaughter was very great."...Dread had taken hold of the country, and village after village was abandoned by the fleeing inhabitants...The war continued, and its atrocities, if possible, increased. New recruits appeared in response to fresh papal appeals, among them six thousand Germans. At the stronghold of Minerve, one hundred and forty of the Albigensian Perfect were put to death in the flames. The ears, noses, and lips of prisoners were cut off.[20]

As I closed the book and leaned back in the chair, I gazed at that book which contained this ghastly secret of the popes, and whispered to myself, "And I thought the Inquisition was bad. This dwarfs it!"

My mind staggered beneath the load of the incredible information I just absorbed. Merely by the wishes of the popes, the Church, for a long drawn-out 574 years, besieged, plundered, ravaged, burned, and murdered people—hundreds of thousands of them—at the command to "fell all to the ground." With heartless cruelty and without the slightest mercy, the Church slew regardless of age or sex, killed people who took the protection of sanctuary within Church walls, and put hostages to death, until the streets were choked with dead bodies. It sounded like a ridiculously exaggerated movie made for warped minds desirous of truckloads of blood and guts in every scene. But this was *true*. It *really* happened! And it was the *popes* who led the Church into this ungodly monstrosity! All because they merely wanted access to visit the land that God gave to the Jews until the time the Church came. But, Jesus did *not* want the Church to slaughter men, sending them to the devil in hell; He wants the Church to *save* men, bringing them to Him in heaven. His commands were *not* for the Church to possess the old Holy Land; His commands were for the Church to proclaim the new Holy Word.[21] It is just as a notable, think-for-himself Catholic who lived during the Crusades boldly declared.

> Humbert de Romanis, general of the Dominicans, in making out a list of matters to be handled at the Council of Lyons, 1274, felt obliged to refute no less than seven objections to the Crusades. They were such as these. It was contrary to the precepts of the New Testament to advance religion by the sword; Christians may defend themselves, but have no right to invade the lands of another; it is wrong to shed the blood of unbelievers and Saracens; and the disasters of the Crusades proved they were contrary to the will of God.[22]

My jaw clenched. *The Crusades a work of God? No way! But, a work of mere men in a man-made office? Yes!*

Yet, not only did the Church inflict casualties, they, too, I read, sustained loss. An enormous loss. "It is computed that nearly two million Christians lost their lives during the crusades."[23] "Two million?!" I gasped. *And we're supposed to believe that God ordered, or even allowed the leader of the Church to have His people suffer such horrific casualties?* I knew, completely opposite of that, when God ordered His leader, Joshua, to take the Holy Land, His people, on a *real* God-sent 'crusade' against *real* wicked people, suffered minimal casualties, if any at all![24] Why? *"Because the Lord God of*

Israel fought for Israel."[25] Unmistakably, God didn't fight for the popes because He did not order it. The popes acted on their own!

Furthermore, of all things, the six centuries of the Crusades ended up a miserable failure!

> The Crusades failed in three respects. The Holy Land was not won. The advance of Islam was not permanently checked. The schism [of the Church] between the East and the West was not healed. These were the primary objects of the Crusades.[26]

God lost?! I furiously struck back. *I'm supposed to believe that God lost?! The same God who led Joshua and the Israelites on an easy walk-through-the-park capture of the Holy Land lost with the popes and the Church?! Yeah, right! I have eyes; I can see.* I knew the Israelites won because their 'crusade' was given to them by God through His leader, Joshua,[27] and God fought for them. But the Church's Crusade lost because it was not given to them by God through the pope, and God did not fight for them. The entire ordeal that wasted two million Christians and at least that many non-Christians, all of which gained absolutely nothing for the Church during almost 600 years under the leadership of 80 popes positively proves: God did not establish the office of the pope, and He does not lead the Church through them. Rather, the papacy was somehow later added to the Church by men. But, when and how?

And then I remembered the book Mr. Babbitt loaned me, in which, he said, lies the answer.

CHAPTER 25
CLASH OF THE TITANS

The unmistakable aroma of warm homemade bread, hot pumpkin pie, and steaming baked turkey, rolled down the halls and spread into every corner of every room in our house. No other meal matched this one. After waiting 364 days, Thanksgiving finally arrived again.

Although Mom created her usual masterpiece of the cookbook-look array of food, artistically designed and bountifully loaded upon plates and bowls laid across the candle-enhanced serving table, my plate of China contained only a meager portion.

Grandma noticed. "Why, you're not eating enough to feed a bird." Grandma lived in Enid, sixty miles north. Dad drove to his childhood hometown to pick her up the day before. The perfect image of a grandmother, she stood five feet tall on a small frame. Always adorned in long and, what seemed to a teenager's mind, old-fashion dresses, she wore wire-rimmed glasses and curled her short gray hair but then stuffed it under a thread-thin, hair-color-matching net. Widowed twenty-three years ago when Dad was a high-school senior, she lived alone in a small, wooden house with a large front porch just across the street from her Baptist Church.

Grandma was right. I hadn't put much on my plate, but it was intentional.

"I'm trying to lose weight, Grandma."

"Well heavens be, Gary, what in land's sake for? There's not a pinch of fat on you!" she declared while squeezing a spot on my waist between her thumb and forefinger.

"Track season begins in a couple months," I began to explain while taking a place next to her. "Last year I ran the short sprints, Grandma, but this year I'm taking on the half-mile and mile races."

"And you have to turn into a beanpole to do that?" She disapproved in a grandmotherly way. Years earlier, whenever I would hop onto her lap, she'd always animatedly say, "Do you have rocks in your pockets? You're heavier and have grown so much since last time." To her, and she was right, this was the time for a young man to grow.

"It's just for one month, Grandma," I said as I shrugged my shoulders and tried to make it sound as if it was no big deal. "I figure I can run faster if I don't have to carry an extra 15 pounds or so for that long of distance." By the sour look on her face, I knew the occupation of a persuasive lawyer was not in my future.

After the family's highlight meal of the year, and after resolving to never again be on a diet on Thanksgiving Day, I went to my bedroom, flopped upon the bed, and waited for the televised Dallas Cowboys football game. As my day-dreaming thoughts jumped from football, to track, to my diet, to my hunger, to agony, to eternal agony, to religion, I remembered the book Mr. Babbitt loaned me. Making a long stretch to my desk, my fingertips, just reaching the corner of the book, pulled it closer until I could grab it without getting up.

"You lazy bum," I scolded myself, "and you're running the mile?"

The title captivated me: *A Debate Over the Roman Catholic Religion.* I hoped Bishop Purcell presented some explanation that would make all this "pope-problem" of the past few weeks just a bad dream, or should I say, nightmare.

The Catholic champion came decorated with high qualifications, evidently the best in America. He held professorship at St. Mary's Seminary and then advanced to its presidency until honored with the bishopric of Cincinnati. Later, when elevated to archbishop, he multiplied the only church in the city to forty, established a college, a seminary, and a charitable institution, all of which ensured half of the residents of Cincinnati as Catholic. Regarded as the second most influential clergyman of the Catholic hierarchy in America, Bishop Purcell stood as my knight in shining armor.

However, his opponent was no slouch either. Described as a careful student of New Testament Greek, an outstanding educator, editor, and author, Alexander Campbell founded Bethany College in West Virginia, published two journals for a combined forty-two years, wrote several books, published a translation of the New

Testament, addressed the United States Congress upon their dismissal of a session in order to hear him preach, and packed all church buildings wherever he spoke. When I read that all religious bodies in the United States had been influenced by this man because he almost single-handedly forced men to re-examine cherished traditions to see if they conformed to the truth of God, I knew this man did his homework and would press Bishop Purcell with his research. *But, hey! That's exactly what I want. No Catholic is going to question a bishop's lecture on the origin of the pope, but how will it hold up when confronted by this Campbell fellow?*

The book contained a gargantuan 360 pages, and since the entire debate involved other issues in addition to the question of the origin of the pope, Mr. Babbitt had referred me to the blank page at the front of the book upon which he compiled an index of the various issues debated. Beside each issue he listed the page number whenever either man discussed it. This enabled me to find their discussions on the origin of the pope much faster than reading the entire book, which I did not particularly savor.

With the focused concentration of a brain surgeon, I read Campbell's first presentation on the origin of the pope. Campbell's evidence, that of an authentic Catholic historian named Du Pin—obviously kept from the eyes and ears of today's Catholics—hit like the Hiroshima bomb and destroyed any hope of survivors to the claim that the Catholic Church has always had a pope, the universal bishop.

> I have examined [referring to his speech up to this point] the proceedings of all the councils of the first six centuries, of which I find about 170, promulgating [issuing] all about 1400 canons. I have read and examined the twenty creeds of the fourth century with all their emendations [revisions] down to the close of the sixth; and I affirm, without the fear of contradiction, that there is not in all these a single vestige [trace] of the existence of a pope or a universal head of the church down to the time of Gregory the great, or John the Faster of Constantinople. [588 A.D.]

I shall now proceed to show from the same learned historian [the Catholic, Du Pin] when this idea began to be divulged. And be it *emphatically observed* that the title of pope in this peculiar and exclusive sense was first assumed by the patriarch of Constantinople [John], and [dis]approved by the patriarch of Rome [Gregory]. Du Pin says in his life of Gregory, chapter 1, "He did often rigorously oppose the title of universal patriarch, which the patriarchs of Constantinople assumed to themselves." Indeed he calls the title, "proud, blasphemous, anti-christian, diabolical," and says, the bishops of Rome refused to take this title upon them "lest they should seem to encroach upon the rights of other bishops." But the following document or remonstrance against the title shows what a novelty the idea of a universal head, father, or pope was even at Rome, A.D. 588.[2]

Campbell then quoted Du Pin, the Catholic historian.

"St. Gregory does not only oppose this title in the patriarch of Constantinople, but maintains also, that it cannot agree to any other bishop, and that the bishop of Rome neither ought, nor can assume it.... [Peter] was not called universal apostle. That the title of universal bishop is against the rules of the gospel [the Scriptures], and the appointment of the canons [the laws formulated at the Church councils]: that there cannot be a universal bishop."[2]

Campbell then resumed his comments.

But at this time [near the end of the 6th century] the patriarchs of Constantinople [John] and Rome [Gregory] were contending for the supremacy [of the church], and while it appeared to Gregory that his rival of the east was likely to process the title, he [Gregory] saw in it, everything anti-Christian and profane. When a new dynasty, however ascended the [Emperor's] throne and offered the title to a Roman bishop, it [the title of universal patriarch] lost all its blasphemy and impiety, and we [then] find the

successor of Gregory can wear the title of universal patriarch when tendered him by Phocas [the new Emperor],
without the least scrupulosity.

It is then a fact worthy of much consideration in this discussion, that John, bishop of Constantinople, first assumed the title of universal head of the whole Christian
church, and that the bishop of Rome [Gregory] did in that
case oppose it as anti-scriptural and anti-christian.

Concerning the reputation of St. Gregory, I need not be
profuse. Of the Gregories he is deservedly called the
Great. Renowned in history as the one who stamped his
own image on the Roman world for a period of five hundred years, yet he could not brook the idea of a pope, especially when about to be bestowed on his rival at Constantinople.

St. Gregory, be it remembered, says Du Pin, did not only
oppose the title in the case of John the Faster, as proud,
heretical, blasphemous, &c., but could not agree to its being assumed by any other bishop; he affirmed that the
bishops of Rome ought not, dare not, cannot assume this
pompous and arrogant title.

Thus stood matters as respects a supreme head up to within 14 years of the close of the 6th century.[3]

Distressed, I wanted to tear out the page and burn it. But I would
only be reacting dishonestly with the established and unchangeable
facts of history. What had happened, happened. I dropped the book
to my chest and stared at the ceiling.

Wow! I thought with astonishment. *No universal bishop until at
least 588 A.D.! And when the first one finally arose, it was only the
result of a power struggle between the two bishops of the two most
important cities of the day.* Unfortunately, a *Catholic* historian
proved my earlier suspicions correct: the office of the pope was created by men, NOT God; and it was created *centuries after* the

Church began. Even Gregory, the bishop of Rome, who would have been the pope if there was a pope, emphatically denied the Church to have a universal bishop over the universal Church. So, Gregory, one of the four most prominent patriarchs of the Church in that day, lets us know **there was no universal bishop in the Church from its beginning unto at least 588 A.D.!**

Then, remembering Mr. Babbitt's advice to observe how Bishop Purcell responded, I made use of his index to read every exchange of both men on this topic. Disappointed, because he was the Catholic champion, but not surprised because even the best cannot overturn the facts of history, Bishop Purcell's feeble attempts to reply bounced away like pebbles tossed at a brick wall.

He first asserted Du Pin was not an authentic historian.[4] Of course, if what Du Pin said cannot be refuted, then try to discredit the author; after all, this is what the Pharisees tried to do with the miracles of Jesus.[5] But the bishop's diversion went nowhere. Campbell read from the front of Du Pin's book the endorsements of notable and scholarly Catholics, the theological Doctors of Sorbonne, which included statements as: this book "never…lays down simple conjectures in place of demonstrative proofs"; "I find nothing to hinder its being printed"; and, "we have found nothing therein contrary to the Catholic faith, or to good manners."[6] In other words, they found nothing wrong with Du Pin's facts. Campbell added that the book was certified by the guardians of the Catholic press.[7] Campbell also pointed out that the bishop of Bardstown admitted Du Pin to be an "authentic historian."[8] Even Bishop Purcell conceded, "I will remark that I consider Du Pin a learned man. I would even select him as a splendid illustration of the strength imparted to the human intellect by the Catholic intellectual discipline. He was truly a prodigy of learning and of precision of style."[9] Campbell pointed out that "other historians record the same fact"[10] as Du Pin had stated which confirmed Du Pin's historical report even more. Bishop Purcell could do no more than toss a mere pebble at this brick wall, but this pebble left not even a dent. Everything established Du Pin to be an authoritative historian, and, thus confirming, in 606 A.D., Boniface III became the very first pope, ever!

The bishop next attempted to discredit Du Pin as a bad Catholic.[11] However, Campbell pointed out that Du Pin was buried in the Catholic Church in consecrated ground, which Bishop Purcell himself, only two or three months earlier, insisted as proof of a man's good Catholic standing.[12] Besides, as Campbell correctly mentioned,[13] even if Du Pin was a bad Catholic, that would have nothing to do with his ability as an authentic historian to report the facts of history. Another pebble fell harmlessly to the ground.

Bishop Purcell was running out of pebbles. He even resorted to the unprovable make-believe: "...they *may* have...,"[14] "...they *might* have been...,"[15] "...the most natural *supposition*."[16] Also, in all of what the bishop said, I noticed he never, as in never-ever, attempted to discredit Du Pin's report of Gregory's denouncement of the existence of a universal bishop in the Church up to his day. Campbell noticed it too, and said, "Can he [Purcell] prove, or has he proved him [Du Pin] unfaithful in stating a single historical fact? Not one."[17] No, the Catholic champion would not discredit Du Pin's facts of history because he *could not*. He could not falsify Gregory's statement because, as Campbell pointed out, "other historians record the same fact."[18] It would have been as foolish for the bishop to deny those statements of Gregory as to have denied all the historians' records of Columbus sailing to the American continents. The bishop knew that; he knew he could not deny the documents of history. Plain and simple: there was no universal bishop in the Church until Gregory's successor, Boniface III, at the very beginning of the 7th century. Historians knew it. Those who read church history knew it.

And now I knew it.

With the book closed and resting on the bed at my side, I laid motionless and again stared at the ceiling. But I didn't see it; my mind was too deep in thought. Angry and confused thoughts. *Why is the clergy keeping all this from us? Could it be that much of the clergy doesn't even know about it themselves? After all, at one time they had all been kept-in-the-dark laity like us, so why should the upper hierarchy tell them after they are ordained and ruin a "good" thing? Has the lower clergy, as well as the laity, assumed everything is okay just because everybody else is assuming everything is okay? Are we just a bunch of mindless dominoes doing what the previous dominoes have done since 606 A.D.?*

I then reflected upon earlier truths I uncovered. First, the papacy was *not* begun with Jesus' statement to Peter in Matthew 16:18. Instead, Peter's name means a small rock and is masculine in gender, but the rock upon which Jesus built the church means a *massive, foundational rock* and is *feminine* in gender. Jesus' specific choice of words makes it *impossible* that the two are the same. In this way Jesus confirmed that Peter was *not* the rock upon which Jesus would build his church, but the rock was rather the fact that Jesus, as Peter just confessed, was truly the Son of God.

Also, I recalled, there are many Scriptures that show Peter was *not* the head of the church.[19]

As I put together all I had discovered the previous few weeks, the pieces began to fall together. The clergy's glamorous picture painted over the papacy dissolved, and for the first time I now beheld the real picture. God did not establish the universal bishop—the pope; *men did*. It evolved from a power-struggle between men, resulting in the first pope in 606 A.D. No wonder then, there had been all those wicked popes living a life of debauchery—God wasn't with them at all; they weren't His; they were on their own. No wonder then, these man-made popes led the Church for centuries in the inhumane Inquisitions of barbaric tortures and ruthless murders of vast multitudes—the office of the pope was not of God, nor did He recognize it after men established it. They had no leadership from God; no guidance; no help. It is plain, they ruled as but mere men in a man-made position issuing man-made decisions because the Almighty, All-Sovereign God, if He had truly established the papacy, would not guide nor even allow the popes to take His precious Church down to such ungodly depths for so long a time.

I realized then why Mr. Babbitt was so willing to loan me the book. But why did my priest incorrectly think our bishop successfully upheld the doctrine of the papacy? Apparently, he believed it, not because he examined it himself, but because others in whom he trusted told him that falsehood. And it always happens: when enough of the others believe something, even the clergy swallows it as the truth. What a perfect trap of Satan! Of this snare, God warned, *"Prove all things."*[20]

Although convinced more than ever of the error of the office of the pope, my faithfulness and loyalty to the Catholic Church stood firm. I knew it started with Jesus and the apostles as told in the New Testament and stood unmovable as the one, true, apostolic Church of Jesus Christ. All denominations rebelled and fell away from the Church, beginning in mass proportions in the 1500s. *True, the papacy is man-made. Yet, that does not change the truth about the one, true Church to which I will steadfastly adhere.*

As I consoled myself, even then, crouched beyond my sight, lurked another monster.

CHAPTER 26
ABRACADABRA

I stepped up the concrete stairs leading to the upper section of the bleachers that rested upon the second floor of the school gym for my daily anticipated moment. The wooden bleachers remained folded like an accordion against the wall so as to provide a roomy area for the wrestling team to practice upon their new Columbia-blue mat.

A little physically spent from setting up hurdles and other equipment for my duties as the fifth-hour helper to the track coach, I routinely grabbed some rest before the grueling track practice. With a soothing smile and an easing exhale, I rolled out upon the absorbing yet dense mat. The large gym, in contrast to the loud ruckus bellowing from hundreds of spectators during basketball games, slept quietly in dormant lighting. I imagined myself floating upon a warm, blue lake at twilight, miles from anyone. Silly? Perhaps. But I needed rest of mind as well as body. In 20 minutes I would push myself in running multiple half-miles.

Yet, as much as I wanted to think about nothing, thoughts about the historical facts showing there to be no pope until 606 A.D. kept elbowing in. "But the list!" I finally recalled. "What about that list of popes I saw in the *Catholic Encyclopedia*? The names go back past 606 A.D. all the way to Peter!"

With a violent leg-thrust that threw me off of my back and onto my feet, I shuffle-footed down the stairs with my feet in a blur. I darted through the network of empty locker rooms and halls looking for the track coach. My eyes locked onto him just leaving the coaches' office.

"Coach Little," I called out.

"What's the excitement, Gary? Did one of the state's fastest milers get kicked off his team?"

"Coach, could I use the phone in the coaches' office?"

"Certainly," he replied as he turned to unlock the door. "Just make sure it's locked when you leave."

"Aren't you coming in?" I asked in puzzlement. Students were not to be in there without a coach, and that by invitation to a serious chewing-out.

"Gary, some guys can be trusted," he said with a wink and left.

As I timidly stepped into the hub of our athletic program, I thought, if sports was a religion this room would be our holy-room. Coaches design plays, evaluate our abilities, and brainstorm game plans. Everything begins and is sustained in this very room.

But, no time to dwell on that. What if one of the other coaches finds me in here? Oh boy!

On the second ring my call was answered. "Hello?"

"Mr. Babbitt, this is Gary."

"Aren't you supposed to be at school? Is something wrong?" he asked with a touch of concern in his voice.

"I *am* at school," I replied. "Do you know there is a list of popes that goes all the way back to Peter?"

"Yes," he answered as he fell back into to his usual calmness. "And you are probably wondering why the historical records reveal the absence of popes for the first 575 years or so."

"Yeah. Why?" I eagerly asked, forgetting about the danger of a coach walking in.

"Gary, I have a general understanding about that, but let me do some research and then we'll get together. Is that okay with you?"

"Certainly," I answered. I did not want to merely be told what to believe. That is what Catholicism shoveled on me. Now, I demanded proof and documentation and I wanted to see it for myself. Where I go for eternity is the most important thing to me.

As I stepped out of the room, big Coach Webb turned the corner at the end of the hallway and walked toward me.

Did he see me? I anxiously asked myself.

My heart beat faster. His huge frame blocked all the light behind him. He approached and said, "Gary, with all that weight loss, you're beginning to look like a wide-receiver." Then he disappeared into the office.

"Phew!"

FIVE DAYS LATER.

I entered the familiar glass doors of the library at the Bethany Nazarene College and spotted Mr. Babbitt. Dressed in gray slacks and a white, long-sleeve button-up shirt, he comfortably reclined in one of the half-dozen lounge chairs of the entry lobby. The previous day, he had called to suggest we meet Saturday at 8 AM when students—what few remained on campus during the weekend—would be slow to begin their homework, if, on their free-day, they did any at all.

"Good morning, Mr. Babbitt," I said high-spiritedly. I looked forward to his findings, and came to expect his thorough research of any subject.

"Good morning young Berean," he bounced back the greeting as he arose and extended his hand to shake mine.

I chuckled. "*Patriots*, Mr. Babbitt. We're the Putnam City West *Patriots*, not Bereans."

Now it was *he* who laughed. His expanded cheeks nearly pushed his eyes shut. "No, no. I am referring to Acts 17:10-11 where Apostle Paul described those in the city of Berea as noble because they '*searched the Scriptures daily*' to find out whether or not what they were being told was true. And that is precisely what you are doing."

My laughter mixed with his. But then I soberly explained my motivation. "I don't want to merely *assume* I'm okay with God, I want to *know* it. It scares me to think about being one of those at Judgment Day of whom Jesus warned—one of those who *thought* they were right with God, but were not!"

"That would be Matthew 7:21-23," he confirmed while nodding his head, and then proceeded, without a Bible, to quote it.

> *Not every one that says unto me, Lord, Lord, shall enter into the kingdom of heaven; but he that doeth the will of my Father which is in heaven. Many will say to me in that day, Lord, Lord, have we not prophesied in thy name? and in thy name have cast out devils? and in thy name done*

167

many wonderful works? And then will I profess unto them,
I never knew you: depart from me, ye that work iniquity.

I responded, "That's it, and that's why. *Anyone* in *any* faith needs no more motivation than that to honestly examine what he has been told.

"Then, may I let you see for yourself what I found?" he invited as he extended his arm toward the reference section which housed the *Catholic Encyclopedia.*

Upon approaching the encyclopedias, all fifteen large, brown volumes stood upright and in order upon one of the many empty tables—evidence of Mr. Babbitt's early arrival. In front of them lay some papers and another book. But as we sat down, me at his left, he began without referring to any of them.

"Gary, do you know what a forgery is?"

I heard that tone of compassion before. Evidently, what he found was going to be tough to take. "Sure. It's like two guys attempting to date the same girl, and one of them writes a 'get-lost' letter to the other guy, and signs her name. So the letter looks like it was from her, but it's not. He forged the letter and her name."

"That is right," he consented, and reached for one of the fifteen volumes of the *Catholic Encyclopedia.* He located the page, put a finger on a paragraph, and pushed the book in front of me with his other hand. "The *Catholic Encyclopedia* describes forgeries with some harsh words. Take a look."

> "Forgery," says Ferraris, who claims that his definition is the usually accepted one, "is a fraudulent interference with, or alteration of, truth, to the prejudice of a third person." It consists in the deliberate untruthfulness of an assertion, or in the deceitful presentation of an object, and is based on an intention to deceive and to injure while using the externals of honesty. Forgery is truly a falsehood and a fraud...."[1]

"So a forgery is a lie," I said.

"Yes. And furthermore," Mr. Babbitt added, "forgeries can be written after a great deal of time has passed. For example, someone today could write a letter on some very old paper, imitate the handwriting and signature of Abraham Lincoln, and attempt to pass it off as authentic."

"So, what are you telling me?" I asked as I gestured with palms up.

A moment or two passed before he could speak. It appeared to be difficult for him to express what he wanted to say. "The list of popes of the early centuries are based upon forgeries."

"Wow! Lies! That would mean there's no real list of popes before 600 A.D.," I said, suffering no little shock. "Of course, you know I want to see it for myself."

"That is why we are here," he said as he reached for the book he brought along. As he turned the pages to locate the book's Foreword, he added, "I came across this book in the library of the Oklahoma Christian College in north Oklahoma City. It is the recorded oral debate between the highly educated Catholic pastor, Dr. Eric Beevers, and Eldred Stevens, a preacher in the church of which I am a member."

Upon finding the page, he pushed the book to me with his age-spotted hand. Tapping the third paragraph with his index finger, he said, "Take a look. You should first realize just how significant this nation as well as other countries regarded this debate."

> After months of preparation, the day for the beginning of the debate arrived and people from twenty states overflowed Stillwater's hotels and tourist courts. Estimates of the size of audiences ranged from 4,000 to 6,000 for each of the four nights. The major national and international news agencies, radio networks, and television interests covered the meeting. Newspapers in every state of the nation and in Canada carried stories about it.[2]

Somewhat awestruck, I commented, "It was like a Super Bowl! And I'll bet those two fellows, being under so much news coverage, had to get ready for everything the other guy might say. Otherwise, if he couldn't answer it, he and his church would be shown to be wrong like a floodlight on thieves. Boy! Talk about pressure! No wonder they prepared for months."

"Exactly," Mr. Babbitt said. "These men were prepared to

respond to everything—if there was a response that could be made."

He kept going, "Now take a look at pages 200 to 202. This is the first time the non-Catholic brings up the forgeries. And Gary," he spoke in his lower and slower compassionate voice and his tender eyes did not move from mine, "I have had second thoughts about showing you this. It will be as painful as anything you have yet discovered. Maybe even more. Take your time and read it."

Like nervously reclining in the dentist's chair for a dreaded cavity drilling, I slowly slid my eyes from Mr. Babbitt to the black print.

Before finishing the first line, I asked, "Mr. Babbitt, what is this referring to? It says, 'whenever these things were brought in...'."

He explained, "Mr. Stevens had just pointed out several practices the Catholic Church brought into the church which were not there in apostolic times."

"Thanks." I began again.

> Whenever these things were brought in, it became very necessary to try to prove that they were Christian in origin, to try to prove that they began with Jesus Christ or with the apostles, and so various things were done in order to try to make them appear apostolic or Christian, actually, in their character. So, forgeries by the hundreds came! Dr. Beevers admitted as much. He admitted that there were many forgeries back there. You take those things that the *Catholic Encyclopedia* admits to be forgeries away from the Catholics and they couldn't prove apostolicity for half the things that they practice in the realm of religion. Take the matter of the "succession of the popes" and various other things. They could not begin even to start to commence to establish a case were it not for all sorts of forged documents. Look at this! (Uncovering Chart No. 10)

CATHOLIC "HISTORY" RIFE WITH FORGERIES AND LIES

Concerning every century
From first to modern times

General Statements
"Quite a trade"

"Not a history in the strictest sense"

"Prolific in Forgeries"

Purpose of Forgeries
"Secure authority of Roman Pontiff"

"Defend Hierarchy"

"To describe many practices as apostolic"

Guilt must be shared by:
Popes, Councils, Cardinals, Monks, "Doctors"

NOTABLE EXAMPLES

Dionysius the Areopagite

Linus

"Apostolic Canons"

"Apostolic Constitutions"

"Acts of Martyrs"

"Liber Pontificiaus"

"Edict of Donation"

"False Decretals of Isadore"

"Symmachien Forgeries"

Clementine Bible

Transforming Popess Joan

I have in my notes—and I have the books to back the notes—hope I'm challenged! I can show you forgeries that were deliberately made by the authority of the Catholic Church and practically every century from the time they started until the present time. the present era.

171

THE IVORY DOMINO

Statements like this, I have lifted from the *Catholic Encyclopedia* (Vol. VI, p. 136), that the making of forgeries was "quite a trade in the middle ages." Monks would often in their monasteries engage in "quite a trade," forging documents to try to make certain practices that the Catholic Church had borrowed from pagans and from Rome [the Roman Empire], appear apostolic or Christian. It was quite a trade!

Then you have "prolific in forgeries." (*Commentary on Canon Law*, Vol. I, p. 27). Forgeries were prolific at various seasons during the development of the apostate religion. Now, what was the purpose of those forgeries? Let's ask the *Catholic Encyclopedia!* Let's let a Catholic authority tell us why they forged those documents. First, "to secure the authority of the Roman pontiff." (*Commentary on Canon Law*, Vol. I, p. 25; *Catholic Encyclopedia*, Vol. XIV, p. 378.) That's a quotation! That's not a Protestant talking! That's a quotation from a Catholic source. Those documents were forged in order to secure the position of the pope at Rome as the supreme authority in the church. He supported it by forgeries.[3]

Completely astonished, I raised my head but still gazed at the page. "Mighty strong stuff," I admitted.

"Like what?" Mr. Babbitt probed.

"Like, he said the *Catholic Encyclopedia* admits the swarm of forgeries."

"Yes, and I'll show you some of those admissions from this very set in front of you," he said, still in his sympathetic tone, which was always. "Anything else?"

"He said there were forgeries actually made by..." I paused. I realized the truckload of starving termites this would release into the Church's foundation of authority and doctrines, "...forgeries made by the deliberate efforts of the authority of the Church."

Taking a cue from my momentary silence, he asked, "Which means?"

I hesitated.

"It means those who controlled what the Church believed and practiced wrote lies. It means, if they couldn't prove their doctrines and practices with the Bible's teachings, or even by their Tradition, they'd just forge up a document."

"Gary, I realize if what Mr. Stevens says is true, this will be very upsetting to you," he said with regret in his voice. "As you read what he said, was there any doctrine or practice in particular you noticed?"

"The one on the authority of the pope," I responded without hesitating, and not without mounting concern. "He said forgeries were written in order to make it look like the bishop of Rome had authority over *all* the Church. So, if they couldn't prove the papacy any other way, they would have to make and use forgeries. In other words, they would have to lie about it! The other thing I noticed was that he said the succession of the popes is based upon forgeries."

At that point, Mr. Babbitt glanced at his research notes and then reached for one of the volumes of the *Catholic Encyclopedia*. "Let us see if what Mr. Stevens said is true. First, he claimed the encyclopedia itself affirms a multitude of forgeries. Here, read it yourself."

The sentence seemed to stand out in large letters right before my eyes. Mr. Stevens had referred to it correctly. "Substitution of false documents and tampering with genuine ones was quite a trade in the Middle Ages."[4] My heart sank with intermingled emotions of heartache and disgust. "How could those early Catholics have done that?!"

Ready with another volume, Mr. Babbitt pointed to a sentence for me to read.

> In all these departments forgery and interpolation as well as ignorance had wrought mischief on a great scale.[5]

He slid another volume in front of me.

> Writers of the fourth century were prone to describe many practices (i.e. The Lenten Fast of Forty Days) as Apostolic institutions which certainly had no claim to be so regarded.[6]

"Mr. Babbitt, this is unbelievable! If it were not in our *Catholic Encyclopedia*, I wouldn't believe it. Mr. Stevens *wasn't* making it up. Those early Catholic leaders *did* make use—*big* use—of forgeries! They *lied* in order to make the laity believe that those new doctrines were actually taught by the Apostles!" I began to understand why Mr. Babbitt hesitated to tell me this—it disturbed me to the core of my bones. Actually, it was downright frightening.

"I am sorry, young Berean." He attempted to console me while at the same time, by using that nickname, encourage me to continue to examine the Scriptures—or, in this case, the encyclopedia—in order to learn the truth no matter where that truth may lead.

"Do you want to stop here?" he asked.

"No," I replied. "This Catholic authority admits the widespread forgeries. I want to see what else it admits."

"Then," he continued as he replaced that book into the set on the table and retrieved another, "take a look at some of those examples of forged documents Mr. Stevens listed on his chart. Here's one, the *Didascalia Apostolorum.*

As I read my astonishment escalated.

> A treatise which pretends to have been written by the Apostles at the time of the Council of Jerusalem (Acts 15), but is really a composition of the third century....we find the whole work incorporated into the Apostolic Constitutions at the end of the fourth century...."[7]

"Good night!" I was appalled. "Some guy who lived maybe 250 years after the apostles, wrote religious documents, forged them to make them out as though they were the actual writings of the apostles, and then the Church swallowed the lie 100 years later and added it to other Church laws!"

Mr. Babbitt added, "And that is exactly what one of those previous encyclopedia articles admitted: later writers created forgeries in the attempt to give a newly invented practice as something taught by the apostles."[5]

"Yeah, and that's exactly what Mr. Stevens brought out in that debate," I said as I pointed toward the book.

"Now look at this one," Mr. Babbitt said while we exchanged

volumes.

> Apostolic Constitutions, a fourth-century pseudo-Apostolic collection, in eight books, of independent, though closely related, treaties on Christian discipline, worship, and doctrine, intended to serve as a manual of guidance for the clergy, and to some extent for the laity...It purports to be the work of the Apostles, whose instructions, whether given by them as individuals or as a body, are supposed to be gathered and handed down by the pretended compiler, St. Clement of Rome, the author of whose name gave fictitious weight to more than one such piece of early Christian literature. The Church seems never to have regarded this work as the undoubted Apostolic authority.[8]

"Man! This is unreal!" I muttered my words, not particularly speaking to Mr. Babbitt. I teemed with bewilderment and anger. Forgeries in the Church quite a trade; made new practices appear apostolic; fooled the Church into false practices for centuries, and apparently, even unto today.

Prepared with the next volume, Mr. Babbitt traded books.

I began reading our encyclopedia's article which confessed the obvious: "No reliance can be placed on the long and fictitious account in the fourteenth-century forgery which is published under the name of Ingulf of Croyland."[9]

"Of course we can't place reliance on a forgery. It's a fake, a planned deception," I said with some heat. "If those doctrines the forgers wrote about were true and had genuine documents, the Church would not have to create forgeries to lie about the doctrines originating with the apostles."

"And did you notice when that forgery was made?" Mr. Babbitt asked, wanting me to detect something else.

I *had* noticed and I replied without looking. "The fourteenth-century. Just as Mr. Stevens told that huge audience, forgeries were made by the authority of the Catholic Church even until the present time." Our *Catholic Encyclopedia's* admissions tore my mind like tiger's claws. I knew, from our own authorized encyclopedia, I could no longer retain my former, and much desired, image of an honest Church.

"Gary, I found so many more admitted forgeries I could show you, and no doubt a great many more remain in these volumes I did not come across. After all, I could not very well read the entire encyclopedia in five days you know. But, there is one more you should see, and a prominent one it is. Even the *Catholic Encyclopedia* declares it a 'huge forgery'."[10]

I read the words in utter dismay.

> Nowadays everyone agrees that these so-called papal letters are forgeries. These documents, to the number of about one hundred, appeared suddenly in the ninth century.[11]

"A hundred!" My wide eyes glared at Mr. Babbitt. "This guy snuck 100 forged documents into the Church! And he was just *one* forger!"

Mr. Babbitt simply nodded his head as though I was about to find out more.

And I did.

> Isidore owed much to the "Liber Pontificalis," or chronicle of the popes. Thus when the "Liber" tells us that such a pope issued such a decree long since lost, the forger noted the fact and set to work to invent a decree for his collection along the lines hinted at by the "Liber."[11]

"What a con-man!" I grumbled with disgust. "Whenever this fella read about an ancient document being lost, that sneak wrote one up and made it to say that the pope of that earlier day had declared whatever the forger now wanted taught. And just think, he wrote a hundred of these, and the Church used these for their doctrines!"

There was even more.

> During the Middle Ages...it was not easy to distinguish genuine documents from apocryphal ones....It must be admitted that Isidore's forgeries increased the difficulty till it became almost insurmountable....And, as a consequence, the Middle Ages knew very little concerning the

historical growth of the rights of the papacy during those first centuries.[11]

"Doctrinal chaos! That's what it was!" I cried to Mr. Babbitt. "When all those forgeries that couldn't be distinguished from the genuine decrees of the popes were all shuffled together, the Church didn't know which doctrines were true and which were false. What a fine mess!"

"Indeed. And did you also notice what the encyclopedia itself admits?" Mr. Babbitt interjected. "Because of that confusion, the church, during the several centuries of the Middle Ages, knew next to nothing about the previous centuries' struggle and rise to universal power of the bishop of Rome to the office of pope."

"Yeah," I responded as I hand-slapped the table. "It all fits together. In that debate-book you loaned me, Mr. Campbell presented to Bishop Purcell the historical fact that there was no pope until around the year 600, and that there had been a long power-struggle to see who would be the first pope. So, during the Middle Ages, the encyclopedia points out, the Church would not have known about all that. Therefore, sometime during the Middle Ages, when the church was finally set up with the pope and his supporting hierarchy, the Church would then *assume* there had *always* been a pope! Then, in an attempt to prove the papacy with the Bible, they twisted Matthew 16:18 into saying what it does *not* say. And so the laity and probably most of the clergy have believed in a succession of popes back to Peter ever since. But it's false as false can be!"

"Gary, I am sorry...."

I stopped him with an upraised hand. "Mr. Babbitt, you're not the one who needs to do the apologizing. But most of those who do are already dead."

"Well then," he said with visual relief, "let us now look at what the *Catholic Encyclopedia* specifically admits about that list of popes."

"Yes, let's," I replied through my agony.

"Do you remember..." He paused. "Well, here. Look at it again." He reached for the navy-blue Stevens-Beevers debate and quickly relocated Stevens' chart on forgeries. "In his list of 'Notable

Examples' is the 'Liber Pontificalis.' The Liber Pontificialis is Catholicism's most prestigious list of the popes. Actually, the *Catholic Encyclopedia* esteems it with unsurpassed honor."

He selected a volume and located the page. My eyes followed his extended finger down onto the page to where he pointed.

> The "Liber Pontificalis," long accepted as an authority of the highest value, is now acknowledged to have been originally composed at the beginning of the fifth century."[12]

"It's just as Mr. Stevens said. It's unsurpassed in its authority, and it's a forgery," I concurred.

Then Mr. Babbitt floored me. "Actually, the Liber Pontificalis is the very list of popes upon which today's list is based."

Flabbergasted, I forgot about the quiet confines of a library and bellowed, "Wow! If the Liber Pontificalis is the highest authority on the list of popes, and if the Liber Pontificalis is a forgery, then today's list is the result of a hoax of the fifth century."

"You are getting it, but tone it down. Remember, we are in a library. Now add to that what the article, 'Book of the Popes,' tells you."

My eager eyes searched the text for pertinent information. I soon found it.

> A great many of the biographies [in the Liber Pontificalis] of the predecessors of Anastasius II [pope, 496-498] are...historically untenable....Liber Pontificalis utilized also [in addition to the unreliable Liberian Catalogue[13]]...a number of apocryphal fragments (e.g. the Pseudo-Clementine Recognitions)...the spurious Acts of the alleged Synod of 275 bishops under Sylvester etc., and from unauthentic sources....[14]

"Mr. Babbitt, I am not familiar with some of those words like 'untenable' and 'apocryphal.' Could you help me out?"

"Certainly. 'Untenable' means not able to be defended. 'Apocryphal' means the authenticity is doubtful. 'Spurious' means not genuine, and 'pseudo' refers to something that appears to be what it is not, and that example, the Pseudo-Clementine Recognitions, is now admitted by Catholicism as a huge forgery as the word 'pseudo' indicates.

I reread the encyclopedia as I inserted those definitions.

"Mr. Babbitt!" I whispered with force. I was fuming. "The Liber Pontificalis is a collection of junk! Some guy—no telling who he was or what kind of a fella he was—in the 5th century gathered up forgeries and all kinds of worthless and phony writings, wove them together, and then passed off the work as a genuine authority. Then its list of popes was gullibly accepted as genuine by the Church in the Middle Ages during the time, as one of these volumes you showed me admitted, 'knew very little concerning the historical growth of the rights of the papacy during those first centuries.' So, when the world knew nothing about there being no universal bishop for the first few centuries, the Church made a forgery to get everyone to believe that there had always been a pope. The list is a sham! It's a monstrous cover-up for a list of popes that does not exist!"

"Gary, you have reasoned correctly with the facts the *Catholic Encyclopedia* itself reveals. Surely this must be difficult for you. I mean, it is human nature to deny the truth when something so important to someone is proven to be false.

"Yes it hurts! But I refuse to be a domino any longer. I no longer accept what others tell me just because they tell me to believe it, or because it's been believed for so long by so many. I want the *real* truth. I want what I believe and what I do to be proven by genuine, authentic authority. I want to be doing what *God* wants me to, not what mere *men* say—lying men at that!"

"Well then, young Berean," he said slowly as he retrieved the Stevens-Beevers Debate book, "would you like to hear how the Catholic scholar who stood before the eyes and ears of the attentive religious world replied to Mr. Stevens' chart on forgeries, and especially the Liber Pontificalis?"

"Definitely. But, with what the *Catholic Encyclopedia* reveals, I don't know what he could possibly say."

"And you are exactly right. Throughout the rest of the debate Mr. Beevers completely avoided that chart. He never replied to Mr. Stevens' argument of the forgeries. Think about that! Mr. Stevens presented the Liber Pontificalis—the document used for today's list of popes—as a forgery, and with the world awaiting his answer, one of the Catholic's best scholars who was fortified with months of preparation *had no answer*! He could not contest what Mr. Stevens presented!"

"That makes it rather clear, doesn't it?" I said as I stared at Mr. Stevens' chart. "Today's list of popes for those first few hundred popeless years comes from a forgery, a hoax used to pass off something that didn't exist."

"Yes," Mr. Babbitt sympathetically concluded.

We both heard a low rumble. We looked at each other.

"Was that your stomach growling?" asked Mr. Babbitt.

"No. I think it was yours," I replied.

Whose ever it was, one of us is hungry. Gary, what do you say we go get something to eat—my treat—and then return here? There is something else you should know."

"It's a deal," I gladly agreed.

But, just what else could he possibly show me?

CHAPTER 27
HOCUS POCUS

A FEW MINUTES LATER

"What else?" asked Mr. Babbitt.

We sat at a four-seat table next to one of a half-dozen open-curtained windows in an old-fashioned café which faced the college as it rested on the other side of the six-lane boulevard of historic Route 66.

"That's all," I replied with a regretful grin.

"A salad?" he said with surprise as he lowered his menu to look at me.

"You sound like my grandmother and her starving birds," I responded with chuckles rippling throughout my come-back. I explained to him about my weight-loss effort for track, but his wrinkled up forehead and drawn-up mouth telegraphed his unspoken, but concerned disapproval.

When the waitress positioned our plates before us, I glanced at my rabbit food of lettuce, carrots, green peppers, and radishes, and then glared at his one inch thick chicken-fried steak that covered half of his plate, a gob of real mashed potatoes and gravy, a plump ten-inch corn-on-the-cob, and two hot homemade biscuits. I began to doubt the sanity of my plan.

Except for a couple of chatting student-librarians behind the entrance desk and a pair of students standing between the outlying book racks—doing more flirting than studying—the library's reference area remained as before. Prior to stepping out for lunch, Mr. Babbitt placed a note upon our table: "Please Do Not Reshelf: We'll Be Back," so the setup survived our absence and we were good to go.

Mr. Babbitt began, but all light-heartedness was noticeably lacking. For once, instead of looking at me when he spoke, his eyes locked onto the tabletop. "I do not know if I have the heart to show you this. All the forgeries you have seen so far dealt with one issue, the pope, and you were already aware of that office to be man-made. Gary, I am so very sorry, but the *Catholic Encyclopedia* reveals so many more of today's Catholic doctrines and practices to likewise be based upon forgeries.

A disheartened, "Really?" was all I could muster. I immediately knew what that meant. If the encyclopedia confirms what Mr. Babbitt just said, then we Catholics believe and practice some things that are *not* apostolic. And if they do not originate with the apostles, then they are man-made. And if they are man-made, then we have a grave problem because Jesus said, *"but in **vain** they do worship me, teaching for doctrines the commandments of **men**."*[1]

"Gary, look again at what Mr. Stevens declared to that huge audience—an audience which included reporters of national and international newspapers—which the Catholic Dr. Beevers could not overturn." Mr. Babbitt spoke with intended clarity as he picked up the book, located the page, and pointed to the paragraph.

> Whenever these things [post-apostolic practices] were brought in, it became very necessary to try to prove that they were Christian in origin, to try to prove that they began with Jesus Christ or with the apostles, and so various things were done in order to try to make them appear apostolic or Christian, actually, in their character. So, forgeries by the hundreds came! Dr. Beevers admitted as much. He admitted that there were many forgeries back there. You take those things that the *Catholic Encyclopedia* admits to be forgeries away from the Catholics and they couldn't prove apostolicity for half the things that they practice in the realm of religion.[2]

Mr. Babbitt, upon seeing I finished reading the paragraph, pointed to another on the facing page and said, "So crucial was this point, Mr. Stevens added this."

> Then [referring to his chart of statements appearing in the *Catholic Encyclopedia*], "Writers of the fourth century were prone to describe many practices (i.e. The Lenten Fast of Forty Days) as Apostolic institutions which

182

certainly had no claim to be so regarded."[3] (*Catholic Encyclopedia*, Vol. III, p. 484). In other words, there were many things that the Catholic Church began to do that were not apostolic and that could not be traced in their history to anything kin to the apostles—and so there was a need to try to make them "appear" apostolic. "Well, let's forge a document." Forge a document in order to make it that way![4]

"Did the Catholic debater have anything to say against that?" I asked with a glimmer of hope.

Mr. Babbitt sympathetically shook his head. "Not one word. I told you this would be as difficult as anything you have yet discovered."

"Well, let's see them," I said in a dismal let-me-see-it-for-myself tone as I pointed to the encyclopedia set. I felt my face turn pale from fear of what I would see.

"There is one right there in what you just read," he said, tapping his pencil on the page.

"Lent?" I said more as an exclamation than a question. "The forty days of fasting and penitence we do before Easter…was invented and made a Church doctrine by *men*? And the encyclopedia *admits it*? And it also says there are *many* such practices?" The room turned cold. No, it was me. An alarmed mind affects the body, and my mind lit up with flares. *Can it be possible? Are we really believing and practicing doctrines that mere men made-up?* I became frightened.

In the corner of my eye, I sensed Mr. Babbitt observing me like a coach examining a player with a possible head-concussion in order to determine whether or not to let the player stay in the game. Mr. Babbitt knew these revelations from our own Catholic authority exploded the origin and validity of many important Catholic practices and doctrines. Mr. Babbitt did not want to crush me; he was the most thoughtful and caring person I had ever met.

"What's next?" I asked, letting him know I was okay and able to continue in the game. I wanted the truth. Yet, the possibility of some of our doctrines being nothing but fabrications of hoaxers infuriated me even more than the discovery of the hoax itself.

With an understanding nod, he glanced at his notes, slid out a volume, found a page, and directed my attention to a location in the article "Clementines."

> The writer [of the Clementine Recognitions] knows a complete system of ecclesiastical organization. Peter sets a bishop over each city, with priest and deacons under him; the office of the bishop is well-defined.[5]

"What does this tell you?" asked Mr. Babbitt.

"The Clementine Recognitions tell us that Peter set up a hierarchy," I answered.

"Gary, this statement is the basis —some say the *only* basis — for today's hierarchy system. But the problem for Catholicism is: the Clementine Recognitions is an admitted forgery. See for yourself," he said as he located the statement for me in the lengthy article, "The Hierarchy of the Church."

> We must nevertheless abandon any attempt to argue from the Clementines, since even the oldest parts betray themselves more and more as a product of the third century [instead of the supposed 1st century]…he is guilty of arbitrary inventions and changes.[6]

"You see," he said, "the Catholic's authority for its hierarchy is the Clementines. But it is a rank forgery containing lies, and, as the encyclopedia itself issued its verdict, must be abandoned for doctrines, including the doctrine of the hierarchy."

He flipped over a few pages in the same article, pointed to a paragraph, and asked, "What do you learn from this?"

> The Divine institution of the threefold hierarchy cannot of course be derived from our texts [1 Cor. 12:28; Eph. 4:11]; in fact it cannot in any way be proved directly from the New Testament; it is Catholic dogma by virtue of dogmatic tradition, i.e. in a later period of ecclesiastical history the general belief in the Divine institution of the episcopate, presbyterate, and diaconate can be verified and thence be followed on through the later centuries. But

184

this dogmatic truth cannot be traced back to Christ Himself by analysis of strictly historical testimony.[7]

"The hierarchy is not taught in the Bible and cannot be traced back to Jesus?!" My voice quivered. "Instead, it was eventually developed by mere men in a later period and has been in the Church ever since?!"

"I am afraid so." Then he asked, "Can you guess when the word 'hierarchy' first appeared?"

"Well, since the hierarchy wasn't in the early church but rather gradually developed, I'll guess the mid-three hundreds."

His pressed lips signaled I missed it. He turned, selected a sheet from his papers, and handed it to me. "I copied this from the *Catholic Dictionary*."

> The word [hierarchy] first occurs in the work of the pseudo-Dionysius (a Greek writer of the fifth century) on the Celestial and Ecclesiastical Hierarchies. ... The signification was gradually modified until it came to be what it is at present.[8]

If I had been an older man, I might have suffered a heart-attack. My body appeared frozen, but my emotions squirmed out of control like a worm freshly hooked. Sitting quietly, Mr. Babbitt added no comments nor asked what I thought. He knew I struggled like a man sinking in quicksand with every hopeful clutch of liberating vines snapping loose from solid ground.

Born into the long-existing and world-engulfing Church with its established hierarchy of priest-to-pope, I never doubted its first century apostolic origin. But here, right here in our very own Church-authorized *Catholic Dictionary*, it admits that even the word "hierarchy" evolved some 400 years after the apostles, and it first appeared in a forgery, attempting—that is, lying—to make it look like the hierarchy had long been in practice. The dictionary also revealed the word to have "gradually modified," which is certainly due to the slow development of the hierarchy, "until it came to be what it is at the present." *Why the forgery? Why not until the 5th century? Why the gradual change?* All this fails to manifest the hierarchy as the handiwork of God. But the *Bible* is not a forgery, yet neither the word "hierarchy" nor its practice appear in the Bible's New Testament of the *first century*. Also, if God had set up the hierarchy, it would have been perfect at its very beginning and in no need of gradual improvement. No, all this instead manifests the work of mere *men* who invented the hierarchy a long time after the apostles died, and then gradually modified it until it emerged as it stands today.

Our encyclopedia and dictionary revealed the truth, and it was not easy to accept. The Bible teaches nothing about a hierarchy. Instead, centuries later, mere men created it, modified it throughout years of development, wrote a cover-up forgery in the attempt to make it look apostolic, and now try to remove it from suspicion by claiming it to be Tradition—today's catchall word for all the not-in-the-Bible practices that early false teachers created of which is too embarrassing for today's Church to admit.

Incredible! Incredibly incredible! I thought as I shook my head in total bewilderment. *But it's undeniable. It's in our own authoritative books. It could not be denied by our foremost debater, Mr. Beevers. The hierarchy, the very organization of the Roman Catholic Church, is built by man, not God!*

Then I remembered what God said. *"But in vain they do worship me, teaching for doctrines the commandments of men."*[1] And, "I testify to everyone who hears the words of the prophecy of this book. If anyone shall add to them, God will add unto him the plagues that are written in this book." [9]

What could I do? I couldn't go to Mom, Mr. Clay, or to the priest, for they were surely unaware of this horrific error. I felt so alone, even scared, as though I was lost in the middle of a dense, dark jungle. I did the only thing I could. I kept searching. I remembered Jesus somewhere promised, *"If you abide in my word, you shall be my disciples indeed, and you shall know the truth, and the truth shall make you free."*[10] Well, I wanted to be free alright, and it takes "abiding," that is, studying. And since Jesus said the truth will make me free, then the false teachings of mere men do *not* make *anyone* free.

I collected myself, looked squarely at Mr. Babbitt, and insisted, although weakly, "What other forged doctrines did you find in the encyclopedia?"

For what seemed like hours—torturous hours—Mr. Babbitt turned to article after article in the encyclopedia in order to allow me to read for myself the admissions of forgery-based doctrines and practices which are still believed and practiced today. They hit like the chest-high waves of the ocean at the beach of Galveston in my childhood, pounding me helplessly and unavoidably off-balance. And when, often even before I regained my footing, another salty wall shoved me over; and then another; and another; and…they were relentless.

In the article, "Symmachus, Pope St.," the encyclopedia revealed,

> The object of these forgeries was to produce alleged instances from earlier times to support…the position that the Roman bishop [Symmachus, 498-514 A.D.] could not be judged by any court composed of other bishops.[11]

This confirmed my earlier discoveries about the lack of a pope in the first few hundred years of the Church. The Church manufactured fake documents to introduce a doctrine that had yet to exist: the bishop of Rome as the supreme universal bishop, that is, the pope.

Next, the article entitled "Forgery" answered my old question. It read, "They had forged, among other documents, a Bull [papal letter] authorizing the priests of Norway to celebrate Mass without wine."[12] My thoughts went back to my first classroom encounter with Mr. Babbitt. Since then, having learned Jesus said "*drink ye all of it*," I wondered why the clergy held back the drink from the laity. Now I knew. Forgeries! We disobey Jesus' command by obeying men's command! I felt cheated, used, disrespected.

Forgeries even covered up, of all things, the origin of the Rosary! The encyclopedia revealed that the documents used to "support the view of the Rosary tradition…have long been proved to be a forgery."[13] My attractive black rosary took a hard hit, as did my heart.

Oh, no! Not this too! my heart begged as I read from Mr. Babbitt's notes from the *Catholic Dictionary*.

> The use of holy water among Christians must be very

> ancient, for the Apostolic Constitutions [a forgery] contain a formula for blessing water that it may have powers "to give health, drive away diseases, put the demons to flight," etc. But there does not seem to be any evidence that it was customary for the priest to sprinkle the people with holy water before the ninth century.[14]

Before lunch, I already observed the encyclopedia's admission of the Apostolic Constitutions to be a forgery that pretended to be written by the very apostles themselves. If the practice of holy water depends upon the Apostolic Constitutions, then it too falls victim to forged, man-made practices.

I detected the pattern. It stood out like a skyscraper on the Kansas flatlands. Originally, the practice was not a New Testament practice; later, men invented the practice; still later, men wrote a forgery claiming the Church has always practiced it; today, the Church is deceived in vainly practicing commandments of men. It was exactly as the debater, Mr. Stevens, had said.

All my life my eyes beheld with Catholic pride the pomp of the clergy's vestures, which underwent a procedure of a special blessing. But, alas, even that fell prey to the forgery pattern. The article, "Vestments," informs:

> On account of the lack of positive information, it cannot be even approximately settled as to the time at which the blessing of liturgical vestments was introduced. The first certain statements concerning the blessing of liturgical vestments are made by the pseudo-Isidore [forgery]....[15]

The information appalled me. Introduced, it admits! The first statements of certainty "are made by Pseudo-Isidore," a forgery of the 9th century, it tells us! Well then, if it was introduced and covered up in the 9th century, then it was introduced by mere men. Even a seven-year-old could see that. The words of Jesus echoed between my ears: "... *commandments of men... vain... vain... vain....*"

When Mr. Babbitt opened a volume of the encyclopedia to "The Sacrament of Penance," I felt my posture droop and my emotional strength, what I had left, fizzle like steam rushing from a teapot. Gathering courage, I read.

188

> Still more explicit is the formula cited in the "Apostolic Constitutions" [forgery]: "Grant him, O Lord almighty, through Thy Christ, the participation of Thy Holy Spirit, in order that he may have the power to remit sins...."[16]

Mr. Babbitt did not have to comment. With such plain statements, he never had to. The encyclopedia made it indisputable: The Apostolic Constitutions, a Catholic-admitted forgery, is still used in the attempt to demand us to believe that the priests and bishops themselves can forgive sins! My mind swirled like an Oklahoma F-5 tornado. *My nervous trips to the confessional to get my sins forgiven by the priest was a practice made up, not by God, but by people!* Then I wondered whether or not God had forgiven me of those sins.

Exhausted and devastated, I confessed to Mr. Babbitt, "I don't think I can take much more of this."

He looked over his list, tenderly put his hand on my shoulder, and softly asked, "How about two more?"

"Okay." I really did not want to continue. I wanted to stay in at least *some* ignorance. But, in this case, the old saying, "What you don't know can't hurt you," was wrong.

I saw the title of the next article. Why not?! I thought in exasperation. All these other doctrines are taught by forgeries. So why not purgatory?! It read:

> ...the Apostolic Constitution [forgery] gives us the formularies used in succoring the dead [in purgatory]. "Let us pray for our brethren who sleep in Christ, that God... may forgive him every fault, and in mercy and clemency receive him into the bosom of Abraham...."[17]

What in the world were those people thinking?! The audacity to make up a doctrine and then lie about it, claiming the apostles taught it! Did they think they could write their own religious doctrine of purgatory to which God would quickly busy Himself to create it? I thought it was God who told us what He wanted, not us who tells God what we want! Which of us is the Supreme Being who made the religion for the other to heed?!

Anger pushed aside my weariness. Adrenaline rushed through my veins like a fireman's hose. I felt exploited, violated, snubbed.

How could those ancient people bring their own religious practices and doctrines into the Church of God Almighty and then blatantly lie, claiming them to be from God?! These must be those who God spoke about when he wrote, *"speaking lies in hypocrisy, having their conscience seared with a hot iron."* [18]

I saw the next article's title.

Fortunate for me my energy returned. I needed it. The last one topped them all. Mr. Babbitt retrieved volume one, located the page, and slowly slid the book to me.

"Impossible! It can't be!" I gasped in complete disbelief. I raised my head and looked at Mr. Babbitt for a moment without saying a word.

It was the Apostles' Creed.

"Mr. Babbitt, do you know what this is?!" My voice exposed my alarm.

"I do."

"Why…, I mean…, this is…, oh man!" Like a person in physical shock, my mind-to-mouth linkage was jangled.

My eyes opened wide and my mind throbbed as I read.

> Apostles' Creed, a formula containing in brief statements, or "articles," the fundamental tenets of Christian belief, and having for its authors, according to tradition, the Twelve Apostles….Throughout the Middle Ages it was generally believed that the Apostles, on the day of Pentecost, while still under the direct inspiration of the Holy Ghost, composed our present Creed between them, each of the Apostles contributing one of the twelve articles. This legend dates back to the sixth century (see Pseudo-Augustine [forgery].)…No explicit statement of the composition of a formula of faith by the Apostles is forthcoming before the close of the fourth century….As a conclusion from this evidence the present writer [of this article], agreeing on the whole with such authorities Semeria and Batiffol that we cannot safely affirm the Apostolic composition of the Creed. [19]

"The apostles didn't write that Creed!" I groaned, and then

irately pressed my teeth tight. They could have bitten through leather.

"Gary, it is not that the doctrines which are taught in the Creed are false, because the Creed does contain biblical truths. But rather the lie is, first, that the apostles wrote the Creed, and second, that the Apostles' Creed is to be an official creed of the Church. Yes, the apostles wrote the New Testament, but they did not write this Creed. If the all-knowing and all-wise perfect God had wanted us to have an Apostles' Creed, He would have given it to us. But He did not."

"No, He didn't. The article pointed that out." My irritation at those forgers and their hoaxes rose like a thermometer poked into a hot baked chicken.

I pursued that discovery. *The Apostles' Creed now saturates the Church because some puny man "loaded" with a minuscule fraction of knowledge and a microscopic speck of wisdom thought he would help God out in His supposed blunder by forging it. The Apostles' Creed, the creed I memorized, recited, and esteemed; the creed that took up nearly half of my Baltimore Catechism that the nuns used to teach me our Catholic beliefs; the creed that gives Catholics our identity; the "mantra" that Catholics throughout the world unite upon, is a forger's lie!*

I felt flattened like a squashed frog on the road.

"Mr. Babbitt, you were right. These forgeries *are* as painful as anything else I've discovered. During these few hours, you told me…"

I caught myself. "No, that's not correct. You didn't *tell* me anything. You *showed* me out of my own Catholic authority, and *it* told me. It told me that the making of religious forgeries—the documents of deliberate lies—was quite a trade that dominated the Middle Ages. It told me that many practices the Church does today are not taught in the New Testament and did not exist in the Church established by the apostles. It told me that many of today's practices were later introduced by mere men, and then hundreds of years later when the practices were deeply rooted in the Church, men resorted to producing lying and deceptive forgeries to cover-up what had happened and to keep the laity from realizing that something was dreadfully wrong."

What a scheme! I thought with contempt. *If we don't have "proof" for a practice, then "Abracadabra, hocus-pocus," now we do! The Catholic Encyclopedia itself makes it as glaring as the sun on a cloudless day: The early Church changed the truth with forgeries, but forgeries changed the truth for the Church.*

Indeed, the articles compelled me to concede, the earlier Christians changed the Church the apostles built into what they wanted. And they got away with it!

"Gary," Mr. Babbitt interrupted my thoughts, "the forgeries tragically affected the church. Without them, the church may have abandoned those man-introduced practices and gone back to the way the apostles originally established it. Also, there never would have been the Protestant Reformation that objected to those man-made practices. Just imagine that! We could have had one, and only one, worldwide church undistorted by all those add-ons of man."

I did imagine it. The thought thrilled me.

Mr. Babbitt continued, "Actually, the Bible foretold those lies."

"Really?!"

"Listen carefully," he said, and then began to quote a Scripture.

> *Now the Spirit speaketh expressly, that in the latter times some shall depart from the faith, giving heed to seducing spirits, and doctrines of devils; Speaking lies in hypocrisy; having their conscience seared with a hot iron.*

"That is 1 Timothy 4:1-2. Apostle Paul told Timothy about something that would happen in *later* times, that is, something beyond the apostle's time. And that something that would happen was first, a *'departing from the faith,'* that is, Christians would depart from God's doctrines and practices, and second, the *'giving heed to deceiving spirits and doctrines of demons,'* that is, the Christians would follow the false doctrines of false teachers. Then, involved in this change from God's doctrines to men's doctrines was the *'speaking lies in hypocrisy,'* which undeniably includes the multitude of the lies in the forgeries."

Upon hearing that God already knew about the man-made changes and forgeries somehow made me feel a little better. It told me God still exercised control. Men could not ultimately thwart

God's plans nor destroy His Church. But this only provoked another question: *What am I to do about it, if anything?*

Outside the library, we exchanged parting courtesies and headed off to different parking lots. After several yards I heard him call me.

I turned. "Yes, sir?"

His voice, weakened by age, required him to cup his hands around his mouth like a megaphone. "Bible class tomorrow? Come with a question. I'll try to answer it."

He knew this information devastated me and gave rise to perplexing questions. He would not leave me shot up and dying on a battlefield. His concern for me, as well as others, accurately fit the definition of "astonishing." And his words, "I'll try to answer it," dripped with humility; he was a walking Bible.

I hollered back, "It'll be a stumper!"

CHAPTER 28
SIMON SAYS

THE NEXT DAY

"**D**oes anyone have a question we need to try to answer before we get into today's class lesson?"

As always, Mr. Babbitt manifested his genuine concern for us. Even if only one of us struggled with a problem in religion, he offered his help. I think he asked this question to the entire class instead of singling me out to protect me from embarrassment—interrupting yet another class to gain answers to my personal questions. His middle name must have been, "Thoughtful."

Surprisingly, the room fell quiet. Kent shrugged his shoulders and Trena focused upon the floor. In that lingering moment of silence, when everybody else either had everything all figured out or were too smart to let the others know they didn't, my tongue let it go: "Is it sinful to teach and do the religious practices that men themselves brought into the Church? Like Lent, holy water, and the hierarchy?"

Immediately, their dormant minds perked. Some looked at me; some looked at Mr. Babbitt; the rest looked at each other.

Was that a stupid question?

Unconsciously, I pressed my back against the chair and began to slowly slide down. A wave of tingling embarrassment crawled over me like a full body rash.

Why did I ask that? I scolded myself. *Nothing like waving my ignorance before everyone.*

In a feeble effort to cover up my blooper with a Band-Aid, I sighed, "I guess that's a stupid question, but I've just found out that in Catholicism we include religious practices that men brought into the Church."

Sensing my humiliation, lightning could not have struck faster than did Mr. Babbitt. "No sincere question can possibly be a stupid question." Mr. Babbitt not only heard what someone said, he also

194

detected why they said it.

"You see," he defended me as he alternately gestured his hands and a pointing index finger, "at some time in every person's past, he did not know the answer to that question or, as far as that goes, to any question. So, at some time everybody must learn the answer. It is just that we all learn the answer at different times. Now, if someone never investigates nor rallies the courage to ask, he will never know. And *that...*," he paused to let it sink into our heads, "...is what is foolish, or, as teenagers say, stupid."

Yanked from the bottom of the ego bucket and flung to the top, I adjusted my neck from whiplash, and thought, *He's right! If I want to know why others believe what they believe, I gotta ask. But more importantly, I ought to know **why** I believe what I believe as a Catholic. Blindly believing what others tell me to believe without knowing why is stupid and dangerous. I've believed what I believe because Mom and the Catholic Church raised me to believe it. Yet, she was raised the same way, as were her parents, and on and on it goes. But why are these things believed? Where is the proof in the Scriptures?*

"Now then, who would like to explain why we do not observe practices like Lent, holy water, and the hierarchy?" Mr. Babbitt solicited with arms extended toward the class.

Like watching a basketball player sink a shot from the other end of the court, I sat amazed at his confidence in the class. *He must have taught this to them before,* I reasoned.

Emerging from a few moments of exchanging who-is-going-to-do-it glances, Kent's voice, at my left, broke the silence. "Gary, have you ever played the game, 'Simon Says'?"

I turned to face him. "Sure," I answered, and then quickly added, "as a little kid. But what in the world does that have to do with Lent?"

"You'll see." He pivoted in his chair to face me directly. "Now tell me, how is that game played?"

I began, hoping I would remember the rules as I went along. "One player, who is Simon, stands in front of all the other players and commands them to do certain things. He begins each command with or without the words, 'Simon says.' If he begins the command *with* 'Simon says,' then the players must do what he told them, because if they don't, they're out of the game. On the other hand, if he begins a command *without* first saying 'Simon says,' then the players must *not* do what he told them, because if they do it, they are out of the game. To stay in the game, you must do what Simon says, and only what Simon says.

"Right!" Kent's display of teeth bettered the Cheshire cat of Alice in Wonderland. "And that is why we do not have Lent, holy water, a hierarchy, and a whole lot of other things that both Catholicism and most denominations have."

"I don't get it," I confessed as I shook my head.

"You see," Kent explained, "God is like Simon and we are to do what He commands."

"I know that. *Everybody* knows that," I said in a slightly objecting tone.

"But here's what everyone *doesn't* understand," he countered. "In the game of 'Simon Says,' as you just explained, when the leader does *not* begin his command with the words, 'Simon says,' then the command is not from Simon, and that means the players are not to do what they were told to do."

"Right," I agreed, nodding my head, yet with a face still broadcasting puzzlement. "They are out of the game because they are not obeying Simon, but, as it were, someone else."

"Exactly. Now apply that to the religious commands people are told to do," Kent said as he leaned toward me extending one hand out, palm up with fingers briskly curling back and forth to encourage me to think.

After a couple of moments of a blank mind—it is kind of hard to think when everybody is staring at you—I said, "I guess you'll have to explain."

"Okay. Listen closely. The religious commands people are told to do are either from God or from someone else, which of course is men. So, instead of the game, 'Simon Says,' we have 'God Says.' That means we only do those commands that God gives us, and *don't* do those commands *men* give us. Otherwise, we're out of the real game of life. And that, Gary, answers your question. It *is* sinful to teach and do the religious practices that man brought into the church."

"Now, I understand your point with 'Simon Says.' But," I fought back, "who says we must think like that with the Bible? I mean, you didn't show me where the Bible itself teaches that. So, all that *you've* said could itself be a teaching of man."

As Kent opened his mouth to speak Richard beat him to it. "Correct."

Kent, Richard, and I sat in a horizontal line with Richard at my right. I swiveled all the way around to square up with Richard.

Now face to face, he resumed. "I'm glad you gave that objection of wanting proof from the Bible. But you see, Kent was simply using that familiar game to illustrate what the Bible itself actually teaches."

"Go ahead, I'm all rabbit ears," I bid.

As he took his Bible, I readied with mine. "Let's look at Colossians 3:17," he said, thumbing through the pages.

"I got it," I said matter-of-factly, and began reading. "*And whatever you do in word or in work, do all in the name of the Lord Jesus.*"

Richard, keeping his eyes on the verse in his Bible, said, "Now carefully look at the words. What does 'whatsoever' include?"

"Everything," I answered.

"Right. Now, what is it in religion we do in 'word'?"

"Our teachings and doctrines," I replied.

"Yes. And what does 'work' mean?"

"That's our religious practices," I answered.

"So," Richard raised his head to look at me, "you're telling me that this verse is referring to everything we teach and practice in religion, aren't you?"

"That's the only thing it can mean," I insisted. "Not a single doctrine or a single practice is an exception."

My peripheral vision caught Mr. Babbitt nodding his head ever so slightly. His attention in the conversation was as intense as a judge listening to a witness in a trial. He made sure everything Richard said was correct.

Richard carried on. "What does the rest of the verse tell us to do with every single one of our teachings and practices?"

"All our practices are to be done '*in the name of the Lord.*' But..." I turned my head toward Mr. Babbitt, "doesn't that just mean that everything we do is to be done to the glory of the Lord?"

"That is taught in 1 Corinthians 10:31," Mr. Babbitt promptly commented, "but the verse Richard is explaining teaches something different. Go on, Richard."

"Gary, what does a policeman mean when he shouts, 'Stop in the name of the law'? Not that an officer ever said that to you," he quickly added.

"Everyone knows it means 'by the authority of the law,'" I answered.

"Right. By the authority of. And the Bible tells us the same thing." Richard began to search in his Bible for another verse. "Here it is. Jesus sent some disciples out to preach and He..., now listen closely, '*gave them power and **authority** over all demons.*' That's Luke 9:1. Then, in the next chapter, verse seventeen, another group of disciples who were sent with the same mission returned and declared, '*Lord, even the demons are subject to us...,*' now, notice what it says, "*in your name.*'"

"Yeah, I see it." I flipped a page back and forth to compare the two verses. "They're doing the same thing, casting out demons. But one verse tells us they cast out demons *by the authority* Jesus gave them, and the other tells us they did it *in the name of the Lord.* How plain is that! To cast out demons 'in the name of' Jesus, means to cast out demons 'by the authority of' Jesus. They mean the same thing."

"So, put it all together," Richard appealed. "What does Colossians 3:17 mean?"

"It means that every single doctrine we teach and every single practice we do must come from the authority of God, not man."

The light bulb in my mind came on and I spun back around to Kent. "I see what you mean with your 'Simon Says' illustration. It's perfect. We are to do in religion only those commands God gives. But if we don't do them, we disobey God and sin. On the other hand, we are *not* to do the commands that *men* create. And if we do, then we also disobey God. So, that means the answer to my question is: Yes, it IS sinful to teach and do the religious practices that men brought into the Church."

"You've got it!" Kent said excitedly as he stretched across the aisle, grabbed my shoulder, and gave it several tugs.

Even though Kent's shaking vibrated my vision, I could still make out Mr. Babbitt pointing to someone behind me.

"May I add something?" asked Marty.

I began to wonder if competition between siblings was contagious. *First it was the Parker girls, then Teresa and Trena, now these two?*

"Let's use this 'God Says' rule with Exodus 30:34-35. These verses are God's instructions to the Jews on how to make the special incense to be used in worship. Gary, you have your Catholic Bible don't you?"

"Yes," I replied as I patted it with my hand.

"Then, how about reading it for us?" he asked.

I found the location and read aloud.

> *And the Lord said to Moses: Take unto thee spices...*

I stopped. "I have no idea how to pronounce those words. Marty, you sneak, is this why you didn't read it yourself?" I joked, and then tried it again as I embarrassingly struggled over each word that must have come from another planet.

> *And the Lord said to Moses: Take unto thee spices stacte, and onycha, galbanum of sweet savor, and the clearest frankincense, all shall be of equal weight. And thou shalt make incense compounded by the work of the perfumer, well tempered together, and pure, and most worthy of sanctification.*

"Look at the first few words," Marty directed me. "It uses the very words, 'the Lord said.' So, this is unmistakably a 'God Says' command, isn't it?"

I looked at the verse again to verify. "No doubt about it."

Marty kept on, "And so, 'God said' make incense out of those four ingredients.

"But, now get this. Later on we read of two priests who did *not* follow what 'God Said' about the incense instructions, and, most importantly, we see how God reacted. Would you read to us Leviticus 10:1, Gary?"

> *And Nadab and Abihu, the sons of Aaron, taking their censors, put fire therein, and incense on it, offering before the Lord strange fire: which was not commanded them.*

"Do you see what that says?" Marty asked with increased excitement and volume. "Notice, these two were God's people. Actually, one of them was supposed to be the next high priest, the most important religious man in all Judaism. They were worshiping, and they were worshiping the one true God. However, it says their burning incense was a '*strange* fire which was *not* commanded them.' Now, whether these two made up their own recipe for the incense, or whether they followed some other man's recipe, they nevertheless did what 'Man Said,' not what 'God Said.' They did something God did not command them, and it was strange and unknown to Him.

"Now, Gary, here's the big question: How did God feel about them doing what 'Man Said'? Go ahead, read verse two."

It was like approaching the climax of a gripping mystery novel. I tilted my head down to the Bible and began reading.

> *And fire coming out from the Lord destroyed them, and they died before the Lord.*

"Wow!" I exclaimed as I snapped my head up.

"Yeah!" Marty agreed as his eyes widened which pushed his forehead into ripples of skin. "This gets it through our skull, doesn't it: We *must not* do any religious practice that man invented. Yeah, I know, nowadays, God does not come right out like that and punish people who are practicing the teachings of men, but it sure does show us how He feels about it and what will happen to them at Judgment Day."

As I tried to grasp how far the effect of this enlightening Bible truth extended, I sat numbed. But it was a mixed numbness. One part was bad and hard to take, like hearing of the death of a good friend. The other was the good numbness of a pleasant discovery, like hearing Dad tell me we were going on vacation to Galveston Island. What an incredible principle I learned from God's own words. Then I thought, *But, does the hierarchy itself not know about this, or, do they know but keep from teaching it to the laity lest we apply "God Says" to Lent, holy water, and numerous other practices, and discover them to be the teachings of mere men —teachings and practices which are sinful before God?*

For the remainder of the class, Mr. Babbitt laid before me other Bible verses which also taught this profound principle. In Deuteronomy 4:1-3, God told His children, if they wanted to enter into the Promised Land, they must heed the commandments *He* gave them. And in case they did not fully grasp what that meant, He explained,

> Ye shall **not** add unto the word which I command you, neither shall ye diminish ought from it, that ye may keep the commandments of the Lord.

In other words, do not make up your own practices and add them together with God's. But if they did add man's practices, they would not be keeping the commandments of God, but of men. Then verse three reminded them of an earlier incident in which 24,000 Jews followed the additional teachings of some man. How did God react? He ordered them put to death! Likewise, if a person today wants to enter our promised land of heaven, he must do what *God* says, and *only* what God says, and abandon men's additions.

Mr. Babbitt then took me to a familiar story. In Joshua chapter six, before the walls of Jericho fell out flat, God told Joshua exactly what the Jews were to do. In verses 3 through 5, God instructed Joshua to march the people around the city once a day for six days and seven times on the seventh day. Precisely at the end of the last march, the priests were to blow their trumpets and the people were to shout. Joshua understood that the people must do only what God said, and he feared that the people might think they could add a shout before the time God so instructed them. This compelled him to order them, "*Do not shout nor make any noise until I tell you.*" The lesson comes screaming through the years into our ears: Do not do anything in religion unless God tells us to do it!

Next, in Jeremiah 7:31-33, I learned about a great number of Jews who did a religious practice *"which I commanded them not, neither came it into my heart."* Consequently, because they did what God did *not* command them, He slaughtered them.

Then, in Acts 15:24 and 28, the apostles condemned some men who taught other Christians to do a practice when the apostles *"gave no such commandment."*

Along with these glaring examples that engraved upon my mind the absolute necessity of conducting ourselves in the church like a child does in the game 'Simon Says,' Mr. Babbitt also introduced me to some verses that plainly teach it.

In Matthew 17:5, when Moses and the prophet Elijah appeared with Jesus, excited Peter blurted out his desire to build three tabernacles, one to each man. But Moses and Elijah disappeared, and God the Father replied from heaven, *"This is my beloved Son...hear ye HIM."* I realized if we are forbidden to mix the Jew's God-given Law of Moses with the Law of Jesus for our commandments to practice, then we sure cannot mix some scrawny man-made religious laws with the New Testament commandments for our beliefs, teachings, and practices!

When Jesus, in Matthew 28:20, issued His orders for the great mission of His disciples, He said, *"...teaching them to observe all things whatsoever I have commanded you."* This verse, like all the others, oozes with 'Simon Says.' It tells us we must do "ALL" Jesus commands us, and, "whatsoever *I*"—Jesus and ONLY Jesus—commands. Not, "whatsoever I *and some men* command you."

Matthew 15:9, which I then knew by heart, reveals what happens when we practice and teach the commandments that men added to God's commandments.

> *But in vain do they worship me, teaching for doctrines the commandments of men.*

What a devastating situation, I thought, *but it's a situation I am in!*

Then, the very last warning of the entire Bible flagged the rules of 'Simon Says' before my eyes.

> *For I testify unto every man that heareth the words of the prophecy of this book, If any man shall add unto these things, God shall add unto him the plagues that are written in this book. And if any man shall take away from the words of the book of this prophecy, God shall take away his part of out of the book of life, and out of the holy city. (Revelation 22:18-19.)*

God could not make it any easier to understand. To "add" to God's Word is to add commandments of men. And to "take away" from God's Word is for men to ignore any commandment of God. To do either results in the loss of heaven and the one-way drop off into the place of horrible plagues.

All these verses left me baffled—*How could I know nothing about this horde of examples and commands that tell us **not** to do the practices men brought into the Church.* I figured I wasn't reading my Bible very much, or, I just wasn't paying attention when I did read, or, I was merely a domino in a long chain, doing and believing whatever I was told and whatever was done by the Church. Truthfully, it was all three.

I dreaded more torture, but I already made up my mind. Heaven is so magnificent and hell is so horrendous, my quest for the one and the evasion of the other drove me to the *Catholic Encyclopedia* to pursue which of the two, God or man, originated our other Catholic practices.

CHAPTER 29
THE BABYSITTER

THE NEXT DAY

The raging south wind shoved relentlessly against me and my track buddies during Monday practice. We fought not only that gale force, but also the sand-blasting missiles of grit that stung our defenseless legs. Thankfully, that battle was behind me—but another stood before me.

Less than a mile from the high school, I swerved Ol' Blue into our driveway to make my special homemade chocolate/peanut butter/honey swirl-in-a-cup before heading off to the Bethany Nazarene College library. I just knew those man-made, forgery-supported practices Mr. Babbitt showed me in the *Catholic Encyclopedia* had to be the extent of them, although that number itself was indeed quite numerous. Yet, I dishonestly pushed that thought into my mind's fade-and-forget-it area. My mission was now set: Stop the bleeding of my Church! Prove to myself that the Catholic Church practices no other man-invented doctrines. Find the statements in the encyclopedia that reveal the apostolic origin of all the rest of our practices.

"Mom, I'm home. But...."

Before I finished my "But-I'm-going-right-back-out" announcement, she interjected, "Good. I have a lot of errands to run, and Kandy is at a friend's. So I need you to stay with Chuck and Danny."

She gave me a kiss on the cheek, and hurried out the door.

At that moment I found out what a fully inflated balloon felt like when released.

After a few minutes of sulking, Einstein Gary got an idea, but without thinking it through. *I'll just take them with me!*

Armed with comics and coloring books, the brothers three set out.

204

"Hey you two, I don't want you getting hungry on me, so how about a hamburger?"

"McDonald's!" Danny yelled, bursting my ears. I think he thought heaven was one huge McDonald's restaurant.

"And fries?" Chuck added his request.

"And fries," I gave in.

As we set foot on the crowded campus, the glitch in my plan struck me: kids don't belong on a college campus! I felt embarrassingly awkward, maybe like sitting in Church and realizing I hadn't put on a shirt. I took them back to the car and waited until the next class session began. When the sidewalks cleared for the most part, I set off with my brothers on the cross-campus trek, hoping to go encounter-free. But, no such luck. A group of five giant upperclassmen emerged from behind a row of tall bushes and headed straight toward us. Upon noticing the two inappropriate intruders, their silent glare expressed their "What do you think you're doing?" thoughts.

"Babysitting," I said with a grin as I shrugged my shoulders. I kept walking, shoving my siblings on.

Getting past the librarian's desk posed another snag. I waited until the two attendants were occupied. Quickly, in single file, we soundlessly walked close to the extra tall, child-concealing counter and zipped out of sight around the corner of the first row of books. All three of us loaded up as many encyclopedias as we each could carry and wobbled up the stairway like ants struggling under objects ten times their weight.

The second floor contained several one-person study rooms that served as my concealment and containment for the little guys while I sat at a table just outside their door. "Here, at last!" I said with a gushing sigh of relief, and promptly got to work.

The first doctrine I looked into confirmed what I had hoped: man did not make up *all* our practices. The doctrine of heaven originated in the Scriptures, not in teachings of men. The encyclopedia even mentioned some Scriptures that teach about heaven.

Next, heaven's counterpart, hell, also checked out as a doctrine originating in the Bible. So did baptism, worship on Sunday, and

Jesus being the Son of God.

Even though these were only five doctrines—five doctrines common to everyone in Christianity—I was on a roll and feeling elated. "What's next for the win column?" I confidently asked myself. And I boldly answered myself, "Let's see. We have big crosses over the altars, and we make the sign of the cross. What about that?"

I located the article, *Archaeology of the Cross and Crucifix*, and began reading. My merry roll abruptly stopped.

> We have seen the progressive steps….in the fifth century the cross began to appear on public monuments, it was not for a century afterwards that the figure on the cross was shown; and not until the close of the fifth, or even the middle of the sixth century, did it appear without disguise. But from the sixth century onward we find many images…historical and realistic of the crucified Saviour….the custom of placing the crucifix over the altar does not date from earlier than the eleventh century.[1]

"The use of the cross began in the 5th century, not with the apostles?" I whispered my surprise as I struggled to believe it. "And the practice developed over several centuries and progressive steps?" I could not deny it, the use of the cross was an invention of man, not God.

My heart nearly burst when I read where the idea of the cross came from.

> The ansated cross of the ancient Egyptian….It often appears as a symbolic sign in the hands of the goddess Sekhet….In later times the Egyptian Christians, attracted by its form, and perhaps by its symbolism, adopted it as the emblem of the cross….Very soon the sign of the cross was the sign of the Christian.[2]

Our dominating displays of the cross, even the cross we put over the altar, did not come from Jesus and the apostles, but was adopted from Egyptian paganism! Gross me out! How could those early Christians stoop so low! And now, when I see those crosses at Mass, I'll know I'm looking at man-made inventions. What a bummer!

The article continued to crush my soul.

It is from this original Christian worship of the cross that arose the custom of making on one's forehead the sign of the cross. …it is not commanded in Holy Scripture, but is a matter of Christian tradition, like certain other practices that are confirmed by long usage.[3]

"Oh, no," I moaned as my shoulders sagged. Not only was the cross adopted from paganism, and from that came the human idea of making the sign of the cross, which is not taught in Scripture, but, the hierarchy has the nerve to say it's okay simply because we've been doing it for a long time! Tradition, they call it.

"How easy is it to see through that!" I smoldered. I had instantly realized, if that was the way to establish Church practices, then nothing, as in **absolutely nothing**, is prohibited from being brought into the Church. Just do it long enough and then it is okay! But, the rules of 'God Says' blows that away like a mobile home caught in a tornado. And the verse, *"whatever you do in word or in work, do all in the name of the Lord Jesus,"* was written, and stands written, long before people brought the cross from paganism into the Church. If they did not act by the authority of God when they brought it in, then we are *still* not acting by the authority of God when we practice it today! And what about those two Old Testament priests who invented that burnt incense which God had not commanded? If God had not killed them, and if they and their descendants had kept on offering that same kind of burnt incense, would it then be okay with God? Of course not! Nor does a practice brought into the Church by mere men become okay with God just because we have been doing it for so long! Tradition—long term usage—is no way to establish Church practices! Tradition, like history books, only tells us what people have been practicing for a long time, regardless whether it is right or wrong. But determining whether a practice is right or wrong is found in the Scriptures.

The article beat me to a pulp, and it further pounded me when it declared, "the sign of the cross…is a matter of Christian tradition, *like certain other practices* that are confirmed by long usage."

"Others? What others?"

Why did I have to ask that!

Celibacy. I avoided that doctrine at triple-arm's length. No way would I become a priest who could not marry. If there was any practice I wished to be a man-made practice that would be reversed, this is the one. I must have had a wish-enhancing good-luck charm in my pocket.

> But we need hardly insist that all this [the article's preceding information] is very inadequate evidence to support the contention that a general rule of celibacy existed from Apostolic times. Writers in the fourth century were prone to describe many practices (e.g. the Lenten fast of forty days) as of Apostolic institution which certainly had no claim to be so regarded.[4]

Wow! It **didn't** *come from the apostles. It's another one of man's doctrines.* My thoughts ran quickly from shock to sadness to anger: *Our poor, cheated priests! If the Church got rid of this wife and family depriving doctrine, I might become a priest. No telling how many good Catholic men kept themselves from the priesthood because of this Church-weakening teaching. And, only God knows how much trouble this faulty practice has and will cause in the Church. When men insert their doctrines into the Church, they only mess things up.*

I glanced at the door which imprisoned my brothers. No banging noises. No yelling. I resumed my research.

Next, remembering our use of candles for religious purposes, I located its article, wholly unaware of the can of worms—make that, tub of vipers—I'd fall into.

> We need not shrink from admitting that candles, like incense and lustral water, were commonly employed in pagan worship and in the rites paid to the dead. But the Church from a very early period took them into her service, just as she adopted many other things…. We must not forget that most of these adjuncts to worship, like music, lights, perfumes, ablutions, floral decorations, canopies, fans, screens, bells, vestments, etc. were not identified with any idolatrous cult in particular; they were common to almost all cults.[5]

I slowly raised my head, drew a deep breath, and softly exhaled.

THE BABYSITTER

"Did I really read that in our encyclopedia?"

I knew I did. I just couldn't think of a way to explain it away. Mainly because there was no explanation. Uncovering this information promptly skyrocketed my distress far beyond hazardous. My stability shook. *These thirteen practices and "many other things" we use today are not only additions to our worship by mere men of the early Church—they were carried over from paganism! Our worship and sanctuaries mostly imitate a jumble of pagan practices rather than the design and commands of God, the Designer and Owner of the Church!*

Fear swallowed me like the encroaching darkness of the setting sun. If I had eaten a hamburger with my brothers, I would have lost it.

The trauma of losing my naïve innocence continued. The images and statues in our sanctuaries—the beautiful works of art depicting Saints and Angels—also came from paganism. The article, "Images," openly states:

> Roman pagan cemeteries and Jewish catacombs already showed the way [for images]; Christians followed these examples with natural modifications.[6]

My deep affection of the images, especially the magnificent ones in St. Vincent De Paul, the Church of my impressionable childhood years in Houston, interwove with my soul. If this disturbing information had not come from our *Catholic Encyclopedia,* I would not have believed it. Even so, I did not want to accept it.

Similar to images, I thought of relics, the objects given reverential respect because of their association with a Saint. I located the article and got a dump-truck load more than I expected, or wanted.

> Few points of faith can be more satisfactorily traced back to the earliest ages of Christianity than the veneration of relics. The classical instance is to be found in the letter written by the inhabitants of Smyrna, about 156 [A.D.] …Nevertheless it remains true that many of the more ancient relics duly exhibited for veneration in the great sanctuaries of Christendom or even at Rome itself must now be pronounced to be either certainty spurious or open to

grave suspicion.[7]

"Few?!" I gasped. "*Few* points of faith can be traced back to the earliest ages of Christianity? 'Few' is a small number, a mere handful. And the article's 'earliest ages' refers to 156 A.D., a time long after the years of the apostles. You mean to tell me that the origin of only a *few* of the practices we do today might, just *might*, go back to a few decades *after* the apostles! Then, what in the world is left of our faith?! Is most everything we do and believe a result of the early Christians *after* the apostle's age, who polluted the Church with their own inventions, many of which were copied off of paganism and made to appear apostolic by lying forgeries?!"

The *Catholic Encyclopedia's* numerous admissions like this one shredded our beliefs and practices from a towering forest of pine trees down to a few toothpicks. Yet, another admission whittled the toothpicks even thinner: "One is forced to admit that the gradual corruption of Christianity began very early."[8] "Well," I reasoned, "if false, erroneous beliefs and practices entered the Church very early, then it's meaningless to look after the age of the apostles to see what the early Christians taught and practiced in order to determine the practices that are authorized by God. Because, what we'd be looking at would probably be one of the numerous and erroneous practices men invented. And then, we'd be acting upon what 'Men Say,' not what 'God Says.'"

I knew, by that very admission, our appeal to Tradition for our authority for what we do in religion was exposed as worthless, even detrimental. Catholicism uses both, Scripture and Tradition. Tradition is claimed to be transmitted through the living Church by what she taught, how she lived and how she worshiped.[9] But, as the encyclopedia "is forced to admit," the "corruption of Christianity began very early," then Tradition, which is the beliefs and practices of the early Christians, *cannot possibly* be today's source of authority for our beliefs and practices! Rather, the source must be the Scriptures. Tradition, the so-called Living Voice of the Living Church, is in actuality, the Man-Spoken Voice of the Man-Altered Church.

Next, I investigated the music in worship. *Surely, that's a "God Says,"* I confidently thought. *Or, is it?*

For almost a thousand years the Gregorian chant, without

any instrumental or harmonic addition, was the only music used in connection with the liturgy. The organ, in its primitive and rude form, was the first, and for a long time the sole, instrument used to accompany the chant. ...In Carlovingian times, however, the organ came into use, and was, until the sixteenth century, used solely for the accompaniment of the chant, its independent use developing only gradually.[10]

The Church had no mechanical instrument for a thousand years?! my brainwaves rumbled. *That means the Church during the time of the apostles did not have them. And, it even means Tradition wasn't passing on this practice. So, that means organs and such are nothing but a blatant "Man Says" practice! Man, oh man! Just think of all the worship assemblies today that use mechanical instruments, both Catholics and Protestants.* Yet, I recollected Mr. Babbitt's church did not use them.

I had a stomach full. Many of our major beliefs and practices slipped through my fingers like water. They were inserted by men, not instituted by God. And the difference makes a difference. An eternal difference. I had come to the encyclopedia to stop the bleeding of our Church doctrines, but our Church doctrines bled even faster in our encyclopedia, teetering on a lethal level. Our authorized *Catholic Encyclopedia*, written by hundreds of Catholic scholars, revealed cold, hard, devastating facts that would never go away.

My day's session ended, but the research kept going. I returned the following day. To my disappointment, the results mirrored the first.

Regarding our use of ashes, I read, "This use of **ashes** is probably older than the eighth century."[11] This is another way of saying that man invented the use of ashes 700 years after the apostles were gone. Another practice bit the dust.

Anxious for an apostolic practice, I hoped in "Confirmation." Instead, I found this:

The Sacrament of **Confirmation** is a striking instance of the development of doctrine and ritual in the Church....It is only from the Fathers and the Schoolmen that we can gather information on these heads.…Even some Catholics, as stated above, have admitted that confirmation "has not any visible sign or ceremony ordained of God"[12]

I knew what that meant. The only information about Confirmation comes from the beliefs and practices of the Church during the time after the apostles when "one is forced to admit" that "corruption of Christianity" existed. *No thank you, I silently reneged. Rather, change that to: No way! Also, it's a **developed** doctrine and practice. That's a sign of it being the work of man, because God, being perfect and doing only perfect works,[13] does not make imperfect doctrines and practices that need improvement by development. A practice that needs development is a practice made by man.*

The article, "**Mass**," punched me square in the face. "The change [of the liturgy of Mass near the end of the 6 century] is radical, especially as regards the most important element of the Mass, the Canon."[14] *Change means development; development means man's alterations; man's alterations means 'Man says.'*

The words in "The **Rosary**" struck another blow. From that time [c.1470] forward this manner of prayer [the use of the rosary] was "most wonderfully published abroad and developed by St. Dominic."[15] *Developed! 1470! The rosary is a man's practice!*

The "Vestments" article offered no let up.

> On account of the lack of positive information, it cannot be even approximately settled as to the time at which the **blessing of liturgical vestments** was introduced. The first certain statements concerning the blessing of liturgical vestments are made by the pseudo-Isidore [forgery] and Benedict Levita, both belonging to the middle of the ninth century, but the oldest known formula of blessing, which is in the Pontifical of Reims, belongs to the end of the ninth century.[16]

Introduced? Forgery supported? Ninth century? Man's fingerprints are all over it!

I found the comforting practice of the priest forgiving us of sins in the confessional booth to have also been made up.

It was not until the scholastic doctrine of "matter and

212

form" in the sacraments reached its full development that the formula of **absolution** became fixed as we have it at present.[17]

Panicking to find another apostolic practice in Catholicism, I rushed to the article, "**Nuns**." But, it states, "at the beginning of the same century [3rd] the virgins formed a special class in the Church."[18] *A special class was formed at the beginning of the 3rd century? Man's, or, in this case, women's invention.*

The encyclopedia also admitted, "**indulgences**, as we now know them, date only from the year 1587."[19]

The article, "Lights," persisted in siphoning my spiritual energy. "It is, at any rate certain that even earlier than this [303 A.D.] the liturgical use of **lights** must have been introduced."[21] *If it was introduced into the Church around 303 A.D., then it's not an original from the apostles around 30-70 A.D.*

In the article, "**Purgatory**," it says, "...praying for the dead is as clear in the fourth century as it is in the twentieth."[21] "Why couldn't the article say it was clear in the 1st century, the age of the apostles?" I indignantly thought. *Because it didn't exist then. Men invented it later!*

"Isn't there an end to this?" I cried. I felt as scared as the last soldier in the foxhole with thirty enemy snipers moving in from all directions. In desperation, I grabbed the library's copy of *Strong's Concordance*—that big blue book in Mr. Babbitt's room that contained every location of every word in the Bible. I scanned its pages for any mention in the New Testament of those practices the encyclopedia admitted as post-apostolic. Nothing showed up. Not rosary. Not confirmation. Not images. Not celibacy of the clergy. Not nuns. Not purgatory. Not ashes. Not musical instruments. Not *any* of them!

"The Encyclopedia printed the truth!" I was forced to concede. And that truth is: Not long after the apostles died, the "corruption of Christianity began very early," which included men in the Church adopting many practices of paganism and, "from a very early period took them into her service." Even more man-made practices were thought up that were "not commanded in Holy Scripture, but [are now] a matter of Christian tradition, like certain other practices that are confirmed by long usage." Today, only a "few points of faith can be...traced back to the earliest ages of Christianity" some of which even originated at a time long after the death of the apostles.

How could those early Christians have done this to the Church! I protested with anger. I wish someone like Kent or Richard would have told them about "Simon Says" and pounded into their heads those verses that tell us that Christians can practice only what God says to do! Otherwise, what we do is vain,[22] and sinful,[23] and makes us lost.[24]

The remembrance of Mr. Babbitt's words rang in my ears, "This will be as painful as anything you have yet discovered. Maybe even worse." He was so right. Learning from our own Church-authorized *Catholic Encyclopedia* of the sheer number of our beliefs and practices that came from unauthorized men, who even stole many of their ideas from pagan worship, is accurately described as painful, even devastating.

"The Church doesn't have to do these practices," I snapped. "We are the one true Church. Can't we just admit that Tradition is a cover-up for the early Christians' add-ons, and stop doing and believing what they brought into the Church? And then get our doctrines and practices from the only source that we know is from God—the Bible? What could possibly keep us from doing that?"

In due time, I would find out.

CHAPTER 30
DEAD MEN SPEAK

T he slender Oldsmobile hood-ornament knifed through the wind as Ol' Blue pushed north on Council Road. Within only three miles from our home, the gray asphalt strip began to stretch through the lazy countryside. The slumbering farms of red barns and black and white cattle were bordered by rusty barbwire wobbling on old tree limbs for posts. I didn't take this tour of isolation often. Only when I needed to think.

Evidently, the mauling I suffered the previous week devastated me deeper than I realized. The *Catholic Encyclopedia's* barefaced admissions of so many of our practices originating from men, which were then defended and retained by merely calling them Tradition, would have been unbelievable—had I not read it for myself. After receiving bad news, human nature normally allows us to emotionally heal over time, but the cruel vice that squeezed my mind tightened more brutally day after day. It should have. Truth outlasts time. Historical facts remain unaltered regardless of the passing of years, even centuries. What happened, happened. And what I want to have happened doesn't change what really happened. Even though I dared to ignore it, that could not change the fact that we Catholics engage in numerous non-apostolic practices that some early negligent Christians swindled off on the Church. *Yes,* I was distressed, and in quite a fix! I was the only monkey on a small island whose lone banana tree just got infested by tree-killing beetles.

After several miles of driving dangerously—thinking about something other than driving—I hung a right on 206th Street, and then another right a mile later on Rockwell to make my southbound back-to-life reentry. As I eventually came to 42nd Street, a sudden notion nudged me to swing left for a short detour by Mr. Babbitt's home. I don't know why. Maybe because…. No, I just don't know why.

"Oh no! He's outside!" I yelped in a panic attack. "Maybe he won't see me. Aww, he's waiving and motioning me to pull in. Just how am I going to explain me being here?! Think Gary, think!"

He approached with a smile that brightened his face even more than usual. "So very good to see you, Gary. You come by to see me about something?"

"Well, uh, yeah," I stammered, rationalizing that that might be my subconscious reason for the wild notion to drive by.

"I am out for a walk through my neighborhood. Are you wearing shoes you can walk in?" He invited in a hopeful tone of voice.

"Always. It's pre-track season," I said as I jumped out of the car, relieved at how nicely my awkward situation turned out. Besides, now I could unload my concern about those Traditions. But before we took off, Mr. Babbitt excused himself into the house. When he returned and stepped down the concrete steps, he folded some paper and stuck it in his back pocket.

The starting-gun cracked and we were off like the turtle and the rabbit. I let up on my pace as I chastened myself, *Where's my head?*

"Now then Gary…what is on your mind?" He spoke in short phrases between breaths.

"Traditions, Mr. Babbitt. It's Traditions that's on my mind. The entire thing rattles me."

"Why does it rattle you?"

Although I suspected he already knew why, I explained. "I've found out 'Tradition' is merely a word given to our practices that, as the encyclopedia itself tells us, are not commanded in the Scriptures, but are accepted only because we have been doing them for a long time. But the problem is, Mr. Babbitt, the encyclopedia admits that soon after the apostles died, the Church began to get corrupted. That means all those new and not-found-in-the-Bible practices that came into the Church *after* the apostles died are no doubt part of that early corruption. But those erroneous practices continue to be used by the Church, and today's hierarchy tell us they are okay to practice because they were introduced so early and we have been doing them ever since. Mr. Babbitt, it is so easy to see: Tradition is merely a hierarchical cover-up for the early Christian's add-ons!"

Mr. Babbitt stopped and stood motionless like a marble-carved statue right there in the street. He gazed toward the concrete pavement a few feet in front of him. I didn't know if he pulled a muscle or if maybe he was having a heart-attack. I wasn't around old people very much, so I wasn't sure what was happening.

"What's wrong Mr. Babbitt? …Say something!"

His words flowed softly from his lips. "I have waited a long time to hear you say that. I knew you would come to that conclusion. I knew *any* Catholic would come to that conclusion after reading what you did in your encyclopedia."

A few more seconds passed. Then he raised his vision up the road and took off again. "Come, let us be on our way. There is more you should know."

Mr. Babbitt waived to a neighborhood couple trimming tree limbs but stayed totally focused on our conversation. "Gary, there are other ways a person can know that Tradition is not a source of religious authority from God."

"Such as?" I asked as I quickly glanced at him.

"What does it mean when a man contradicts himself?" he asked. "For example, a man tells one person he spent all day in his downtown office, but he tells another person he spent all that day in his boat fishing at the lake."

"Oh, that's obvious," I replied. "Both cannot be true. One is a lie and that makes him a liar and his word unreliable."

"Now, what if Tradition contradicted Tradition?"

"Well, same thing," I reasoned with consistency. "Tradition would be unreliable. And if it's unreliable, it certainly would not be from God."

"Gary, listen to me carefully. What the laity is being told by today's hierarchy about the need of using the Scriptures *and* Tradition, is not at all what the early Church Fathers taught. Those early Church Fathers, as they are called, were preachers and bishops who stood in the lead of the church during the first three to four hundred years. And, now get this, they are the very ones from whom today's hierarchy gets its earliest source for their doctrines of Tradition."

He then reached for that paper he had stuffed into his pocket and said, "I knew you would again someday confront this problem of Tradition. When I saw you drive up, I figured that day may have arrived. So I brought this along just in case. Here are some quotations of those Church Fathers I found in one of my books.[1] Most of it is information Mr. Campbell collected but did not use in that debate with Bishop Purcell. Here, take a look at what those Church Fathers—the Tradition of the early church—declared about the Christian's source of religious authority."

He held the paper in front of me. I took it, unfolded the paper and saw, in small but neatly printed letters, several quotations set off one from another by a blank line. I read aloud so Mr. Babbitt would know what quotation I was reading.

> *Tertullian* (about 200 A.D.):—Let this man's school show that it is in the Scriptures: if it is not in the Scriptures, let him fear the curse against those who add to or diminish.[1]

"Wow!" I bellowed like a mediocre student staring at straight A's on his report card. "This is not what today's Tradition says! Tertullian says doctrines must be found in the Scriptures and we cannot add to it. That's Scriptures *only*. Today's Tradition contradicts the original Tradition! But, since God does not contradict Himself,[2] then Tradition is not from God! And that can mean nothing other than the doctrines taught by Tradition have been added to the Scriptures by man—just as Tertullian said we cannot do!"

Mr. Babbitt maintained his steady pace looking down the street and said, "Tertullian was referring to Revelation 22:18, *'If anyone adds to these things'*– the Scriptures –*'God will add to him the plagues that are written in this book.'*"

"And, Tertullian was right," I conceded. "We can't add doctrines beyond what is in the Scriptures. And those not-in-the-Bible teachings of Tradition do just that!"

I read another one.

> *Basil* [head of a monastic community], (born 326 A.D.):—The hearers that are instructed in the Scriptures must examine the doctrines of their teachers; they must receive only those things which are agreeable to the Scriptures, and reject what are contrary to it.[1]

"Basil agrees with Tertullian," I remarked. "To *hear* 'doctrines of their teachers' can only refer to *oral* doctrines. And he says the

218

oral doctrines—Tradition—*must* agree with the Scriptures; but if they don't, then reject the oral. That means Basil taught the Scriptures are the only authority. That also means, today's Tradition contradicts the original Tradition."

"You are catching on," he said, and then looked at me with an approving squint of his eyes.

I went on to the next three.

> *Chrysostom* [Bishop of Antioch, and later of Constantinople], (345-497 A.D.):—…continually busy yourselves in reading the Holy Scriptures; which practice also I have not ceased to drive into them which privily come to me….The Canon [the authoritative list of New Testament books] ceases to be the Canon if anything is added to or taken away from it.[1]

> *Jerome*, (born 340 A.D.):—But the word of God smiteth the other things, which they spontaneously discover, and feign as it were, by an apostolic authority, without the authority and testimony of Scripture….[1]

> *Irenaeus*, [Bishop of Lyons, France in the last half of the 2nd century]:—[in a condemning manner said] They gather their views from other sources than the Scriptures.[3]

"All these are head-on collisions with what today's Tradition says!" I said with spunk. I was getting aggravated at the hierarchy's erroneous, misguiding trump-card of Tradition. Those Church Fathers were Scripture-only and anti-Tradition crusaders!

The next one topped them all.

> *Athanasius* [Patriarch of Alexandria], (about 340 A.D.):—If you are the disciples of the gospel, speak not unrighteously against God; but walk in the things that are written. But if you will speak anything besides that which is written, why do you contend against us, who are determined neither to hear nor to speak anything but that which is written? The Lord himself says, If you continue in my word, you are truly free! …For the holy and divinely

inspired Scriptures are of themselves sufficient for the discovery of truth.[1]

"Mr. Babbitt, how can anybody miss that?! 'Hear and speak nothing other than the *written*'; 'walk in the *written*;' 'don't 'speak besides the *written*;' '*the Scriptures themselves are sufficient for truth*.' Athanasius teaches Scriptures only!

"Mr. Babbitt, there's several more quotations on your paper, but I get the point. During the first 400 years or more, the Church Fathers—the main source for our Tradition—taught that our authority is the Scriptures *only*. But today the hierarchy teaches that Tradition says our authority is Scriptures *and* Tradition. That makes Tradition contradict itself! But God does not contradict Himself. So that means Tradition is not from God!"

"Exactly," Mr. Babbitt said like a coach complementing his player. "And, to look at it another way, people will either accept and use Tradition as a source of religious authority, or they will not. If they will not, then that's the end of Tradition for their authority. But, if they do accept Tradition, then they will have to denounce it and stop using it because the true, original, fact-of-history Tradition teaches to use *only* the Scriptures for religious authority. So, no matter what, Tradition fails to be the religious authority."

I shook my head in amazement of his simple logic. "You make it so understandable."

"My young friend, this is all so apparent, but the hierarchy is certainly not going to show you these things. Now, read the next statement by Jerome and see if you can detect a second contradiction with today's Tradition."

> As the Apostles wrote, so also the Lord has spoken—that is, by the Gospels; not in order that a few, but that *all may understand*.[1] (emp. added.)

"Are you kidding?!" I pulled the paper closer and read it again. "That's the exact opposite of what we are being told by today's Tradition. I can still feel my Catholic teacher branding my mind, 'If anyone is not a pope, a bishop, or a priest, then he cannot understand the Scriptures.'" I gave special emphasis to the word "cannot."

Mr. Babbitt prodded me on. "Take a look at what Irenaeus said."

Therefore, the entire Scriptures, the prophets, and the Gospels, can be clearly, unambiguously, and harmoniously understood by all.[4]

"This is unbelievable!" I spoke out without lifting my eyes from those words. "Today's teaching about this is completely foreign to the Church's original teaching."

I eagerly went to the next one.

> *Polycarp* [one of a small number distinguished from the rest as *apostolic fathers*], (116-117 A.D.):—Paul...did write an epistle to you, into which, if you look, you will be able to edify yourselves in the faith that has been delivered to you....I trust that you are well exercised in the Holy Scriptures and that nothing is hid from you.[1]

"Yep, same as Jerome and Irenaeus," I consented. "He says we can look into the writings—the Scriptures—and learn them ourselves with none of its teachings left hidden from our understanding. Mr. Babbitt, do you know what this means?!"

He kept looking down the street as he simply nodded his head, leaving the explaining to me.

I spoke with audible disgust, "Not only does it mean Tradition contradicts Tradition, which proves Tradition is *not* from God, but it also reveals that the later hierarchy changed the early Traditions to fit and cover-up the new man-made doctrines that differed from the Bible! Also, it means two of the hierarchy's tightest headlocks on the laity—the laity can't understand the Scriptures, so just believe and do what the clergy tell you to believe and do; and, the laity must do what Tradition says—are false! They are deceptions! They are lies!"

Outraged, I again had to slow my pace. But my controlled guide calmly said, "There's more. Read on."

I located the next one while hoping all this reading as I walked would not give me motion-sickness. "This one is from the *Catholic Dictionary*. 'It would of course be a monstrous anachronism...' Now there's a word I don't hear every day. What does it mean?"

"Anachronism means something is out of place in order of time. Like saying our country had a president in 1650, when our first president did not take office until after 1776."

I began again with the modification.

> It would of course be a monstrous misplacement in order of time were we to attribute a belief in Papal Infallibility to the Anti-Nicene Fathers.[5]

"Look at that!" I snapped as I slapped the paper with the back of my hand. "Papal Infallibility was not taught in Tradition back then as it is today. Yep, another contradiction. And, since the only authority for Papal Infallibility comes from Tradition, another big-time doctrine is erased!"

"Actually," Mr. Babbitt added, "Papal Infallibility was not taught until 1870. As a matter of fact, earlier, in the Campbell-Purcell debate of 1837, Bishop Purcell himself denied Papal Infallibility. I included his words in the next quote."

I read with sheer astonishment.

> Appeals were lodged for the Bishop of Rome, though he was not believed to be infallible. Neither is he now. No enlightened Catholic holds the pope's infallibility to be an article of faith. I do not; and none of my brethren, that I know of, do.[6]

"What can I say? Since it wasn't an article of faith in the Scriptures, or in the Tradition of the early Church Fathers, or in the Tradition of the Church until only one-hundred thirty years ago, then there's no doubt about it, it's just another man-made, man-wanted, man-inserted doctrine. Like I said before, Tradition is not the 'Living Voice of the Living Church,' it's 'The Man-Spoken Voice of the Man-Altered Church.'"

We were only a few houses away from Mr. Babbitt's home, giving me enough time to read the last one.

> Although Josephus tells of the wonderful effects produced in the Temple by the use of instruments [by the Jews], the first Christians were of too spiritual a fiber to substitute lifeless instruments for or to use them to accompany the human voice. Clement of Alexandria severely condemns the use of instruments even at Christian banquets. St.

> Chrysostom sharply contrasts the customs of the Christians [the non-use of instruments] at the time when they had full freedom with those of the Jews [the use of instruments] of the Old Testament. Similarly write a series of early ecclesiastical writers down to St. Thomas.[7]

"So the Church Fathers taught against using musical instruments in worship," I muttered in disgust. "Well, once again, the early Tradition contradicts the Tradition of today, showing it not to be from God. And, not only did the early Church Fathers, the so-called Tradition, not use the musical instruments, they severely condemned their use. Musical instruments have no Scripture, no Church Fathers, no nothing until 1000 years later when men pushed in the organ and said 'it's okay, it's Tradition.' What a rebellious scam against God's will!"

"So you see it then," Mr. Babbitt observed. "Catholic Tradition contradicts Catholic Tradition."

"As bright as the low-lying winter sun that's shining in our eyes," I replied as I held his paper for a sunshade.

"And since Tradition contradicts Tradition…" He halted for a breath.

I jumped in to finish his words, "…then Tradition *cannot* be from God because God does not contradict Himself."

"That is correct. And Gary, Tradition not only contradicts itself, it also contradicts Scripture. However, if both were from God, then God's teachings in the Tradition would not contradict God's teachings in the Scriptures because God cannot contradict Himself. Yet, Tradition contradicts the Scriptures by teaching: the clergy cannot marry,[8] the Scriptures are not our sole source of religious authority from God,[9] the everyday Christian cannot understand the Scriptures,[10] and many, many more crucial contradictions of critical doctrines."

"So," I said as we walked up his driveway, "Tradition contradicts both, itself and the Scriptures. That's like a solid 1-2 punch from Mohammed Ali for a cold, send-for-the-doctor knock-out."

He chuckled. "I guess that is one way of putting it."

Worn and wearied, Mr. Babbitt steadied himself with the metal guard-rail as he made it up the three steps to his raised porch that extended to the left behind the row of evergreen hollies that ran the length of the concrete deck. Loaded with thousands of bright red berries, the shrubs were quite an eye-catcher to those who passed by. We each took a seat on the matching white metal chairs that soothingly bounced. Thoughtful and pleasant as always, Mrs. Babbitt brought us each a mug of hot peppermint tea, and returned into the house.

We sat quietly. He, no doubt, waited for me to speak first so as to discover what pressed most upon my mind. As he sipped the steamy tea and watched a couple of children play in the yard across the street, he would have to wait patiently several minutes while I pondered the cruel, inescapable facts.

I knew what our talk during our walk meant. It was just that I did not want to accept it. But how could I not? I could stop being honest, but what good would that do? I'd be like an atheist who learned God actually exists but did not accept the truth. But, just because he would not accept God's existence does not change the fact that God exists. No. Failing to accept the truth that our Tradition is not a God-given source of authority does not somehow make it so. Not only would it do me no good to continue believing it is, it would also do me tremendous harm—I would be worshiping and living by commandments of men, which is vanity.[11] Yes, the facts of truth must be accepted, no matter where that truth may lead.

Anger seethed within my chest at whoever was guilty of coming up with the idea of Tradition as a source of religious authority. This deception of Christians and damage to the Church must surely rank as one of Satan's most ingenious schemes of corruption. My mind rehearsed what I had learned. *There's so much against it, just how can we miss it?! Tradition contradicts Tradition. Tradition contradicts Scriptures. Church Fathers taught Scriptures only. Tradition authorizes itself—which is worthless circular reasoning. Revelation 22:18-19—do not add to nor take away from what is written. 2 Timothy 3:16-17—the Scriptures by themselves are all we need to be complete, perfectly instructed for every aspect of Christian living and Church function. Indeed, how can we miss it! How can we not see that Tradition is not from God! Have we stopped thinking? Are we each but one piece in a domino chain taking our turn at falling just because all the dominoes before us and around us did? Do we not examine what we are told? I mean, my goodness, our eternal destiny is at stake!*

"Mr. Babbitt." It must have relieved him to finally hear me speak. "There's no way Tradition is another source of religious authority from God."

Without breaking his casual watching of the children across the street, he finished his sip, lowered the mug, and calmly said, "No, Gary, it is not."

"Then what is Tradition?" I asked as I raised my mug-free hand, palm up.

He turned to face me eye to eye. "It is simply a needed invention by the hierarchy in order to create a make-believe source of authority that would fool the laity into believing that all those man-made teachings and practices were actually from God."

"But they are not from God! The *Catholic Encyclopedia*, written by the scholars of Catholicism, makes that crystal clear!" I said, and then gritted my jaw as I churned in fury.

"No, they are not from God," he softly echoed.

"No wonder they tell us not to read the Bible, but rather just let them tell us what to believe!" I said explosively. "Otherwise, we'd see the contradiction between what we read in the Scriptures and what we are taught by the clergy's Tradition, and we'd know something was wrong. *Terribly* wrong!"

Keeping firm eye-contact, Mr. Babbitt seemed to choose his words carefully and speak in a manner as though he felt personally connected to them. "When an unsuspecting person stares at his test results which reveal indisputable evidence of a fatal cancer existing in his body, the news shatters every fiber of his being. He denies it. Thinks it a mistake. Wants to go on as before. But, what is, is. And he better do something about it. Gary, so it is with you and the 'cancer' you now know exists in your spiritual body, the Catholic Church."

Ol' Blue's hood-ornament did not cut the wind as sharply as I drove home. Not even on the mile stretch of Route 66. Emotionally exhausted and spiritually distressed, my snail-paced driving reflected my inner turmoil.

What a mess some of those early Christians made for me, I wailed in thought. *And what a nightmare they made for the Church! But, perhaps it should not be so unexpected. I recall God's people often got led astray into man's teachings by weak leaders.* I took a moment to scan my memory of the Bible stories I knew. It happened in the incident with the golden calf at Mount Sinai, the report of the ten spies of the Promised Land, idol worship when living in the Promised Land, and the tradition of the Jewish elders during Jesus' time. In all these, God was angry and He furiously punished them. But, since the Church has likewise been led astray into many God-angering doctrines of men, just what am I going to do?

CHAPTER 31
"THE REASON FOR THE SEASON"

It was Christmas Eve. Days earlier, Mom whisked her magic wand around the living room and crafted an enchanting atmosphere in Christmas decor. A huge poinsettia showcased its rich red petals from the center of the round, black, low-setting table positioned in the middle of the room. A host of 15-inch white candles on silver lampstands, crystal angels trimmed in gold, various figurines, Christmas cards from previous years, deep-green holly, and a large, hand-painted, ceramic Nativity scene harmoniously adorned the room. Chuck and Danny especially liked the wooden statues on the glass-top dinette table: Santa, Rudolph, and Frosty. No piece of furniture, no wall, no lamp lacked ornamentation. A burning candle under a small bowl of liquid cinnamon embellished the air with its satisfying aroma. Completing the enchanting mood, orchestra renditions of *Silent Night, Hark the Herald Angels Sing*, and many other seasonal songs softly, yet richly, flowed from the stereo. Also on the glass table, Mom set a variety tray filled with her large, thick homemade peanut-butter, oatmeal, and chocolate-chip cookies. But, why did she have to leave the note: "Limit: 3 per day"?!

The Christmas tree stood out among all else. Not even displays in stores could compare. Placed in front of the off-white, ceiling-to-floor patio door curtains, Dad's bleach-white, completely snow-flocked tree appeared like royalty with its mirror-like gold bulbs and a couple hundred tiny lights glowing like a campfire in the dark. Mom was a holiday genius.

Christmas Eve also brought along the yearly Christmas Eve Mass at midnight of which every serious Catholic attended. Mom, Kandy, and I, being serious Catholics and dressed in our best, headed for the door while Chuck and Danny, too young for the late hour, stayed with Dad, a Baptist.

Chuck, in a somewhat taunting manner, said, "Don't fall asleep in Church." Danny quickly added his jab with even more dare, "And remember, when you are trying to stay awake, we are sleeping in our soft beds."

"Yeah," I countered, "but when I get home it will be tomorrow, and tomorrow is Christmas, and Mom said there's no three-cookie-limit on Christmas, so I'll eat all the cookies!"

They looked at each other with a shocked, wide-eyed expression like they'd seen the Ghost of Christmas Past.

Kandy elbowed my ribs as we walked away and whispered, "Good one, brother, good one."

During the drive to St. Patrick's Church, Kandy interrupted our playful prying into what each other got Dad and the two elves for Christmas. "Mom, why does Christmas Eve Mass begin at midnight? I mean, that is so late."

"Well, I don't know," she honestly admitted. "My parents always took me, and the Church has done this for who knows how long. I just never felt the need to ask why or question it."

My precious mother's words tore my heart like the claws of a cat. The domino effect petrified Mom into a non-thinker.

My thoughts returned to Kandy's complaint of the late hour. Fully aware of the way the hierarchy changes practices due to what men want, I said, "Don't despair Sis, the day may come when the time is changed to an earlier hour."

Even though we arrived thirty minutes early, the parking lot already swelled to half full and the incoming river of headlights meandering through the blackness showed no end in sight. I dropped off Mom and Kandy near the entrance and then maneuvered through the hastening pedestrians and creeping cars to park Ol' Blue. Swiftly scuttling to the sidewalk, I came upon an elderly, slightly bent-over woman clenching a cane in each hand to support her feeble legs and ill-balance. She hesitated at the six-inch-high curb. For her, it presented a dangerous obstacle.

"Here, ma'am, please, let me help you," I implored.

"Oh thank you, honey," she replied with noticeable relief.

"Glad to help, and maybe one day somebody will invent a curb-less, paved slope at these spots," I said sympathetically and then hurried on to find Mom.

Arriving at our meeting place by the corner of the great bell tower, the three of us passed through the tower, dipped our finger-tips in the basin of Holy Water, made the sign of the cross, took a seat as guided by one of the ushers, visually scanned all the extra Christmas paraphernalia, and waited for midnight as we watched the people come in.

As the two hands of the clock approached straight up, the pews in the inner glass sanctuary bulged with laity like Elvis fans at a concert. Ushers then directed all subsequent arrivals to the hundreds of folding chairs set up in the expanse between the glass walls and the outer concrete walls embedded with those fifty, 36-foot-tall images of angels. A sense of pride filled my soul to see the multitude of loyal Catholics. I felt secure in the one, true, original apostolic Church.

When four priests, adorned in tall, tear-shaped headpieces, and cream-colored robes trimmed in fancy, four-inch wide gold-colored material affixed along the long flowing sleeves, collar, and front opening from neck to foot, assembled themselves with several older altar boys at the back of the center aisle, I knew Midnight Mass had arrived.

As the procession paraded down the center aisle toward the altar, which was bordered by poinsettias at its base and lit by candles on top, one attendant hoisted a three-foot, finely decorative golden cross mounted upon a golden pole. One of the priests swung a golden censor attached to a chain, releasing white-smoke incense from its several small dark windows encircling the censer. Upon approaching the altar, each took his position and then his part of the spectacular ceremony.

All during Mass, the people's devotion to God and the occasion could not go unnoticed. I could see it in their faces, feel it in their responsive readings, hear it in their boisterous singing and playing of instruments. While all throughout the neighborhood houses not a creature was stirring, not even a mouse, inside the sanctuary the Church heartily praised the one, true, living God.

The Eucharist, reserved for the last, highlighted the Christmas Mass. The ushers, row-by-row, directed the laity into the two lines formed in the center aisle. Step-by-step, I moved steadily toward the altar, watching the back of the person in front of me. When that now familiar back moved off to the right to return to his seat, I stood face-to-face with the priest. I opened my mouth and extended my tongue while he placed upon it a white, round wafer, which almost completely dissolved before I returned to my pew. As I knelt on the knee-pad, I meditated upon Jesus and the body He sacrificed.

But then, my thoughts slid to His commandment to eat of the bread *and* drink of the cup.

The cup! Drink of the cup! The priests drank of the cup, but Jesus commanded, "Drink ye ALL." I've been cheated from half of my communion with Jesus because of some man-made, Church-changing doctrine of mere men! I was furious.

The Mass ended when the priest raised his hands and proclaimed, "Go in peace."

"Yeah, right," I grumbled. "How am I to go in peace when I know the hierarchy depraves us laity like this? It's more like, 'Go in vexation.'"

I asked Mom to drive us home, and I let Kandy sit shot-gun while I sunk into the back seat, disturbed and insecure, again. Slapped sober by the no-cup communion, and removed from the brain-blunting pomp and excitement of the occasion, all the previously discovered man-made practices of the night began to surface in my mind. Altogether, I counted thirteen of them, eight of which were copied off of ancient paganism. I felt like I just came from a pagan worship. It was disgusting.

Yet, the laity is blindly led into all this because it's said to be Tradition, something we've done for a long time so it's supposed to be okay with God. But Tradition, which is really inventions of men covered up by forgeries, does not determine truth. Instead, truth is determined by the Scriptures of God. And the Scriptures do not command us to do any of these things taught by Tradition. Furthermore, the Scriptures even command us not to add to what is written. Like "Simon Says," the worshippers are only to do what "God Says." Man, what a mess!

The next two weeks passed ever so slowly. If, as it is said, time flies when you're having fun, then somewhere there must be a Law of Science that says time drags when you're in anguish. Day after day I racked my brain to figure out what to do about the Catholic Church's use of so many practices and doctrines which, even our *Catholic Encyclopedia* openly admits, originated from mere men, even pagans. And, since God's voice in the Scriptures forbids the performing of man-made religious practices and doctrines—or else be lost to the devil's hell—then yes indeed, non-stop anguish filled my mind to capacity.

"What am I going to do?" I asked myself a hundred times a day. "No way am I leaving the Catholic Church, it's the one, true, apostolic Church. Where else could I go?"

After developing, and then shooting down, a dozen ridiculous ideas, a workable solution finally emerged. Relief swept through my soul like the surge of cold air from a freezer's open door. The seven-ton elephant fell off of my back.

"I am a Catholic. I will go to Mass, but I will ignore the man-made practices and not participate in them. But, since almost all I ever hear taught is Tradition, then, to learn what the Scriptures teach, I will go to Mr. Babbitt's class and also listen to Mr. Young's sermons. Give 'em credit, that church teaches nothing but the Bible."

But, wouldn't you know it, that very next Sunday Mr. Young preached a sermon I would have rather not heard.

CHAPTER 32
LIKE FATHER, LIKE SON

I f I had believed in omens, the bitterly cold and windy January morning would have signaled danger. Without a clue to what lay ahead, I cut through the Arctic blast to Mr. Babbitt's church. Indeed, as lethally cold as it was outside, inside, Roy Young's sermon was as lethally hot.

As he stood behind a large wooden pulpit mounted upon a raised platform and faced nearly a full-house of eager ears, Mr. Young introduced his sermon. "Soaring far above most other doctrines in the grand realm of Christianity looms the well-known doctrine of Original Sin."

Original Sin? I know all about that, I boasted to myself. *That's where Adam and Eve's sin was passed on to their children, and their children's children, and so on until today. That's why I was baptized when I was six weeks old—to get rid of that inherited sin.*

My attention turned back to Roy's preaching.

"Many precious souls believe the doctrine of Original Sin, and many precious souls do not. However, as you well know, both cannot be right. Either a dear child is born with it, or he is not. He cannot be born in both conditions."

Well sure, I silently agreed.

He went on. "And, hear me now and hear me well, you ought not cast your precious faith in a doctrine just because you inherited that belief, no matter how treasured your predecessors may be. Reason with me friends and brethren: Is a Muslim's belief correct just because he grew up on the other side of Earth with loving Muslim parents in a Muslim community?"

He paused to let the obvious answer sink in.

"So it is with the doctrine of Original Sin. Listen! You're chances are 50-50 that *you* could be the one who inherited the wrong belief! Rather, and because of this epidemic problem of 'inherited beliefs,' our loving God commands us, for our own good, to '*prove all things*,' 1 Thessalonians chapter 5 verse 21. So, we shall promptly do what our Maker tells us. We shall ask the question, 'Is the doctrine of Original Sin true or false?' And we, as God-adoring seekers, shall test this vital doctrine with the Holy Spirit-delivered Scriptures to learn our Creator's answer."

That's music to my ears. I've learned the hard way: Don't place your eternal state in inherited and unexamined beliefs, but rather get God's answer from God's Word. And then we'll know we are born with sin.

"First," Roy emphasized as he proceeded in orderly fashion, "we shall hear from ancient recorded history as to when the popular doctrine of Original Sin began. Those who make it their work to research the writings of the early Church Fathers inform us, although Tertullian at about 220 A.D. and Cyprian at about 250 A.D. merely toyed with the concept, the doctrine of Original Sin is not found in any of the existing works of the Church Fathers. Yet, time continued to pass until, in the early 5th century, Augustine became the first man recorded to proclaim the idea of Original Sin. The doctrine grew in acceptance until many in the church began to believe that babies are born *with* sin, while multitudes still maintained babies are born *without* sin. The growing contention finally erupted into a blistering head at the Catholic Council of Orange in 529 A.D. in which the Council sided with the views of Augustine. The Catholic Church then changed from its ancient, apostolic doctrine, and ever since then the church has believed in Original Sin."

With limp arms and sagging shoulders, I sat like a drooping stick of taffy in a hot oven. *I've heard this song before*, I moaned. *Surely, Original Sin is not another man-made doctrine! There are just too many people who believe it, including a host of non-Catholic denominations.*

The preacher, as he went on, must have read my mind. "Nearly 1,000 years later a distinguished Catholic named John Calvin began his staunch opposition to several Catholic doctrines which inflamed the historic protestant movement against the Catholic Church known as the Reformation. Yet, now hear me friends, Calvin never denounced Original Sin. Thus, his teachings included that doctrine which then became a major part of the beliefs of the vast and diverse protestant movement which eventually produced hundreds of denominations which believe in Original Sin."

Well, so much for my "but the majority believe it" reasoning, I conceded. *The denominations believe it because the Catholic Church believed it; and the Catholic Church believes it because the Council believed it; and the Council believed it because Augustine believed it. Boy! If that isn't a classic case of inherited doctrine!*

Mr. Young advanced to his second point. "Next, brethren and dear friends, it shall be our task to examine what the Holy Bible of God the Almighty teaches about the doctrine of Original Sin so that we may learn whether the doctrine is true or false. The first of two verses we shall hear comes to us from God's faithful servant and majestic Law deliverer, Moses. In the 24th chapter of the beautiful book of Deuteronomy, verse number 16, we read:

> *The fathers shall not be put to death for the children, neither shall the children be put to death for the fathers; every man shall be put to death for his own sin.*

"Brethren and cherished friends, I ask of you, is our holy and wonderful God a hypocrite? Certainly not! God is not a sinner! Well then, beloved, since God is not a sinner, then, of course, He cannot be a hypocrite. And if God cannot be a hypocrite, then He will not tell His precious creatures, as He did in this verse, *"the children shall NOT be put to death for their father's sin,"* and then transgress His own perfect law by punishing children in hell, or even some so-called Limbo, because of the sin Adam committed! No, no! God is *not* a hypocrite! Therefore, neither does God put children to eternal death in hell for sins that Augustine, Calvin, and subsequent priests and pastors erroneously claim to be inherited!

"Furthermore, this significant passage of the marvelous Word of God makes it indisputable, since *every* man shall be put to death for his *own* sin, then, until a soul *personally* sins, he is NOT to be put to death! This means, the innocent babies—who have not committed any sin of their own—are not to be put to death for Adam's sin! And, look at the verse again, for the verse makes it just as undeniable: He who personally sins shall be *personally* guilty—he and he *alone*, WITHOUT passing the sin to his descendants! This means, Adam's sin is *not* passed on to all humanity! So, first of all—are you listening?—the doctrine of inheriting Original Sin is false because:

The Bible teaches that everyone is accountable for his *own* sins, *not* the sins of Adam!"

Wow! I was never shown that verse. No wonder!

I kept listening.

"Our second Scripture from the Holy Word of our blessed God is spoken by none other than Christ, the Master Teacher. In the Gospel of Matthew, chapter 19, the 14th verse, it is recorded for all time and for all people to hear:

> *But Jesus said, Suffer [allow] little children, and forbid them not, to come unto me: for of such is the kingdom of heaven.*

"Now, my attentive audience, we have heard the words from the mouth of Jesus, and before anyone automatically applies his 'inherited interpretation' to what our Lord said, I beg you bear with me for a quick and simple explanation of monumental importance of which Augustine and Calvin sadly overlooked. I wish to take you back nearly 2000 years ago to the original language in which Matthew wrote as he penned that particular word which the King James Version translated, 'little children'. The Holy Spirit inspired Matthew to use the Greek word, *paidion.* As you can see in the verse, it took two English words to properly translate the one Greek word. This is because the English word, 'child,' does not completely translate *paidion.* Therefore, the word, 'little,' is needed to describe the age of the child as is included in the word, *paidion.* The children, in our verse, were toddlers—not teenagers!

"In addition, take special note of this: *paidion* is used six times by Matthew in chapter 2 verses 8 through 14. This is the world-famous account of the new-born Savior entering into the world. Listen to verse nine.

> *When they [the wise men] heard the king [Herod], they departed; and, lo, the star, which they saw in the east, went before them, till it came and stood over where the* **young child** *was.*

"You may be thinking, 'Preacher, what is your point?' My dearly beloved, it is this. Since the word, '*paidion,*' means *newborns*—like the infant Jesus—and *young* children, then, when Jesus Himself said, the kingdom of heaven includes *paidion*, He was saying that some souls in heaven are those who died as newborns and young children! And that means: Since sinners cannot enter heaven, and since newborns are of the kingdom of heaven, then *children are NOT born with sin!*

"I would wish all sensible people would think for themselves as to what Jesus here declared. When He said, 'of such is the kingdom of heaven,' He *cannot* mean that a man must become like a child who is totally depraved in sin in order to enter heaven! But that is precisely what the doctrine of Original Sin has the words of Jesus teaching!

"Secondly, then—are you listening?—the doctrine of inherited sin is false because: Jesus Himself unequivocally teaches that children are born pure and without sin."

Oh, man! This is tough to take! I thought as I rallied enough strength to continue sitting erect. *Roy explained it unmistakably though. The verse definitely means we are born without sin. But, why hadn't I known about that verse? I've read the entire New Testament within the last few weeks, but I didn't notice that verse. I think I better start reading much slower and pay closer attention to what I read.*

Mr. Young began his third and last section of his sermon. "Finally, brethren and friends, we would be unwise and unfair to fail to address the verses of which those who believe in Original Sin claim to so teach it. But, be it known, verses in the Bible cannot contradict each other because God Himself wrote the Bible and God cannot contradict Himself. Therefore, when there *appears* to be a contradiction in the Bible's verses—as it appears with today's topic, that is, some verses for and some against the doctrine of Original Sin—then the contradiction is instead between man's *correct* interpretation of those verses and man's *incorrect* interpretation.

"We shall endeavor to examine the two passages of Holy Writ most prominently presented in the feeble effort to teach the unscriptural doctrine of Original Sin. The first of which is Psalm 51:5. Listen to it my friends, *'Behold, I was shapen in iniquity; And in sin did my mother conceive me.'*

"Let me now illustrate the trap into which multitudes fall when interpreting, or should I say, *mis*-interpreting this verse. Here is the story: A crime was committed of which three men, Al, Bob, and Curt were possible suspects; and, without investigation or trial, but due to the townspeople's minds already being made up, Al was taken and hanged to his death in spite of the fact he had the evidence to prove his innocence. Now I ask you, my fair and just listeners, was your reaction that of appalling disgust? I'm sure it was. All good people quickly see the townspeople's erroneous procedure of attempting to select the correct criminal. No investigation. No trial. No allowance for the man to prove his innocence. Instead, just pick whoever you want. Pick the one everyone else picks. Blindly pick and hang. I'm quite sure, under such a pathetic method of selection, you would not relish the thought of having been one of those three suspects, would you?

"Good people, that is exactly the method many use in interpreting Psalm 51:5! It appears to me the good folks who believe in Original Sin do not know there are at least three possible interpretations of Psalm 51:5."

What? I thought in near disbelief of Roy having said that. *This verse might mean something other than Original Sin? How could it?*

I continued listening with the sensitivity of the ears of a bat.

"The first possible interpretation, as we already know, is the opinion that this verse teaches the doctrine of Original Sin. The second possibility is that the psalmist, David, was pure and innocent of sin, but was born into a world full of corruption and iniquity. Such a phrase is used in Acts 2:8, which says that people were born in a language. Therefore, just as babies are not born already speaking a language, but rather are born into a country of a certain language, so can Psalm 51:5 correctly mean a child is not born with sin, but rather is born into a world of sin and corruption. The third possible interpretation of Psalm 51:5 is that David's ancestors were under a curse of sin. Follow with me in the Scriptures, folks. If a man was born illegitimate, his descendants were under a curse up to the tenth generation, Deuteronomy 23:2. Pharez was an illegitimate child, Genesis chapter 38, and David was the tenth generation from Pharez, Matthew 1:3-6 and Ruth 4:18-22. Therefore, Psalm 51:5 may very well be referring to David's conception and birth under the curse of the sin. There you have it, three very real and very possible interpretations of Psalm 51:5."

He's right! I admitted as I sat in astonishment. *There are other possible meanings of this verse. That means it just may not teach Original Sin after all!*

I eagerly turned my attention back to Roy.

"So, how do we know which possible interpretation is correct? Do we use the faulty method as was done with Al, Bob and Curt? Just blindly pick one due to what we favor, or due to what the multitudes pick? Or, do we investigate? Do we look for evidence that either proves or disproves any of the three possibilities?

"So, my friends, my fellow believers and lovers of God, in the process of elimination, is there any evidence that disproves any of the three possible interpretations? Oh, yes, there is indeed, and we have already seen the evidence. Remember, Jesus Himself made it incontestable in Matthew 19:14, children are born pure and without sin. Therefore, the possibility of Psalm 51:5 teaching that children are born depraved and with sin is *NOT a possibility!* Thus, the correct meaning of the verse must be one of the other two possibilities, neither of which teach Original Sin. My good friends, please do not believe in Original Sin. It is a *mis*-interpretation of Psalm 51:5."

Man! The clergy never even hinted at the possibility of another possible interpretation. Instead, they told me what to believe and I was not to question it. However, Mr. Young ripped that verse from their hands. The verse doesn't teach it at all!

Roy preached on. "This brings us to the other passage most often used in their attempt to teach Original Sin, and this will close our sermon from God's heavenly Word. Hear Romans 5:12 and 19.

> *Wherefore, as by one man [Adam] sin entered into the world, and death by sin; and so death passed upon all men, for that all have sinned:*

> *For as by one man's [Adam's] disobedience many were made sinners, so by the obedience of one [Jesus] shall many be made righteous.*

"From these precious passages, the claim of Original Sin is

advanced by those who so believe in it. But, my friends, as you are about to see for yourselves, the verses teach no such thing! Rather, trusting souls have read these with minds pre-told by others what to believe."

And I am one of those trusting souls, I added, feeling duped again.

"Please notice, as I am sure you did during your hearing of the passages, these two verses, as well as the entire section from verse 12 to verse 21, are concerning a comparison of what Jesus did and what Adam did. Adam's deed brought sin and spiritual death; Jesus' deed brought freedom from sin and gave spiritual life.

"Return your attention, if you would, to verse 12. The last half of the verse declares: *'death passed upon all men.'* Knowing this, we must then ask, *how*? HOW is spiritual death passed upon all men? Is it by *inheriting* Adam's sin? Or is it by committing our *own* sin? Our helpful God gives us the answer within the verse itself. Take note of the verse's very next word, 'for.' 'For' is an explanatory word. That is, the meaning of the words that occur before the word 'for,' are explained by the words that follow it. Let us together return once more in our Bibles to verse 12 and look to see if it reads in this manner: *'death passed upon all men, FOR that all have **inherited** sin'*? No! No! It does *not* so read. But that is the way it must read in order for the verse to teach Original Sin. But, I emphasize, IT DOES NOT SO READ!"

He's right! The truth forced me to concede as I inspected the verse. *I have been **assuming** it read "inherited." But it doesn't!*

"Well then," he pursued his point, "just how *does* it read? It reads like it always has, and always will: *'death passed upon all men, FOR that **all have sinned**.'* Do you see it, friends? A person enters spiritual death only when he *himself* sins. It is HIS sin, not Adam's; HIS breaking of God's law, not Adam's, 1 John 3:4; HIS disobedience to God, not Adam's, Hebrews 2:2. It is just as the powerful prophet Ezekiel proclaimed in the 20th verse of his 18th chapter: *'The soul that sinneth, it shall die. The son shall not bear the iniquity of the father.'* No, no, no! Romans 5:12 does not even come close to teaching Augustine's and Calvin's erroneous doctrine of inheriting sin. The good people of today are being misled into believing this 5th century, man-made false doctrine!

"'But,' we may be asked, 'what about verse 19?' Let us refresh our minds to its words.

> *For as by one man's [Adam's] disobedience many were made sinners, so by the obedience of one [Jesus] shall many be made righteous.*

"I remind you of the comparison between Adam and Jesus that is being presented in these God-inspired verses of 12 through 21. It is a comparison between the two regarding what each did for mankind. And take special notice, the comparison is between two deeds that produced effects on equal scale. That is, as verse 18 distinctly points out, what Adam did 'came upon *all* men,' and what Jesus did also 'came upon *all* men'. What each one did was *universal* for *all* men. Neither of the men's deeds affected only a portion of mankind.

"Now, this comparison is keenly emphasized in our verse 19 by its word 'so.' That is, as Adam did, *so* did Jesus. And this is how God provides sufficient information for any alert and honest student of His Word to know assuredly that Original Sin is *not* taught here. And, what is that information? Reason if you will. If, as the doctrine of Original Sin claims, *all* men are automatically made sinners by the disobedience of Adam, then, due to God's comparison on equal scale, SO are *all* men automatically made righteous by the obedience of Jesus! But, we well know it is *false* that *all* men are automatically made righteous by the obedience of Jesus to His crucifixion because numerous are the verses which teach that all men are *not* righteous, that is, all are *not* saved. Therefore, it is false that this verse is teaching that all men are automatically made sinners by Adam. You see, do you not: if sin is imputed to all, and not to just a portion, SO is justification imputed to all, and not to just a portion; if *all* men are automatically lost because of Adam, SO are *all* men automatically saved because of Jesus; if one is universal, SO are both; if one is 100% of mankind, SO is the other."

I see it! I teemed with excitement like solving a mystery novel before reading the last chapter. *Of course! And it was in front of my eyes all the time; I just didn't see it. If Adam's deed automatically made 100% of mankind sinners, then likewise, Jesus's deed automatically made 100% of mankind saved. But we know Jesus's deed didn't do that because most of mankind are still lost. Likewise, then, Adam's sin does not automatically make mankind born as sinners. Come on, Gary. Read, pay attention, and use your head!*

Mr. Young preached on. "My dear attentive hearers, you now know, do you not, this verse is not teaching the erroneous doctrine of Original Sin! What, then, you ask, is it teaching? Very briefly, it is this: Just as Jesus makes people righteous *by providing the **conditions** to become righteous*, which is by His crucifixion and His glorious good news of what to do to be saved, so did Adam introduce and expose people to sin *by providing the **conditions** to become sinners*, which occurred right after his sin when his and Eve's *"**eyes were opened**, and they knew they were naked, and they sewed fig leaves together, and made themselves aprons,"* Genesis 3:7. With this changed trait of the original male and female, their children and all humanity thereafter would likewise have 'open-eyes.' Brothers and sisters, and cherished friends, are you listening? The Bible is revealing to us, at the very moment Adam and Eve sinned, mankind's naïve innocence was lost! Their 'opened eyes' now knew there was right and wrong, and that is why they immediately realized they were naked. God Himself declared this change brought about by Adam in verse 22 of this same chapter in this manner: '*Behold, the man is become as one of us, **to know good and evil.**'"

"My good people who love God and His soul-enriching Word, are you still listening? It is because of Adam and Eve's sin and this change they brought upon the human race, that now their children, which is all mankind, inherits this 'opened-eyed/to know good and evil' CONDITION—*not the sin!* And, sadly, in this difficult 'opened-eyed' condition, all men, when severely tempted to choose evil, by their own freewill often choose the evil, and thus, sin, James 1:14-15.

"So then, my friends, as we bring to a close our sermon on this marvelous Sunday, what have we learned? We first learned that the doctrine of Original Sin was brought into the church, not by Jesus or the apostles, but by a man much later in the 5th century. Second, we learned from God's Holy Word that each person is responsible for his own sins—*not* his father's, Ezekiel 18:20; and, that Jesus Himself teaches that babies are born *innocent* and *without sin*, Matthew

18:3. And third, the verses which are claimed to teach the doctrine of Original Sin do not teach it at all. With this firmly established, I plead with every fiber of my being to all good and honest hearts: Do not be a victim of this false doctrine fabricated by man as devised by the deception of the devil himself."

Mr. Young stepped down. A song was sung; a prayer was led; and worship concluded.

I crept along with the crowd toward the exit doors. *Phew! After getting cooked by that sermon, when I step outdoors the cold won't bother me at all. Who would have ever dared to doubt the doctrine of Original Sin? Well, not me, I just believed what I was told to believe and didn't read the Bible—just like the clergy and nuns trained me.*

I was infuriated. I took being deceived personally. Being regarded as just a dumb sheep among many dumb sheep to be herded about where ever the hierarchy cared to point its staff insulted me to the max. I loved the Father, the Son, the Holy Spirit, the laity, and whatever good clergy there might be. But the clergy who, whether due to dishonesty or ignorance, brought in or sustained these false doctrines in God's precious Church, disgusted me to no end.

"Poor Ol' Blue, sitting in this frigid weather," I said sympathetically as the engine struggled to kick over. As I waited for the motor to warm up before heading off to Mass, I thought over those verses which teach children are born without sin.

"GOOD GRIEF!!" I said with a blast. "Since I didn't have any sins as an infant, and since I was baptized as an infant for forgiveness of sins that I didn't actually have... then what does that mean about my infant baptism?!"

CHAPTER 33
ON MY OWN, ALMOST

TWO HOURS LATER

I hate to do this, but I hate not knowing even worse. I stood to the side of the broad flow of priest-greeting laity exiting the sanctuary from the morning's Mass. Eventually, the last few hand-shakers trickled out and I forced myself to step toward him.

"Sir?" I beckoned as the priest turned to re-enter the sanctuary.

"Yes?... Oh! It's you, my earnest inquirer. Tell me, my son, your last question—the pope's potential for sinning—is it resolved in your mind?"

"Completely," I said, and added in concealed thought, *but not the way you wanted.*

"Then, there must be something else you are wondering about?"

The lines I rehearsed over and over unrolled flawlessly. "We Catholics baptize infants, and I was baptized as an infant. As a matter of fact," I turned and pointed to the baptismal basin, "right there, only four years ago, you baptized my youngest brother while I served as his godfather. So, what I want to know is, where do the Scriptures tell us to baptize infants?" I closed my lips and braced for a scolding for inexcusable ignorance.

The prolonged eye-lock with a corpse rattled me. I wanted to run—I knew he couldn't catch me. Just before I suffered permanent emotional damage, he said, "I thought I told you before, all you need to know and do is told to you by me and the rest of the clergy. You, the laity, do not need to be concerned with what the Scriptures teach. Nevertheless, my inquisitive child, I shall satisfy your curiosity."

My ears perked. My heart pounded. My thoughts focused. I knew the clergy's answer would be quite revealing, one way or the other.

"In Mark 16:15, Jesus said, '*Go into all the world and preach the gospel to every creature.*' 'Every creature' includes infants. So, there you have it. Infants need to be baptized."

What?! True, I favored infant baptism, but I struggled to hold back an honest burst of laughter. *"Every creature" also includes cats and dogs. Are we to baptize them?! Besides the "creature" is to be preached to, and it's absurd to preach to infants who do not understand what is said, and God does not command us to do absurd things. No way does 'creature' include infants. The clergy's reasoning with this verse has a hole big enough to drive Ol' Blue through!*

"Furthermore," he added, "there is no verse in the Bible that says, 'do not baptize infants.'"

You got to be kidding! Scattered thoughts flashed through my head in microseconds. *Then we can sacrifice an elephant on the altar during Mass—the Bible doesn't say don't do it! And we can spread peanut butter and jelly on the Eucharist wafer—the Bible doesn't say not to! As much as I want infant baptism, I won't stoop to absurd reasons. Besides, I've read for myself the Bible's warning to not add to the Scriptures,[1] and baptizing babies merely because "the Bible doesn't say not to" is adding to the Scriptures. And the Bible says to do only what God tells us to do[2]—like "Simon Says." No wonder the church has so many false practices—the clergy tells the laity to take their word for what the Bible teaches, but they themselves do not know how to interpret the Bible, and it shows!*

"Now, young man, do you have something to write with?"

I felt in my pocket. "No, I'm afraid I don't."

"Well, in this robe, neither do I. No matter, this is easy to remember. In Acts 16, Acts 18, and 1 Corinthians 1:16, there are four examples in which entire households were baptized. So you know that would include even the babies."

"Entire households?"

"Entire households."

"And that was Acts 16, 18 and what is the other?"

"1 Corinthians 1:16."

"Okay. I'll check them out," I assured him, and hoped he might now have something in spite of his first two ridiculous reasons.

"And one more thing," he added, "in Colossians 2:11-13, baptism took the place of the Old Testament practice of circumcision.

244

Now remember, circumcision put them into the Old Testament kingdom of God. So, in the New Testament, that which puts infants into the kingdom of God is baptism."

After thanking him for his time and answers, I made my way to Ol' Blue, repeating those verses to etch them in my memory. I was not going to forget them, not after losing five years of my life due to the stress it took to get them.

All in one motion, I flipped on my desk lamp, pulled out my Bible, and plopped onto the chair. I repeated the verses for the thousandth time, "Acts 16, Acts 18, and 1 Corinthians 1:16." But, my mantra for the day calmed no anxiety. These verses held my answer to whether my baptism as an infant was of God and saved me, or was of man and worthless. I already decided not to call on Mr. Babbitt, at least, not if I could help it. I needed to Sherlock Holmes this myself. After all, God tells us *"when you read, you may understand,"*[3] and God doesn't lie.

"'Four cases of entire households baptized,' he said. The first is Acts 16." I began reading the chapter in desperation for a Scripture to validate my infant baptism. "Here, this must be it."

> *And a certain woman named Lydia, a seller of purple from the city of Thyatira, who worshipped God, was listening; and the Lord touched her heart to give heed to what was being said by Paul. And when she and her household had been baptized, she appealed to us and said, "If you have judged me to be a believer in the Lord, come into my house and stay there." And she insisted upon our coming. Acts 16:14-15.*

But there's no mention of children. It can only be assumed, and assumptions never prove anything. It's putting words in the Bible's mouth by forcing it to say something it doesn't say. Assumptions only bend the Bible to teach something we want it to teach.

But, favoring infant baptism, I argued back. *But, surely most households have little children. Ours does.*

Yeah, but our neighbor's don't, I countered myself. *Neither does the house on the other side of him.* I took a quick census of the households down the street. The tally revealed far more households without little children. *Not only is it an assumption, the percentages are heavily stacked against it.*

Still looking for loopholes, I read the verse again. *Uh, oh. This settles it. Those who were baptized were those who heard, believed, and heeded to what the preacher said. But, infants can't do any of that. This means only matured people were baptized, not infants. No, there were no infants baptized in this household.* The first case flew away. A feeble assumption proved wrong by the verse itself. Expecting better in the other three, I located the next one.

> *And they spoke the word of the Lord to him and to all who were in his household. And he took them at that very hour of the night and washed their wounds; and he and all his family were baptized immediately. And taking them into his house, he set food before them, and rejoiced with all his household over his faith in God. Acts 16:32-34.*

Rats! This one doesn't teach it either. Those in the household rejoiced over the occasion, but infants can't do that. This one also describes adults being baptized, not infants.

I noticed a tension in my chest and shallow breathing. I forced deep breaths while searching for the third account.

> *But Crispus, the president of the synagogue, believed in the Lord and so did all his household, and many of the Corinthians heard Paul, and believed, and were baptized. Acts 18:8.*

Man! It does it again! The verse identified those who were baptized as mature people. They understood and believed what they heard. No infants in this household either!

Only one possibility remained, and the odds stood against me. Biased for infant baptism, yet loyal to truth, my fingers fumbled through the pages. I located my last hope.

> *I baptized also the household of Stephanas. I am not aware of having baptized anyone else. 1 Corinthians 1:16.*

This could be it! There's nothing here that infants can't do—no rejoicing, no responding, no understanding. Just that the household

246

was baptized. Surely, out of these four households. one had infants.

Hold on Gary. My mind split again. *You are assuming, not proving. And remember, you're biased. You want this verse to teach infant baptism.*

While my other half searched for a reply, I noticed at the end of the word, "Stephanas," a small, italicized letter "*g.*"

"A footnote?"

The footnote referred me to 1 Corinthians 16:15-17. I obliged.

> *Now I beseech you, brethren—you know that the household of Stephanas and of Fortunatus are the first-fruits of Achaia, and have devoted themselves to the service of the saints—to such as these do you also be subject, and to every helper and worker. 1 Corinthians 16:15-16.*

The knot at the end of my rope unraveled. Those baptized in the household of Stephanas were made of *helpers* and *workers* who *devoted* themselves to serving others—something only grown people can do, not infants. No, there were no baptized infants in this household either.

With elbows on desk, my face sunk into my palms. *Four cases. The hierarchy tells us infant baptism is taught in each of these four cases. But not one single solitary case does! And it's so simple to see that they don't. Good grief, I'm not a Bible guru, but I see it!* The darkness in my palms matched the devastation in my heart. I pushed against the surrender that banged at my door. Give out and despondent, for a few moments I drifted empty-minded.

My head shot up with eyes open wide. "Colossians 2:11-13!" I had forgotten about the last verse the priest gave me.

As I flipped the pages, I recalled what he told me: As circumcision put infants into the kingdom of God in the Old Testament, so does baptism remove sin and put infants into the Church today because it replaces circumcision. With hope renewed, I located the verses.

> *In him, too, you have been circumcised with a circumcision not wrought by hand, but through putting off the body of the flesh, a circumcision which is of Christ. For you*

were buried together with him in Baptism, and in him also rose again through faith in the working of God who raised him from the dead. And you, when you were dead by reason of your sins and the uncircumcision of your flesh, he brought to life along with him, forgiving you all your sins. Colossians 2:11-13.

Ho, boy. This is a little deep. I better read it again.

After the sixth reading without enlightenment either for or against infant baptism, I conceded, *I guess I'll call Mr. Babbitt. He's always honest in his explanations. Maybe he can help.*

The phone played its seven digit tune as I punched his number.

"Hello?" greeted Mr. Babbitt in his always gentle tone. He exemplified a true follower of Jesus—a lover of people, and a student and teacher of His Word.

"Mr. Babbitt, if I'm not interrupting anything, I have a Bible question."

"Gary," he recognized my voice, "even if I was busy, I would stop to try to help you. What is it, young Berean?"

"Since the circumcision of infants in the Old Testament put them into the kingdom of God, doesn't Colossians 2:11-13 mean…"

"Hold on, Gary. Who told you circumcision in the Old Testament put infants into the kingdom of God?"

"My priest; the hierarchy."

"Circumcision did *not* put them into the kingdom of God."

"It didn't?"

"No. As Romans 4:11-12 makes plain, Abraham was righteous *before* he was circumcised, and circumcision was only a *sign* of his righteousness."

"So, Abraham was righteous and in the kingdom of God before circumcision, huh?" I asked, wanting verification.

"Correct."

I immediately knew what that meant: baptism did *not* replace circumcision as my priest told me. Baptism, which puts a person into the kingdom, could not replace circumcision which did not. The two were not parallel. What my priest told me was wrong!

248

ON MY OWN, ALMOST

His words pierced my soul. That knotless rope slid through my hands. I felt myself falling, not knowing when or where I would land. The priest gave me the best the hierarchy had, but none of those verses taught infant baptism. They never have.

I thanked Mr. Babbitt for his help, then crawled back to my room and crumbled upon the bed. *No inherited sin. No infant baptism.* I felt like I blasphemed for even thinking that. But it was only the life-long indoctrination of those man-made doctrines taunting my conscience into such unjustifiable guilt. The truth stood firm. The Scriptures not only fail to teach those two doctrines, it proves them false.

"What do I need to do?" I moaned in isolation within a dark pit of horror I never knew existed. *Am I still lost? Have I only been thinking I'm saved? Am I one of those who that haunting verse is talking about—people at Judgment Day who think they are saved, but are not?[4] Man! I don't want to be in hell forever! Do I need to be baptized? Or, since I believe in Jesus, am I already saved as most denominations teach? I want answers. I want the right answers!*

CHAPTER 34
NO PAIN; NO GAIN

My head slid through the extra sweatshirt and pushed out at the hooded top. The dam, concealed under the night's blanket of darkness, revealed its more than quarter-mile length by a few distantly spaced lampstands stretching into the blackness of the West. I turned to look behind me. The faintly lit horizon promised the sun soon to rise for my eight mile Saturday run around Lake Overholser.

I needed a break. The relentless thoughts of the worthlessness of my baptism pounded my heart to putty. A good, long run around the peaceful lake would give my mind that release. Or, so I thought.

After stretching, I warmed up in a trot to cross the dam. Picturesque and historic, the renowned Mr. Ambursen built the buttress-type dam in 1918 using mules and steam shovels. As I jogged the concrete walkway over the chain of twenty-two water-gates that extended the length of the dam, each gate's fully exposed lifting machinery—huge, fifty-inch geared iron wheels with twenty-seven-foot axles—passed by on my left, appearing to grow in size in my slightly bouncing vision until disappearing behind me. Entering into the sixty-foot span of the truss bridge, I glared into the dark between the triangularly connected steel beams to catch the pale image of the spillway's crashing white-water nearly seventy feet below, and then gazed overhead at the silhouette of crossbeams against the now lightening, yet still star-studded sky.

After the warm-up crossing, I picked up the pace. The lake was all mine. No cars. No bikers. Not even fishermen. After all, it was cold. *Only an idiot would be out here,* I thought, incriminating myself.

The run supplied me what I hoped it would: distraction and relief from the disturbance that wrung my mind. The serene scenes surrounding me demanded my every thought. At snail's pace, the night slid westward, pulling its black blanket with its ever dissolving edge. Its departure uncovered pastel shades of blue and orange painted in cotton-candy clouds, and the rising artist splashed brilliant gold linings around each plume. Hundreds of thousands of tiny, isolated waves bounced in the one-and-a-half mile wide mystical expanse to create a dancing water-spectacle of the colors above. A song of a winter-hardy sparrow sliced the silence of the crisp air. Encouraged, a scattered chorus of its cousins soon provided me a continuous serenade from the sixty-foot oak trees surrounding the lake's shoreline.

Ahhh. I needed this. That thought arose often during the therapeutic run.

After forty minutes of vacation, I crossed Route 66's old truss bridge spanning the North Canadian River and approached the seventh mile mark. This mile would hurt. I intended it to. Already spent, I would run it hard, as though running to a burning house to save my mother. The maniacal exertion of a six mile worn-out body would increase my strength and endurance for my upcoming track races. But it would come at a grueling price. A price I consented to pay.

The imaginary starting-gun cracked and I took off. In moments, my heart pounded harder and my lungs drew deeper. But I pushed the pace—Mom was in that fiery house. With increasingly rapid and harsh breathing, the cold air began to burn my throat and lungs. My legs, devoured by fire, begged me to stop. Doubt raised its defeatist head, "You can't make it." I fought back. *I must! Mom's in that house!* That vision propelled every step. I pushed into the final 300 yards. Everything hurt. My head hobbled. My shoulders slumped. My chest bent forward. Even my arms agonized from their successive strong strokes. My tortured body fluttered above unconsciousness. *This must be what dying feels like.* A hundred yards to go. Bellowing groans of anguish with every breath, I gave it all I had.

I intended, without stopping, to slow down to a jog to cool off during the final mile, but I couldn't keep going. I flung my hands behind my head, stood erect, and sucked in as much air as my panting allowed.

Even if hell is merely that, I do NOT want to go there! I howled to myself.

That taste of torment kept on rattling my thoughts as I resumed jogging the last mile to the dam. Maybe that's one reason God has us feel pain, so we won't want to exist forever in something far worse. I mean, the Holocaust of those few minutes was madness, but it's dwarfed in comparison to hell.

Something Jesus said then popped into my head. It's one of those verses you don't forget.

> *Then he will say to those on his left hand, Depart from me, accursed ones, into the everlasting fire which was prepared for the devil and his angels.*[1]

*A fire! Hell is a fire! My legs and lungs burned during that insane mile all right, but not like **real** fire.* I then recalled how I once held my hands inches from a wood-burning campfire, but yanked them back in extreme pain. I then stared at the pile of bright orange charcoals pulsating with intense heat and imagined hell as positioned between three or four of those coals in the size of cars. *If I trembled at that, I sure do not want to go to hell.*

And, it's everlasting! I knew the pain of that mile would last only a few minutes. But what if it never ended! What if my palms began blistering at the campfire, but I couldn't pull them back! Ever! What if I were between those coals, for ever and ever! Hell is horrible!

And, if that wasn't enough, hell has no light at all! I remembered Jesus also said:

> *...cast him forth into the darkness outside, where there will be the weeping, and the gnashing of teeth.*[2]

Not moon-lit darkness, but, as Mr. Young said many times, "blackness of darkness."[3] I flashed back to a youthful walk through Alabaster Caverns with my grandfather. In the twisting cavern's deep belly, the guide switched off the lights. I waited for my eyes to adjust. But they never did. All I ever saw was black. Pure black. My eyes searched all around. I turned my head to and fro. I wiggled my fingers in front of my eyes. Nothing. No objects. No movement. Not even different shades of dark gray. I stood in pure blackness!

Within a minute of that wide-eyed stare into total blackness, I craved light. Anxious alarm mounted as the seconds ticked off. How could I possibly handle eternity? It is even said, within a few months

252

of blackness like that you go mad.[4] That moment in the cave branded my mind—maybe for such a time as this. *I do not want to go to hell, even just because of that!*

Hearing myself think of the "burning torment" triggered my memory to Mr. Young's explanation of "*the lake which burns with fire and brimstone.*"[5] Brimstone is flammable sulfur, and when burning, emits a repulsive, suffocating odor. *Gross! I've caught whiffs of the stench of dead, rotting animals. I've opened lids of putrefying, maggot-filled trash-cans in the hot summer. It's hideous!* When that happened, I would spew out the air, hold my breath, dash away, and then spit and spit and spit. But in hell, there's no place to get away from it! You never pull your head out of the trash-can full of vomit! Hell is horrible!

I stood by Ol' Blue. The lake's lengthy shoreline merited only a quick glance at my accomplishment. Something far more important demanded my concern. *Hell is so horrible, I'm going to do whatever it takes to avoid going there! No matter who I disappoint, I've got to do what God says. Hell is torment, and it's never going to end. It's a fiery furnace.[6] The excruciating pain makes you grind your teeth and scream; how hideous then must be even the sound in hell! It's total, maddening blackness. It's repulsive stench. No wonder Jesus said:*

> *If thy right eye offends thee, pluck it out, and cast it from thee: for it is profitable for thee that one of thy members should perish, and not that thy whole body should be cast into hell.*[7]

I contemplated those words. *I'll take that to mean, hell is so horrible, do whatever it takes to not be put there! Other people may think they'll not go to hell if they just do and believe what others do and believe. But that's nothing but being a domino in a long line of dominoes who merely assume they're in the right line and doing the right things. But not me! I'm not going to be naïve like that anymore. I want only that which can be proven by the Scriptures. After all, that's what I'll be judged by.[8] Eternal hell is too horrible to take any chances!*

CHAPTER 35
MISERY LOVES COMPANY

Whizzzzz…, ker-plunk.

After tossing a cast, Bruce sat on the ground a few feet from me. Winter fishing usually wasn't a good idea, but, with the abnormally warm and sunny day, we figured the fish might crave a big, juicy worm dangling between their eyes.

"Why so down in the mouth, my friend?" he asked as he faced the lake, watching his red and white bobber sway peacefully upon the tranquil, blue surface.

"Sorry, Bruce. I didn't realize it showed."

"Yeah? Like, you haven't cracked a smile or said much of anything since we got here. That's not my energetic pal. So, what's eating you?"

"Bruce…" I paused to think how I would tell him. "What if our baptism as babies wasn't God's teaching at all? What if it's a practice man made up? That would mean our baptism wasn't any good, wouldn't it? And that would mean we have never done what God said to do to get our sins forgiven. It would mean we're lost, Bruce."

I went on. "Last Saturday, when I ran around this lake…"

"You what!" Bruce cut in. "You ran around Lake Overholser?!"

"Yeah, and man it hurt. I felt like I went to the edge of hell for a few minutes. Bruce, I'm telling you, I would not want to run in that pain for eternity, and I *sure* don't want to be in *hell* for eternity."

"You got that right! But look, you said 'what if.' Gary, there's no 'what if' about infant baptism. Good buddy, infant baptism *is* God's teaching."

"I asked our priest about that. He gave me six verses, but not one of them teaches it. It is only *assumed* infants were in those baptized households. But Bruce, all those who were baptized did things infants can't do, which means, there were no infants baptized. I got to admit, the Bible doesn't teach it."

"Hey, man. Don't bend yourself out of shape trying to understand those verses. Remember, Mr. Clay told the both of us, only the clergy can interpret the Bible, and all we have to do is believe what they tell us it means."

"Aw, Bruce, we talked about that, remember? That's circular reasoning, and reasoning in a circle never proves anything. It can't. It's a logical fallacy. You see, the clergy tells us: 'The Bible can only be correctly understood by the clergy, so you laity must believe and do what we tell you.' But, we ask: 'How do we know *that* is true?' They say: 'Because the Bible says so.' And we ask: 'But how do we know the Bible says so?' Then they answer by repeating their first statement; and then their second; then their first; their second; first; and on and on it goes. Reasoning in a circle: it deceives, but proves nothing."

"But, creepers! I can't understand the Bible."

"Bruce, what if God said you can?"

"Well, I, uh… But He hasn't told me that."

"Yes, He has. You just don't know it because the clergy has kept you from it. You wanna hear it?"

"What, is God going to speak through you so I can hear Him tell me?" he joked.

"No. He speaks through His Scriptures, and, I add, very clearly and very simply. Listen, part of the God-inspired Bible was sent to the faithful in the city of Ephesus, that is, the normal, everyday Christians. That's in the very first verse. Then, in very simple words that need no smart interpreter, God tells you, '*when you read, you may understand*.' Bruce, you know there's nothing complicated about that. '*When you read, you may understand*.' It's telling you that normal Christians *can* understand the Bible when we read it! '*When you read, you may understand*.' So, what Mr. Clay told us is wrong. It's not true that only the clergy can interpret the Bible and all we are to do is just believe what they tell us, like they do about infant baptism, which is not found in the Bible at all."

"But, you're forgetting about…*Tradition!*" He thundered the word like Poppa in *The Fiddler on the Roof*.[1] We both cracked-up laughing.

Bruce slapped a cupped hand over his mouth. His big, brown, wide-opened eyes signaled, "Oh, no! I forgot!" His hand transformed into a fist with his upright index finger pressed against his lips. We always sat quietly on the bank. He insisted our talking scares away the fish. We took our optimum fish-catching mode: two good friends quietly watching two bobbers while sharing the moment.

I think Bruce was glad he got me to laugh. So was I. But neither laughing nor ignoring solved my problem—a problem, as Bruce noticed, that vexed my soul. So much of Catholicism, as I read in our own books, depends upon dirty secrets that, if known, would demolish the foundation of many of our doctrines and practices. *And Tradition's no help,* I silently groaned. *It's merely the clergy's tight leash around our necks. Tradition is **not** from God, as they claim. It not only contradicts the Scriptures, it contradicts itself! And, since God doesn't contradict Himself, then Tradition **can't** be from God! On top of that, there's the verse that declares the Scriptures themselves give us every instruction we need in order to be religiously perfect.[2] That means there are no other teachings from God for Him to give. My goodness, the clergy's claim about the need of Tradition makes God out to be a liar!*

And today, because of the lies of Tradition, the Church is deceived into vainly believing and practicing many things that were made up centuries ago by mere men, and, for doing so, He will add to us eternal punishment.[3] What a fine mess!

My lowered eyes glanced up at my bobber. I longed to see it plunge with a pop. Fighting a hefty catfish would certainly halt my depressing thoughts. At least, temporarily. But it sat motionless as if in a tranquil tub of water.

The pope, I grumbled to myself. *Even the papacy exists because of Tradition. It's not taught in the Bible. The particular words Jesus said make it impossible for Peter to be the rock. Besides, many of the popes have been some of the most despicable characters ever to walk the face of the earth!* It gnawed on me like a starving rat to think of those sixty popes who committed such hideous evil. They murdered, committed adultery, robbed, bribed, and so much more. And there are the six centuries of popes who used the Inquisitions in ruthlessly torturing hundreds of thousands in the most repulsive and inhumane methods, and then burned many thousands roped helplessly to a stake. All the while, God said in the Bible that the most He allows the Church to do to heretics is to kick them out of the Church. So there's no way God was leading all those popes to do that!

And the Crusades! The papacy created and fueled the 600 years of the ungodly, brutal Crusades that left four million people dead in spite of Jesus declaring His kingdom is not to do that.[4] No sir! God was not leading six-hundred years' worth of popes to rule contrary to His own will!

Sinfully corrupt! Inquisitions! Crusades! If God had established the papacy, He would not have let all those popes take His precious Church down to such ungodly depths for so long a time. My! It's obvious to a ten-year-old, the popes are not from God nor are they led by God. Rather, the papacy was created by men and covered up by Tradition. When Bishop Purcell, with the ears of the world listening, could not deny those historical facts the other guy in that debate presented—the facts that show the first pope not to have appeared until around 600 A.D.—then the truth that men, not God, thought up the papacy, glared blindingly.

*And they had the audacity to lie about a chain of popes spanning those first few pope-less centuries through forgeries! Just what in the world do they think they were doing? But not only that, they made up a host of forgeries to cover up numerous practices men brought into the Church. Important things! The hierarchy. Lent. Holy Water. Mass with the fruit of the vine held back from the laity. Penance. Purgatory. Rosary. And, yes, even the Apostle's Creed. Forgeries! Lies! Deception! And there are yet many more of our practices the Catholic Encyclopedia admitted as new inventions of men. The cross. Making the sign of the cross. Celibacy. Confirmation. Nuns. Instrumental music. The mind-blower is our encyclopedia's statement that only a few points of faith that we practice may be traced back to within a few decades of the apostles. So we have only a few of the things we believe and do that might be what God says?! And the rest are man's doctrines?! And what does God say about that? "**In vain do they worship me, teaching for doctrines***

257

the commandments of men."[5] *And, do not add to His Word, or He will add to us the plagues written in the Book.*[3]

I looked at my friend, who seemed to not be bothered by the contradictions and cover-ups of our mutual religion. *Yeah, Bruce, I haven't cracked a smile or said anything. I'm worried. Yes, I'm scared. Man has corrupted God's Church. And man has told me my infant baptism saved me when it didn't! I don't want to go to hell, but, I don't know what to do!*

I drove Bruce to his home after our catch-less fishing trip. We didn't talk about religion. I didn't want to, and I don't think he did either.

"Let's do it again sometime, big 'un," I said as he slid out of the car.

"You're on. But let's go when the lake is frozen. We'll ice-fish." He joked.

As I arrived home, Chuck burst out the door and dashed to the car. "Somebody came by wanting to see you. He left you this note."

I opened it.

"Give me a call. Mr. Babbitt."

CHAPTER 36
PANDORA'S BOX

As I hung up the phone I sensed something was wrong. Mr. Babbitt insisted he and I meet for Bible class tomorrow in the church library while one of the other men in his church taught his high school class. I felt privileged for the personal tutorial, but both, the arrangement and his disposition were way out of his character. I knew something was wrong.

"Come on, Ol' Blue, don't quit me now!"

Sputtering and spattering up Rockwell Avenue, the fuel-gauge teetered on empty. She sipped the last drop and fell asleep. With what little momentum remained, I crept onto an empty parking lot a mile from Mr. Babbitt's church.

"Great! Just great! Now I've got to walk and I'll be late. Mr. Babbitt will think I cut out on him." The thought of disappointing Mr. Babbitt hurt me.

I zipped up my coat and set off for the church, hoping my legs in the thin Sunday slacks would soon warm up.

HONK!

Behind me, a car slowed down and pulled alongside me with its window rolling down.

"Car problem?"

My gloom flipped to exhilaration. One of the men in Mr. Babbitt's church spotted my predicament.

"I ran out of gas," I replied as I grinned in embarrassment.

"Hop in. We will get you some gas after church."

"Thanks!" I said as I opened the door and gratefully slid in.

"I'm Ralph," he introduced himself. "My wife, Lorene; and our daughters you are sharing the seat with are Cindy and Martha."

The little girls with the giggly faces looked the age of my brothers.

"I really appreciate you picking me up. I didn't want to be late for Mr. Babbitt's class."

Ralph and Lorene turned their heads ever so slightly toward each other and caught momentary eye-contact. I recognized a we-know-something-you-don't movement when I saw it. And I just saw one.

A nervous tingle rippled through my body. Emptiness rose in my chest. Without realizing it, a fondness had developed during the past few months for the gentle, honest man who sacrificed so much of himself in order for me to discover religious truth. I knew it might not be good manners to ask about the secret, but I just had to know.

"Sir, is there something wrong with Mr. Babbitt?"

Lorene, as before, glanced at her husband, but this time he maintained his stare straight ahead. Procrastinating a response, Ralph finally broke the stressful silence. "Mr. Babbitt has cancer."

"*Cancer!?*" I cried out in disbelief. The war against cancer offered little to no hope in those days. It was essentially a death-sentence. I personally witnessed its life-extinguishing progression when Mom's mother died with cancer. A cancer victim possessed precious little time. I yearned for either Ralph or the doctors to be mistaken.

Then Ralph added, "He has been fighting it for a while, but it took a turn for the worse."

I sat stunned. My eyes glared outside, seeing only the blur of objects darting across my side window. If Ralph said anything else, I did not hear it—I was sprawling in agony by the spear that ran through me. No, he wasn't family. No, he wasn't a close school buddy. No, I hadn't known him for years. Nevertheless, Mr. Babbitt, by his teachings and by his example, forged an incredible impact upon my life, and knowing what cancer did, Ralph's words devastated me.

A spherical curtain drew around me and shut out the world while thoughts of the past few months scrolled across my mind. *Mr. Babbitt has had cancer ever since I've known him. But he didn't let on when he extended his large hand and greeted me with one of his big smiles, "Hello, I'm Loral Babbitt." He was struggling with cancer in body and mind when I rudely told him off about him not*

260

using Tradition. Yet, he responded with kindness and patience. He was fighting the weakening effects of the deadly illness when he exerted himself to meet me, an angry young whippersnapper, for an hour before further pushing his ailing body in teaching his Sunday class. But he did not object. And when he should have been thinking about himself, he thought about me as he kept my Catholicism secret from the class. He was suffering from cancer when he, without regard for himself, promptly invited me into his home when I had telephoned about Peter, and later, about the Inquisition. And no wonder he had difficulty breathing when we walked his neighborhood as he taught me the truth about Tradition—he strained with cancer. His research and guidance through the Catholic Encyclopedia at the Nazarene college, his special Bible classes—at least a half dozen—specifically prepared for me, his answering my Bible questions when I called—all done during the trauma of cancer!

Cancer, but I couldn't tell it. He's cheerful, not sad and despondent. He doesn't talk about his problem, instead he asks us about our accomplishments and our religious questions. When cancer, especially at his age, should have withdrawn him to self-concern and self-survival, he longed to help others learn the Bible and do right. He taught me with respect by guiding me to my own discoveries instead of demanding conformity to what he could have easily told me. He showed earnest concern for my feelings when I learned things that shattered my Catholic beliefs. And he did all that for me while knowing his own candle was flickering out. I've never known anyone so helpful, so caring, so Christ-like.

I just never imagined Mr. Babbitt would soon be gone.

Chapter 37
When All Else Fails,
Read the Instructions

I wiped the tears from my eyes as inconspicuously as possible while Ralph maneuvered the car into a parking slot between two other cars. I thanked him for the ride and then headed toward the church's building.

Why does Mr. Babbitt want a class with just me? And, now that I know he is dying, how should I act?

As I approached the door, each step waded through thicker uncertainty. I was even uncertain of the location of the church library.

A wooden door with a six inch square window allowed me to detect a room with bookshelves. But, was it the library, or was it Mr. Young's study? I inched my nose closer to the window for a better view.

"You are not afraid of a library, are you?"

The voice came from behind my back, but I knew it anywhere, although it sounded weakened. I decided to mirror his behavior, whether sad or otherwise, and his spirited humor signaled normality—the secure and glad-to-serve-God Mr. Babbitt. The man feared not death. The words, *"For me to live is Christ, and to die is gain"*[1] found a heart in which to live.

"Only *school* libraries," I returned the jesting.

After turning the cold, metal doorknob, I stepped into a room of huge, fully loaded bookshelves butted up one to another and towering from floor to ceiling. The wooden sentries surrounded me into a bookworm's dream. One bookshelf, instead of books, contained various Bible maps and charts affixed to removable horizontal poles like the hanging newspaper racks at public libraries.

These people are serious about learning the Word of God, I thought as I took a seat upon the slightly cushioned chair at the middle of the eight-foot oak table resting in the center of the room.

Mr. Babbitt intentionally selected the chair facing me on the other side. This special class was his doings, so I waited on him to speak. But, for a few moments, he too said nothing. By his kind eyes and peaceful expression, he appeared to relish the moment.

"Young Berean, you impress me. In the last few months you have learned and verified several devastating truths about your Church, truths so serious that most others would have quit religion completely. But you remained firm in your faith in God and in your search for answers. Neither have you reacted as did the Pharisees to the words of Jesus in their blind prejudice by ignoring the undeniable. Nor have you, like so very many do, run to their priest or pastor but never give a fair examination to honestly see whether what they tell them is really true or just cover-up talk. However you must surely have many questions, and, before long, you will graduate from high school and go off to college and I will not be able to help you."

Perhaps, Mr. Babbitt, I sadly considered, *but I know the real reason why you soon will not be able to help me.*

"So," he spoke on, "I made this arrangement to see if I can be of help."

His words thrilled me. A question-and-answer session, and, man, I swam in questions! And he probably knew it.

"That's great, Mr. Babbitt! Thank you!" I felt my face squeeze into a big smile.

His smile, better controlled than mine, likewise revealed his delight.

"But, your answers are going to come out of the Bible, aren't they? I mean, I want your answers to be proven by the Scriptures, not by your church's creed-book. You know I have been misled by man-made doctrines before, and I'm not going to let that happen again." I hoped I did not insult him, but his broad grin eclipsed mine of that moment earlier and I knew what I said pleased him.

"Gary, we do not have a creed-book…well, I take that back. We do. It is the Bible and *only* the Bible. Besides, other than looking in the *Catholic Encyclopedia* to see what Catholicism teaches, have I ever shown you anything other than the Scriptures?"

"Never." I felt embarrassed.

"And neither shall I now. So, what is foremost on your mind?"

"It is this, Mr. Babbitt. I know the Catholic Church is the one, true, original Church that began with the apostles right after the crucifixion of Jesus, and I also now know that Jesus' Church had a lot of vain, man-made doctrines and practices added to it during those first few hundred years that we Catholics still believe and do today. What I want to know is, what was the Church like originally, *before* man made a mess of it with a bunch of vain practices that God does not accept?"

His hands, clasped together upon the table with fingers alternatingly shuffled together, unfolded, reached for, and slid his Bible in front of him. "Actually, and probably in contrast to what you are thinking, the answer is quite simple."

"Simple sounds good to me!" I said as I opened my Bible, and waited to turn to his first announced verse.

"Gary, there are three major aspects of the church presented in the New Testament everyone ought to know. The first is the church's creed-book—its religious authority for everything it does. As I said a moment ago, and as we have talked before, the only creed-book of the church is the New Testament Scriptures. Now, I am going to put you on the spot: do you remember why this is so?"

"Do I remember? After I was the battered ping-pong ball between you and my Catechism teacher, how can I forget! Second Timothy 3:16-17 says the Bible has *everything* we need for our beliefs. That means we do not need additional creed-books. And on the last page of the Bible it says we cannot add to or take away from the Scriptures. So, we are also prohibited from making and using creed-books. That means the Bible, and *only* the Bible, is the sole religious authority."

"Exactly," Mr. Babbitt concurred. "And the church at the very beginning knew that. That is why you can read through the New Testament and see all the churches teaching and practicing the same things. Oh, yes, here and there you come across some Christians teaching something different, but they were quickly rebuked. There was none of today's 'You believe what you want, and I will believe what I want because everyone is entitled to their own opinion.' For instance, instead of tolerating that which was different from the apostle's teachings, five of the seven churches in Revelation 2 and 3 were rebuked and told to get back to the right way. And, the Christians in Galatians chapters 1 and 5, who merely added their own opinion of the religious practice of circumcision, were accursed and cut off. Even Peter, of all people, was correctly rebuked by another Christian."[2]

"So," I interjected, "at its beginning, the church was united in its beliefs and practices because they used only the Scriptures and stuck to it?"

"Yes. They could visit any church in any town and find all of them believing and practicing the same things."

"Wow! How nice that would be!" The thought enthralled me.

"I think others would agree with you. But you see, that is the way it was in the church's beginning because they understood they were to *all speak the same thing and that there be no divisions among you; but that ye be perfectly joined together in the same mind and in the same judgment.*"[3]

I leaned back in my chair. "Mr. Babbitt, do you think that could happen today? I mean, this *is* God's Word, and this *is* what He wants. So, why couldn't it happen today?"

"Because, Gary, people have free-will to choose, and the vast majority seem to always choose wrong because people feel there is safety in going with the majority or in what they grew up with. But, that should not stop you, should it?"

That was a strange question. What did he mean by that? What could I possibly do to get the Catholic Church to use only the Bible? That will never happen! Did he mean something else?

He turned some pages in his Bible. "This brings us to the second major aspect of the church you need to know: how it worshipped."

"Good. With all those articles I read in the *Catholic Encyclopedia* that admit so many things we do were made up by men, I don't know whether or not what I'm doing in worship is what God told me to do. And it's scary."

"Because of Matthew 15:9?" he asked as he kept looking for the verse he wanted.

"Yeah." I knew what he was talking about. That verse sat on my shoulder and yelled in my ear during every Mass.

His pages settled down. He looked at me and said, "Gary, the way God tells us to worship is wonderfully rich, yet so very simple. He instructs us to worship Him by only five acts. No more, no less. Now, due to our limited class time, I am going to show you only one verse for each, but be assured, there are many more verses for each of the five."

"I'm more than ready," I said with my fingers perched on the edges of the pages of my Bible. The thrill of seeing for myself God's pure instructions for the manner of acceptable worship unleased a cage of butterflies into my stomach.

He began. "First, turn to Acts 20:7."

"Just a sec…. Okay, I got it. You want me to read it aloud?"

"Please."

> *And upon the first day of the week, when the disciples came together to break bread, Paul preached unto them, ready to depart on the morrow; and continued his speech until midnight.*

"I see it, Mr. Babbitt. It was the first day of the week, Sunday, and in the assembly Paul *preached* to the church. Good. So preaching is not something men added to worship."

"Right. That is one of the five. And the verse mentions a second," he said as he pointed a finger at my Bible and gave a slight head-nod.

I re-read it and answered in puzzlement. "The only thing I see is something about breaking bread."

He noticed my confusion and replied with a slight chuckle. "That does not mean to merely tear apart a loaf of bread as an act of worship, but rather, it refers to the Lord's Supper, or communion, or, as it is familiar to you, the Eucharist."

"The Catholic Church does that!" I said in an exhale of relief. Another part of our worship was right.

"And," he added, "Catholics do it *every* first day of the week, which is something you have always done without man changing it. Every week has a first day, and on the first day of the week the Christians are to eat the Lord's Supper. It is just like the Jews who understood the commandment, *'Remember the Sabbath day, to keep it holy,'* meant *every* Sabbath. Every time the seventh day of the week came, they were to observe it. Likewise, every time the first day of the week comes, we are to observe the Lord's Supper. However…"

"Yes, I remember," I cut him off. I never forgot our first meeting. "Catholics don't drink of the cup like Jesus tells us."

"Unfortunately, no," he said in a sympathetic tone.

"Yeah, I even read about that man-made change in our own encyclopedia." I knew the clergy was wrong to hold back the cup from us.

"For the Scripture's third act of worship, turn to 1 Corinthians 16:2."

Again, I read aloud.

> *Upon the first day of the week let every one of you lay by him in store, as God hath prospered him, that there be no gatherings when I come.*

"What do you observe in this verse," he asked.

"It's the first day of the week again, and we are to give in the collection."

"Correct," he assured me. "Many people do not get it, but giving money to God's work is worship to God."

"And we do that, too!" Knowing our numerous vain add-ons, discovering our correct acts overjoyed me.

"Do you have any questions so far?" He peered across the table awaiting my response.

"Nope. I'm ready for the fourth one."

"Then, when you find it, read Acts 2:42 and tell me what you see."

> *And they continued steadfastly in the apostles' doctrine and fellowship, and in breaking of bread, and in prayers.*

"Well, it has a lot in it, but I notice the breaking of bread which is the Lord's Supper of Sunday's worship, and then there's praying."

"Right."

"That's four out of four…well, without the cup of the Lord's Supper, three and a half out of four things we do right!"

He again began turning his pages as he said, "The last act of worship is found in Ephesians 5:19, and as you read it, carefully notice what it *says* and what it does *not* say, remembering that we cannot add to nor take away from what it says."

As I flipped through the pages, I wondered why he said that. I found the verse and read.

> *Speaking to yourselves in psalms and hymns and spiritual songs, singing and making melody in your heart to the Lord;*

"And?" he asked.

"We are to sing."

"Anything else?"

I looked at the verse. "We are to speak to ourselves in psalms, hymns and spiritual songs."

"That is another way of saying we are to sing. If you speak by songs, then you are singing. See anything else?"

I looked again. "Make melody in your hearts."

"Which means put your heart into your singing. Anything else?"

Since he asked me again, I figured there must be something else. But I couldn't see it.

He gave a me hint. "Does it say anything about the playing of mechanical instruments, like guitars or pianos?"

I examined it word by word. "No, it doesn't."

"Precisely! Gary, in *all* of its twelve verses on this subject, the New Testament instructs the church on earth to worship Him by *singing*, but *never* by *playing* pianos and such. Mechanical instruments are *not* the instructions of God, but are the inventions of *men.*"

"Yeah, I remember the *Catholic Encyclopedia* said the Church worshipped for 1,000 years without any instruments until the organ was added. So, it's not in God's instructions for the Church, and it's not in the worship of the Church for 1000 years. How transparent can it get? The instruments were added into the worship by man!"

"And Gary, you know what God says about that, do you not?"

"Uh, huh. It's vain worship, and God will punish those who add to His Word with the plagues written in the Book. That's what bothers me, Mr. Babbitt, and that's why I asked you what the one, true, original Church was like *before* man messed it up with all those changes."

"Well, that is the way it worshipped," Mr. Babbitt summarized. "Preaching; the Lord's Supper of the bread and the cup on every Sunday and only on Sunday; the contribution; praying; and singing without the instruments. Nothing more; nothing less. Nothing added to God's Word; nothing taken away."

"But we've taken away the cup and added the instruments," I groaned. "And men in the first few hundred years also added Holy Water, candles, incense, making the sign of the cross, images, and other things." I shook my head as I stared through the table.

"Now," he said with liveliness—no doubt in an attempt to lift my spirits—"the last major aspect of the church: its organization. Are you familiar as to how the Catholic Church is organized?"

"Yeah. There's the priest of the local church. Then we have bishops over several priests. Next are the archbishops over several bishops. And then there's the pope over everybody, and he uses advisors called Cardinals. I think there are more offices, but that's the basic hierarchy."

"And you want to see how God set up the organization of the church before, as you say, 'men messed it up?'"

I nodded.

"Then take a look at Colossians 1:18."

We both flipped through the pages. He got to it first, but I arrived only a second later and then read it aloud.

> And he is the head of the body, the church: who is the beginning, the firstborn from the dead; that in all things he might have the preeminence.

I raised my head. "Can't miss it. Jesus is the head of the church. He makes the rules; we follow. But, He is in heaven. What do His rules say about the church's organization on earth?"

"He set up an organization that is very simple and extremely efficient by the installation of only two offices. You will find the first in Acts 14:23."

I located it and read.

> *And when they had ordained them elders in every church, and had prayed with fasting, they commended them to the Lord, on whom they believed.*

"Notice," Mr. Babbitt began, "Apostle Paul ordained elders, or, as some versions translate it, presbyters. Whichever is fine, there is no difference. But every time this word is used in the Scriptures, it is *always* plural, elder*s*, except twice when a single elder in the group of elders was addressed. And, this verse you read says there is to be a plurality of elders in *every* local church."

"Mr. Babbitt, I have never even heard of elders," I sheepishly confessed.

"Actually, you have, but by one of their other titles. Go to Titus 1:5."

He waited until I stopped flipping through the pages and said, "We find the same thing here. Apostle Paul appointed Titus to '*ordain elders in every city.*' Then, Paul lists the qualifications these elders must have, and, in verse seven, he calls these elders by the term, 'bishop'."

"Bishop?!" I perked up, hoping Catholicism had it right.

Mr. Babbitt was quick to read me. "But not like you are thinking. Like I just explained, the way Jesus set up bishops was to have a *plurality* over *each* local church. But Catholicism has *one single* bishop over *several* churches."

"Men changed it, huh?"

"I am afraid so. Also, one of the qualifications of those bishops is that they were to be married and have children, as verse six demands, and as does 1 Timothy 3:2."

I looked at both verses. "Yeah, and our bishops *aren't* married." I always knew celibacy was a rotten requirement. "But what are elders supposed to do? What's their job?"

270

"Elders, like shepherds, are to oversee, guard, and feed the flock, which are the members of their local church. This is taught in 1 Peter 5:1-2. In verse one, you see that Peter was addressing the elders, and then told them in the next verse, *'Feed the flock of God which is among you, taking the oversight thereof.'* To 'feed the flock' means they had the responsibility to make sure the church had the right spiritual food, not false doctrines or false teachers. And, to 'take the oversight' means they were appointed by God to plan the work of their local church and make sure everything was done scripturally and according to their plans."

"So, the elders don't make doctrines or creed-books, right? But they do make the decisions for the church as to *how* the church will do what the Scriptures tell it to do. Is that right?"

"Exactly, young Berean. For example, the Scriptures instruct the church to assemble for worship on Sunday, but God allows each local church to decide the time and place that is best for them. So, whether the church owns a building, rents a facility, or meets in the home of a Christian, someone has to make the decision, and God gave that authority to the elders."

"So the Scriptures tell us what to do, and the elders decide for their own local church how to do it. No hierarchy, no politics, no power-struggle. You're right, Mr. Babbitt, God's way *is* simple and effective."

"By the way, the words, 'to feed the flock,' actually refer to the elders working like a shepherd or a pastor of sheep. And in Ephesians 4:11, that is precisely what these elders are called—pastors. Which means the denominational concept of a pastor is way off."

He continued, "Now, the second and only other office Jesus set up in His church is that of the deacons. Go back to 1 Timothy 3 where we looked at the qualifications of the elders. In verses 8-13, we have the office and qualifications of the deacons. Deacons are servants, which is what the word means. They serve the church by working with the members, or even by themselves, in carrying out some task the elders decided needs to be done.

"And, Gary, that is it. That is God's organization for the church, and that is how the church was organized at the very beginning before men started changing things."

"That's it?! Elders and deacons? That's all?"

"I told you it was very simple, but extremely effective."

"So, without adding to or taking away from God's instructions, that's it? That's how the original church was organized before men messed it up?"

"Yes. A plurality of men, who met the qualifications, had the authority of the oversight of the work and spiritual welfare of their own local congregation with deacons to serve them in carrying out the works. It is as simple as Philippians 1:3 declares, *'Paul,'* a preacher; *'...to all the saints,'* that is, the local church of the Christians at Philippi; *'in Christ Jesus,'* the head of the church, *'which are at Philippi, with the bishops,'* the elders/presbyters/pastors, *'and deacons.'* So, Gary, *any* religious group who is organized *any other* way has added to or taken away from God's instructions. And, from what God declares in Revelation 22:18-19, they better make some changes real fast and get back to what God wants and accepts."

Mr. Babbitt closed his Bible and leaned back a little from the table into a posture-perfect position. I took it as a sign that class was about over. After all, the five-minute-till-dismissal-bell, which sounded more like a tiny jack-hammer than a bell, clattered in the hall a few moments ago. The dying old gentleman, donned in his grey suit with matching, neatly combed hair, faced me only four feet away. In that lingering pause, my mind awoke from thinking about myself and what I was learning from him, and instead fixed upon him and what he was sacrificing for me.

Out of the prolonged quiet that filled the room, he slowly asked, "Have I satisfactorily answered your question, 'What was the church like originally before men began to change it?'"

"Yes, sir. Thank you so very much."

"Well then, let us see how good your teacher is," he said with a crafty grin. "What picture do you have of the original church you read about in the Scriptures?"

Teacher? I mused. *That's good Ol' humble Mr. Babbitt. He's more like a guide. For the most part, he just directed me to the Scriptures, and then allowed me to see for myself what they taught.*

"Mr. Babbitt, the Bible reveals the church—the church as

directed by the apostles at its very beginning—to be only one world-wide church that had all of its Christians united in their teachings and beliefs. And the reason they were united in their teachings and beliefs was because they used only the Bible —no divisive creed-books. And because of that, they all worshiped the same way in those five acts you showed me—no more, no less, and, no partial. And, they were all organized the same way with only elders and deacons—no additions, no subtractions."

"Good. You see it, just like anybody else would if they put forth the effort to read the Instruction Book and think."

The miniature jack-hammer rattled again. Class was over.

"But, Mr. Babbitt, what happened to that Church after the apostles died? Why is the Catholic Church like it is now?"

"Gary, that story will have to wait until next Sunday."

CHAPTER 38
THE GREASED SLIDE

All that week the sun crept along its daily course across the broad blue sky. At least so it seemed. That strange trick that time plays on the mind when anticipating an important day taunted me as I awaited Mr. Babbitt's explanation of what happened to the Church after the apostles died.

"A lot must have occurred," I'd tell myself every time I thought about it, "because the Church is so different today from what it was with the apostles in the New Testament."

The answer would come tomorrow.

Ol' Blue's fuel tank nearly burst with gas. I made sure of that, although dad had to pay for it. For once, I arrived in the room long before Mr. Babbitt. "Must be my anxiety," I surmised.

While scanning over the book titles on one of the library's bookshelves, Mr. Babbitt's aura filled the room. "Great morning, Gary!"

Great morning? I thought in amazement. *"Great morning" and cancer is eating him up?!* His remarkable attitude flowed naturally from his deep faith in God and complete conviction of going to heaven.

"Yes sir. Great morning," I responded in likeness.

"Still wondering what happened to the church after the apostles died?" he asked as we settled into our chairs.

"I couldn't sleep all week." I exaggerated, but only by a little.

"Good. But first, review for us what the church was like at its very beginning—the way the God-inspired apostles set it up."

"Piece of cake, Mr. Babbitt. I've rolled this over and over in my mind all week." I quickly summarized the organization, the creed book, and the worship of the Church as set up by the apostles in the Bible.

"And you want, like Paul Harvey[1] says, 'the rest of the story'?"

"Yeah, what happened to the church after the apostles died?"

274

"You are probably not going to like it," he warned with his head tilted slightly down and eyebrows raised.

"Maybe. But what happened, happened. Besides, I've already seen the admissions in the *Catholic Encyclopedia* itself where men changed and added practices."

"And that is exactly where I get the information you are about to hear. That and Schaff's, the work you already noticed to be endorsed by your church's encyclopedia. I also used another work just as prestigious, the twelve-volume encyclopedia of McClintock and Strong.[2] Actually, any reliable book on church history, whether Catholic or non-Catholic, will tell you what occurred in the church after the apostles died. So here is what happened."

My forearms upon the table felt the increase of weight as I leaned closer.

"As you said, Gary, the apostles left each of the local churches with a plurality of qualified men functioning as elders. And when these men had their meetings to discuss the affairs of their local church, one of the elders served as the chairman. And there is nothing wrong with that; however, it was not long until the same elder chaired *all* the meetings. Then, over several decades, this chairman naturally began to be regarded as more important than the other elders. He also assumed the lead in opposing false doctrines, and was expected to take charge in times of problems and dangers. By 150 A.D., this prominent elder of each church was called the bishop, while the others maintained the reference of elder, or presbyter. In time, since the bishop was doing everything the eldership was set up by Jesus to do, there was no need for the eldership, and it became extinct."

"So that's the first step man took in changing the organization of the Church!" I butted in.

"Precisely. And it didn't end with that. Once a change occurs, there is no stopping another, and then another. Here is what happened next. The bishops of the larger city churches would help the development of the small country churches. The country churches, leaning so heavily upon the city bishop, eventually came under his authority, and then those bishops in the country churches, no longer needed, disappeared. The area over which the city bishop ruled was called a diocese. Gary, in this step, I am sure you can see, the bishops extended their authority beyond that of their own local church. And that is something the Scriptures do not allow even an entire eldership."

"So *that's* why there's one bishop over several churches today." The information captivated me in spite of the fact it exposed the early Church-corrupting changes that we still use today.

"Next," Mr. Babbitt picked up where he left off, "by the end of the second century, each bishop of the city churches or dioceses began to meet with the other bishops within a reasonable geographic area to settle disputes over doctrines and practices. The bishops of the largest cities had the greatest influence, became the chairmen, and were eventually called the Metropolitan Bishops. These meetings, called councils or synods, were soon viewed as meetings in which their decisions were to be designated as laws for the entire church. All the bishops would then return to their own local church or diocese and enforce the decisions of the council."

"So the same struggle for supremacy that occurred within the eldership also happened among the bishops," I remarked.

"Yes, and it was far from over. With the increasing authority of the bishops, they began to think of themselves as the successors to the apostles. Also, during all this, the New Testament preachers evolved into man-made priests, imitating the abolished practice of the Old Testament. Now, only the priests could baptize and serve the Lord's Supper, which, of course, gave the priests and bishops incredible control over the people because their salvation and their blessings from God could be obtained only through the priests—or so they were unfortunately led to believe. And it was during this time of the development of priests, bishops, and the bishop's lawmaking councils that the clergy-laity division came into being."

As Mr. Babbitt unrolled all this mess before me, I kept thinking about the original setup of the church by the apostles: a local Church in which some of their own members were elders—a *plurality* of men with only the authority over their *own* local church—and serving deacons, and someone to preach. The changes men made to Jesus' Church burned me up. *Wasn't God's way good enough? Did they think they were smarter and wiser than God? Did they think they had to help God with His "feeble" design? Did they not know or care that God warned against adding to or taking away from His orders, and that at Judgment Day they were not going to get away with it?*

But, what Mr. Babbitt told me next shifted the changes into high gear.

"Gary, during the time of these latter changes, the Roman Empire, which was the land in which the church thrived, suffered tremendous disunity because of different men fighting for the emperorship. One of them, Constantine, used Christianity to help him gain the throne. He ordered the persecution of Christians to be stopped; outlawed the empire's old state religion of paganism and replaced it with Christianity; and encouraged the church to build elaborate buildings at the empire's expense. Of course, the Christians, who consisted of multitudes of citizens throughout the empire, were thrilled and thereby gave their support to Constantine which secured his position as emperor and united the empire."

"Boy, what a smooth move," I remarked.

"Yes," he said with a touch of remorse, "but look at what it did to the church. The Christians, in their deep indebtedness to Constantine's tremendous benevolence, and in fear of losing his favoritism, allowed him to have his way in the affairs of the church."

"Uh, oh." I knew that would not be good.

"Later, when Constantine heard the church itself was dividing over a religious issue, he knew it likewise threatened the unity of the empire, and perhaps his throne. To solve the issue and obtain unity of the church, he called, and controlled, the first general counsel of the church in the city of Nicaea in 325 A.D. After discussing the issue, the council made a ruling, and that decision was written into a creed. Constantine then had the audacity to declare that the creed was 'sanctioned by the Divine will.' In other words, the council was said to be speaking for God."

I saw the error of that in a flash. "I guess Constantine did not know that 2 Timothy 3:16-17 means there would be no more writings or revelations from God."

"Obviously not. And remember, he was not even a Christian. Nevertheless, he controlled the church and he led it into the permanent addition of church-wide general councils and man-written creeds that were claimed to be the Divine Will. Furthermore, since Constantine was using the church and this meeting for his need of unity, a new name was issued to the church—'Catholic,' meaning, universal. So those who accepted the new Nicene Creed were Catholics, but those who rejected it were not Catholic."

I dropped my hands flat on the table with a thud. "So that's where the name 'Catholic' came from!" I had never seen it in the Bible.

"Gary, as if Constantine and this council had not already accomplished enough damage to the church, there is one more thing. The bishops of the cities of Rome, Antioch, and Alexandria were exalted as patriarchs, and later, the bishops of Jerusalem and Constantinople were added to make five. These patriarchs were given charge over the church and all the bishops in each of their five respective territories called provinces, which, by the way, were identical to the Roman provincial government."

"Five supreme leaders of the entire church, huh? Well, I bet I know what happened next: a fight to become the one, ultimate leader. After all, that is what's been going on since one man became the bishop over all the other elders. Am I right, Mr. Babbitt?"

"Indeed you are. The struggle lasted a long time, but it came down to the patriarch of Rome and the patriarch of Constantinople. If you remember from reading the Campbell-Purcell Debate, this is the very struggle Campbell presented from a Catholic historian."

"I remember alright, it branded my mind. It was the patriarch of Rome who won."

"Correct. Boniface III became the first pope in 606 A.D."

"And then forgeries made up a fake list of popes going back to Peter," I added from another branded memory.

"Right again. So, Gary, there you have it. You now know what happened to the organization of the church after the apostles died."

"Yeah, and maybe now I wish I didn't," I said as I leaned back in the chair and crossed my arms. I stewed in a mix of anger and

278

helplessness. Anger because mere men who, due to either ignorance of the Scriptures or disrespect of God's Word, freely changed God's Church. But, helplessness because I knew I could not change Catholicism back.

Mr. Babbitt watched me for a moment. I suppose to see if I was going to break down, or even explode. Convinced of my stability, he pressed on. "At the same time these gradual changes in church organization occurred during the first few centuries, men were also slowly changing church practices."

"Why not?" I said scornfully with a sour face. "If they had the nerve to change the organization, why not change the practices too?!"

"I will mention a few of the many inventions of men," he said as he removed a folded sheet of notebook paper from his Bible. I could see even from the upside-down angle that it was a list of doctrines and dates. "You will probably recognize some of these; you already read about them in the *Catholic Encyclopedia* when you and I spent that day at the Nazarene college library. In the 2nd century, along with the addition of one-man bishops, came the use of holy water. Water was blessed by the bishops to supposedly give it special purification abilities. The New Testament does not teach this practice, but it seems to have been carried over from the old Jewish practice as Jews were converted to Christianity. Also, Penance began to be practiced in the 2nd century. But notice this, at the end of the 12th century, men virtually changed its complete doctrine."

"I suppose they thought God had it wrong for 1,000 years," I said bitterly.

"In the next century, the baptizing of infants began to be practiced here and there. It gradually caught on until it was generally practiced in the 5th century. Also, due to serious illnesses, an occasional baptism by pouring or sprinkling was performed. But these methods did not come into wide-spread use until the 12th century and were finally declared indifferent to immersion in a council at Ravenna in 1311 A.D. The 4th century saw the introduction of the doctrine of Purgatory. Also, as you just saw, the hierarchy began to take form, but was not fully established until centuries later. In the 5th century, celibacy was added to the church, but was not strictly enforced until 1074 A.D.”

"Hold on!" I interrupted as I raised my hands off the table to signal him to stop. "I see a pattern here. These practices began on a very small scale long after the apostles died, and then continued to gain acceptance among others until finally practiced by *all* the Church. Man! I'd have to be blind not to see that this shows they are nothing but new, man-made practices that were added to the Church!"

He nodded and then proceeded. "Extreme Unction, one of your seven sacraments, began in 588 A.D. In 606, as the Campbell-Purcell debate proved, came the first pope. The 8th century, ashes. The 9th century, transubstantiation, which finally became sanctioned by the church by the 4th Lateran Council in 1215 A.D."

"Same grow-until-accepted pattern," I muttered.

"In the 9th century, the priests sprinkled holy water on the laity. With the 11th century came the introduction of the organ, then later, other musical instruments. In the 12th century, Penance was given a near complete change in doctrine. The confessional came in 1215. The laity was denied the cup of the Lord's Supper by the council of Constance in 1414. The Rosary, 1470. Apostolic indulgences, 1587. And many, many more. As I said, these are but a sample of the host of changes and additions men made to the practices of the church as was set up by Jesus' apostles. Additions, as Revelation 22:18-19 declares, that were *not* to be made."

Mr. Babbitt's list crushed me. Although the list on the paper was written by a non-Catholic, I knew it was true—I had seen many of them for myself in our encyclopedia. I silently conceded, *We Catholics, undeniably, practice an incredible number of doctrines invented by men. And those who practice them, Matthew 15:9 tells us, God rejects. We're a house corrupted by the work of ancient termites.*

"Gary, now that you know how men changed the church in both, organization and practices, it will be simple to see how it changed from using only the Bible for its religious authority to its addition of creeds and Tradition."

As I shifted in my chair to brace for another chapter from the disturbing history lesson, the wooden chair groaned with a creek which seemed to sympathize with my strained head.

"Remember, by the 2nd century, the one-man bishops of nearby local churches assembled together to discuss doctrines, and then demanded their decisions to be accepted by all the churches of those bishops. Then Constantine took this procedure to the next level when he assembled the church-wide council at Nicaea in which the Nicene Creed, the first man-created creed, was written."

"And that opened the door for many more creeds to be written in the years to come?" I asked, suspecting it so.

"Indeed it did. Those men would write their man-made creeds to self-approve their own man-made practices which then became mandatory for the church to practice. Quite a controlling operation, I would say. Eventually, those men felt the pressure to prove God's acceptance of those practices. Since they were unable to do so from the Bible, they resorted to two devious maneuvers. First, they wrote numerous forgeries. You recall what forgeries are, do you not?"

"Sure do. They are documents written decades, even centuries *after* they claim to have been written, by a man *other than* the one it claims as its author, stating that doctrine such-and-such was being practiced. Those documents are nothing but deceptive lies that tricked the Church into thinking those man-made practices were from God."

"And sadly," Mr. Babbitt added, "it worked. Then their second maneuver was the introduction of the false authority of Tradition. With this they claimed that the things the church in the early centuries taught and practiced are supposed to be our authority for what the church is to teach and practice today."

"Yeah, I remember all about that. But that's kind of dumb. I mean, to look at the Church at a time when it already had a lot of *man*-made practices, and then think that whatever they were doing is what we are supposed to do too, is not very smart. What if we are imitating one of those *man*-made practices? And by what our encyclopedia reveals, we're imitating a lot of them!"

"Exactly!" Mr. Babbitt pointed his finger at me with a jolt and snapped it back. "Man's invention of the so-called authority of Tradition is just another scheme to self-approve whatever practices men themselves brought into the church. The assumption is: 'They did it in the 2nd or following centuries, so it must be what we are supposed to do.' And the assumption is wrong."

"No wonder Tradition contradicts the Scriptures!" I continued to put together the pieces of the puzzle.

"Gary, you wanted to know what happened to the church after the apostles died so you could understand why the Catholic Church today is so different from the church set up by the apostles of Jesus in the New Testament. Now you know."

"You were right, I *don't* like it." But I couldn't deny it, history recorded the fact: men changed the Church from what Jesus established. And the changes started only a few decades after the apostles died by the very leadership of the local churches, the elders. But, when one elder assumed superiority over the others, they took the first step on the long road that lead to the hierarchy and councils. Then the hierarchy in the councils formed man-made laws so the laity would have to accept all their man-made practices that had grown into Church-wide usage. And today, Tradition is used as an authority equal to—even greater than—the Scriptures in order to cover up all the mess the early Christians got us into. And what a rotten mess it is!

When the last warning of the Bible resurfaced in my mind—do not add to nor take away from the Scriptures—my anger at those who changed the Church gave way to fear. Today's heavy involvement of the Church in those many man-added doctrines scared me. I did not want to be worshipping in vain. I did not want to die and be put in the place of plagues that God will cast upon those who added to His Scriptures. *But the Catholic Church is the one, true, original Church. So, what do I do?!*

"Gary!"

His firm voice startled me. Then I realized he had been trying to get my attention for the previous few moments.

"Sorry, Mr. Babbitt. I guess I was deep in thought."

"I should say so.

"Gary, I think it is time you should see a particular set of verses God put in the Bible. But unfortunately, our class-time is up. You will be here next week, will you not?" he asked with observable concern.

"Same time, same place," I assured him.

As I rose from the table, I thought, *Ho, boy! "It is time I should see a particular set of verses" he says. Don't know if that sounds good or bad, but I'll find out.*

CHAPTER 39
THE BOTTOM OF
THE GREASED SLIDE

NEXT SUNDAY

"Find in your Catholic Douay-Confraternity Bible, 2nd Thessalonians chapter 2."

Mr. Babbitt began class promptly. The fluorescent lights, still warming up with its bee-hive hum, were dim.

"Okay…I'm there."

"Take your time and read the first twelve verses."

Putting my finger on verse one and sliding it down to each succeeding verse, I read the passage aloud.

> *¹We beseech you, brethren, by the coming of our Lord Jesus Christ and our being gathered together unto him, ²not to be hastily shaken from your right mind, nor terrified, whether by spirit, or by utterance, or by letter attributed to us, as though the day of the Lord were near at hand. ³Let no one deceive you in any way, for the day of the Lord will not come unless the apostasy comes first, and the man of sin is revealed, the son of perdition, ⁴who opposes and is exalted above all that is called God, or that is worshipped, so that he sits in the temple of God and gives himself out as if he were God.*
>
> *⁵Do you not remember that when I was still with you, I used to tell you these things? ⁶And now you know what restrains him, that he may be revealed in his proper time. ⁷For the mystery of iniquity is already at work; provided only that he who is at present restraining it, does still restrain, until he is gotten out of the way. ⁸And then the wicked one will be revealed, whom the Lord Jesus will slay with the breath of his mouth and will destroy with the brightness of his coming.*

⁹And his coming is according to the working of Satan with all power and signs and lying wonders, ¹⁰and with all wicked deception to those who are perishing. For they have not received the love of truth that they might be saved. ¹¹Therefore God sends them a misleading influence that they may believe falsehood, ¹²that all may be judged who have not believed the truth, but have preferred wickedness.

"Whoa! That's a little scary, Mr. Babbitt."

"Indeed. Now, let us see what this is talking about. Look back to verses 1 and 2. There were those who thought Jesus' Second Coming was just about to happen. But verse 3 informs them that before Jesus comes again something else must happen first. Do you see what that is?"

"Yeah. It's the apostasy, uh, which is…?"

He turned his King James Version around and pushed it to me with his fingertips.

"Falling away?"

He nodded his head and explained, "That is when Christians forsake the teachings of God, which results in God removing them from the church. They have fallen away from God's commandments and therefore, away from God. You can see that in verses 10 and 11. They rejected the truth and followed falsehood."

I took a moment to reread those two verses. "Mr. Babbitt, I see something else. Those Christians in this apostasy are perishing and are not saved."

"You read it right. And verse 12 says they are judged, meaning, as the King James has it, damned. Also, verse 9 tells us this apostasy is the workings of Satan, the enemy who strives to lead Christians away from God and into hell. So you see, those swept away by this apostasy, without realizing it, have been deceived and are led away from the church by Satan and are lost. True, verse 10 says those in the apostasy are being deceived, but verses 10, 11, and 12 inform us they are still responsible for believing the falsehoods."

Wow! A section of verses foretelling the Reformation and the formation of the denominations that fell away from the one, true, original Church! It's just as my Catechism teachers told me. But, doesn't Mr. Babbitt realize that he and his denomination are part of the apostasy?

"Now, Gary, take special care in noticing verse 3. The apostasy is described as '*the* apostasy.' It is not '*an* apostasy,' which means one of many, but it is THE apostasy. One so massive, it needs only to be referred to as 'the apostasy' in order for everyone to know what He is talking about. It dwarfed any other group that fell away and caused them to pale to insignificance when compared."

Well sure, the Reformation was one big apostasy!

"It is popularly taught that this apostasy is the Reformation. But this is impossible."

"What?!" I did not intend to speak out, but his words shocked me.

"Look at verse 7. The words, '*the mystery of iniquity is already at work,*' makes it certain that the apostasy was already beginning when this was written. However, the Reformation did not begin for another 1500 years! So, THE apostasy this passage is writing about cannot possibly be the Reformation."

He's right, the Reformation can't be the apostasy. So, just what falling away began to work so early?

He pushed on. "It is also said that this apostasy was the Gnostics, or some other such group, that fell away from the church in the early centuries. But, these too, are not the apostasy of these verses."

"And you're going to tell me why, right?"

"The Gnostics, Montanists, Novatians, and the like began early, but they died out in the 5th and 6th centuries. But look what verse 8 declares. The apostasy of this passage will still exist at the Second Coming of Jesus."

I saw what he was saying. "So, Mr. Babbitt, those groups with the weird names ended too early to be THE apostasy, and the Reformation began too late. Well, what is this great apostasy God is talking about?"

"Gary, if you think about what God said in this passage, you can figure it out for yourself. Look in the verses at the identifying clues of the apostasy. What is the main feature of the great falling away?"

I scanned over the verses. "It has a very powerful leader."

"Right, and most of the verses of 3 through 9 are talking about him. So, what does it say? It says he is 'the man of sin,' that is, he transgresses God's Law. So, his actions and laws do not follow God's Law. He is also 'the son of perdition.' Perdition means destruction. And that means he destroys the church, which, of course, is what an apostasy does. So, by his replacing God's Law with his laws, the Christians are led away from what the church is supposed to be, resulting in their spiritual destruction."

Although I knew the Catholic Church certainly was not the apostasy, that swung too close for comfort. After all, numerous laws made up by men—laws and practices which did *not* follow God's Law—flooded into the Church in the first few centuries.

"Now, Gary, what identifying trait of this leader do you find in verse 4?"

I read verse 4 again. The toxic description repulsed me. "This man makes himself out to be God!"

"Yes, and his traits are quite prominently expressed. Now, verses 6 and 7 declare that this exalted, worshipful leader did not yet exist when this letter was being written because something or someone restrained him from taking that 'as-if-he-were-God' position."

"So, this position took time to develop?" I asked.

"Correct. Now, the last thing you need to notice is in verse 8. What do you see?"

"It says Jesus will slay him at His Second Coming. But, Mr. Babbitt, how can that be? If verse 7 tells us the apostasy and the development of the leader were already beginning back in the 1st century, how can he still be alive at the Second Coming?! Nobody lives for several centuries!"

"Of course not. But a *position* which is occupied by a *succession* of men, does."

Well, sure. That's the only possible answer, unless I want to say God made a big mistake in what He wrote.

"Gary, those are the identifying marks of 'the man of sin' and the apostasy." Mr. Babbitt spoke a little slower and as gently as he

THE IVORY DOMINO

could. "When you identify 'the man of sin,' then you will know the identity of this great apostasy. So take a moment, put it all together, and think it through. You can figure it out."

From past experience with his shift in tone, I sensed his concern for me. I knew what he must be thinking, but I also knew the apostasy *wasn't* Catholicism. More concerned now about proving to myself that the apostasy was not Catholicism than I was concerned about finding out what church was the real apostasy, I attacked those identifying marks to show that they did *not* describe the Catholic Church.

Can't do anything about "the man of sin" though. I mean, his man-made laws certainly cause us Catholics to worship in vain. Matthew 15:9 makes that clear. And then there are all those popes who lived in sinful immoralities of adultery, murder, robbery, and on and on. Also, there are those five to six centuries of popes who plagued humanity with the Inquisition and its insane tortures and stake-burnings. And there are the five centuries of popes who led the Church into the ungodly Crusades that plundered, ravaged, and murdered hundreds of thousands of people. As much as I don't want to admit it, "the man of sin, the son of destruction" fits the popes far better than any other man in all of history. I took a deep breath to relieve the uneasiness creeping upon me.

What was the other clue? Oh, yeah, succession. "The man of sin" is a succession of men. My anxiety returned in a flare-up. And this succession will continue until the Second Coming, which means "the man of sin" and "the apostasy" exists right now!

Aw, come on! I shouted to myself. *Surely **something** doesn't fit!*

Let's see, what else do the verses say? Oh, yeah, "the man of sin" took time to develop. Man! It can't be! Another perfect fit! Going from elders, to a congregational bishop, to archbishops, to patriarchs, to pope definitely took time to develop.

My heart beat as rapidly as in a track-meet race. I panicked for any clue that did *not* fit our pope.

Verse 4! What about verse 4? It's the one most descriptive of "the man of sin." Surely it doesn't fit. Let's see.... Yes, that's it! "He sits in the temple of God!" We don't have a temple like that! Not like the Jews did in Jerusalem. The pope doesn't fit!

I felt my shoulders relax. Relief returned. The alarm shut off. No longer fearful of the apostasy being the Catholic Church, I asked Mr. Babbitt where that temple of God was located and what religious group owned it. Then I would know who the apostasy was.

"Gary, I can tell you where that temple is located, but first you must understand what the temple in Christianity is." He pointed to my Bible and said, "See what 1 Corinthians 3:16-17 says."

While I turned the pages, I wondered, *Why find out **what** the temple is? It's a building of bricks or rocks and mortar, isn't it?* But I then found out why he wanted me to read it.

> *Do you not know that you are the temple of God and the Spirit of God dwells in you? If anyone destroys the temple of God, him God will destroy; for holy is the temple of God, and this temple you are.*

"Well, Mr. Babbitt," I said with a struggle and without looking up, "the temple is the people, the church."

"You see," he caringly said, "in Christianity, the temple of God is not some building like it was in the Jewish religion, but it is the church. So, 'the man of sin,' verse 4 informs us, is set in the highest position *in the church*, that is, what is *thought* to be the church because it is really the apostasy."

The tension returned so swiftly I almost got back and shoulder cramps. My heart raced and my shallow breathing quickened.

"Gary, when I borrowed your Catechism several weeks ago, I read what it says about the pope. I am sure you and every Catholic throughout the world already know this, but, to its question number 496, 'Who is the visible Head of the Church?,' it answers, 'Our Holy Father the Pope, the Bishop of Rome, is the Vicar of Christ on earth and the visible Head of the Church.'"

He didn't say it. He didn't have to. I knew the pope fit this clue. And he fit it perfectly.

"And the rest of the verse says...." He pointed at my Bible, indicating I was to read it.

> *"...and gives himself out as if he were God."*

"Gary, if you were to tell someone that it is a religious law to go to worship on Sunday, what would you be doing?"

"I guess I'd just be telling him what God's law in the Scriptures tells us."

"That is right. God wrote His law in the Scriptures, and you are merely pointing it out to someone else. But, if you were to tell someone that *you* say it is a religious law for the church to sacrifice a rabbit during Sunday worship, who would you be making yourself out to be?"

"Well, since that's not in the New Testament, I would be giving a new religious law, and since only God gives religious laws, then…" I paused, "I'd be making myself out to be God."

"And you are correct. As long as you are teaching what the Scriptures *already* teach, you are but a teacher, something all Christians are to be. But when you make laws that are *not* taught in the Scriptures, you make yourself out to be God. You see, when a person claims rights only God can claim, he sets himself forth as God."

"I see Mr. Babbitt." But I wish I didn't. My one loophole unraveled, and I knew what was coming next.

"And Gary," he spoke even more tenderly, "you have already seen the many laws the popes have made that are not taught in the Scriptures."

"Yeah, I know," I somehow managed to whisper.

The pursuing silence agonized me. Perhaps Mr. Babbitt waited for me to speak first. But I wasn't going to. I wasn't going to admit it. Even if we had to sit in silence for the rest of the class, I wasn't going to admit it.

Mr. Babbitt sensed my locked lips, and my agony. Mercifully, he spoke. Then again, maybe it wasn't so merciful. "This 'man of sin,' this succession of men who are exalted above everyone else in the church and make themselves out to be God when they add their own man-made laws, is the identifying mark of the great falling away—the apostasy that began in the 1st century and will continue to exist until the Second Coming of Jesus.

"Gary." He stopped mid-breath, as though regretting to continue. "Of all the religious bodies of people in Christianity, there is only one that fits the description of this verse. And it fits it perfectly."

He did not say which one he meant. He did not have to. I knew the facts all fit—I had been discovering them for weeks.

He then turned several pages in his Bible. "Listen to this in 1 Timothy 4, beginning with verse one."

> *Now the Spirit speaketh expressly, that in the latter times some shall depart from the faith, giving heed to seducing spirits, and doctrines of devils; Speaking lies in hypocrisy; having their conscience seared with a hot iron; Forbidding to marry, and commanding to abstain from meats, which God hath created to be received with thanksgiving of them which believe and know the truth. For every creature of God is good, and nothing to be refused, if it be received with thanksgiving.*

"This too," Mr. Babbitt gently explained, "tells us that sometime after this letter was written there would be a departure of Christians from the church. That departure occurred because they followed man-made doctrines. God labeled those teachings as '*doctrines of devils*' because the added doctrines were not His. Two of the doctrines are identified: the first, 'forbidding to marry;' and the second, 'abstain from meats.'"

Double bulls-eye. Celibacy and fish on Friday. Guess who.

"Gary, the group who restricts God-approved marriages and meats and has an exalted one-man head of the church that makes laws like he was God is the group that is the apostasy."

My thoughts pounded within my head like the interior of a huge bell. *Okay! Okay! Okay! It's true, the Church did depart from the elders and created a hierarchy of positions with an exalted, one-man leader—the pope! And true, the Church did add numerous man-made doctrines—doctrines of devils, the Bible calls them—that we still practice today! And it's a fact, forgeries were made to make it look like those practices were done by the original church! And it really happened, Tradition was invented to make it look like God authorizes all those practices that can't be found in the Scriptures!*

*Yes, it's true! The Bible identifies **us** as the one who fell away!! **WE** are the great apostasy!!*

CHAPTER 40
HELD TOGETHER BY A THREAD

MOMENTS LATER

The door burst open as my shoulder struck it and, after a moment of silence, the pop of the door slamming against the brick wall shattered the outdoor silence. As I positioned my Bible under my left arm like a leather football, I silently griped that the class had not revealed to me what I expected. I wasn't mad at Mr. Babbitt; how could I be? He, with deep consideration of my feelings, let me see the truth—truth that is concealed from us trusting Catholics. But I just needed to leave. I didn't stay for worship. I didn't go to Mass. I needed to think.

The rocks ground and popped against each other under the weight of Ol' Blue's tires as I navigated the shrub and tree-concealed quarter-mile gravel road built upon the dike that separated the North Canadian River from Lake Overholser. Obscured from sight and public knowledge, the hideaway provided the solitude I craved. As the engine hushed its mechanized roar, the soothing flow of water rolling over the shallow spillway calmed the air.

Standing at the front of Ol' Blue, I propped my forearms upon the spillway's metal railing. With the toe of my black leather shoe, I nudged a rock over the edge of the cement wall, but did not bother to watch it dive into the spillway lying ten feet below.

"Never in a million years would I have imagined this," I bemoaned. But I could not deny it. All the discoveries of the previous few months snapped together into a vivid picture. A picture in which many influential post-apostolic church leaders added practices of their own with the early church at large following them, just as God foretold in the Scriptures. And those permanent additions slowly, but drastically, moved masses of people away from the God-given organization, practices, and source of authority—a departure, and a picture, which God did not, nor does He yet, nor will He ever, accept.

"There's no pope. Just a forged list and twisted verses to make it look like there's supposed to be one." My life-long belief in the pope as the God-established leader of the Church made me feel like I just blasphemed. But, in reality, I blasphemed when I had exalted him as *he sat in the temple of God.*"

"And there's no hierarchy. Just the result of the power-struggle of men for prominence.

"No celibacy, confirmation, purgatory, piano, indulgences, infant baptism…. Just numerous *man*-made practices.

"And no Tradition. Just the man-made cover-up to self-endorse the man-made practices of the early Church."

Most of those changes occurred in the first few centuries, and ever since then people believed and practiced those changes because that is what their parents and the Church—rather, the apostasy—believed and practiced. We each became a single domino in a long train of falling dominoes, imitating the one before us and influencing the one after us. And we take our turn without questioning who pushed the first domino: God, or man?

"*But the difference makes a difference!* And God lets us know that." I reached through the open passenger side window for my Bible, leaned my back against the car, and read again those unforgettable verses.

> *In vain do they worship me, teaching as doctrines the precepts of men. Matthew 15:9.*

> *I testify to everyone who hears the words of the prophecy of this book. If anyone shall add to them, God will add to him the plagues that are written in this book. Revelation 22:18.*

> *Let no one deceive you in any way, for the day of the Lord will not come unless the apostasy comes first, and the man of sin is revealed, the son of perdition. 2 Thessalonians 2:3.*

> *Not everyone who says to me, "Lord, Lord," shall enter the kingdom of heaven; but he who does the will of my*

father in heaven shall enter the kingdom of heaven. Many will say to me in that day, "Lord, Lord, did we not prophesy in thy name, and cast out devils in thy name, and work many miracles in thy name?" And then I will declare to them, "I never knew you. Depart from me, you workers of iniquity!" Matthew 7:21-23.

"How blind I have been! I *assumed* we were the right church and that all was well. But God has been warning us all along. We *can't* follow doctrines of men—doctrines which men added. Otherwise, we apostatize, *thinking* we're the one, true Church, when all the while we're lost and headed for a horrible shock at Judgment when Jesus looks right into our eyes and declares, '*I never knew you; depart from me.*'"

But my resolve stood firm. I determined to do whatever it took to avoid going to hell.

My vision lifted across the river and fastened upon the very stretch of road where I tasted stifling pain during my run of that seventh mile. For a few moments my mind relived that excruciating agony, and then thought, *Hell is no joke! It's real and it's coming. Hell is a fiery furnace of torment; everyone screams in anguish; the stench is horrific; the darkness is maddening; and, it's **never** going to stop!*

The thought of being captured by the headed-to-hell apostasy infuriated my soul against those wretched men who, due to their selfish lust for prominence and their rebellious additions, led the Church away from God. "Irresponsible! Wicked! Devilish! If you warp-o's wanted to go to hell, then go ahead. But why did you deceive millions to go with you?!"

As I wiped the tears from my cheeks, I knew I wallowed in a desperate situation. The verses Mr. Babbitt showed me shattered my world. Insecure and scared, I did not know what the true church was. Or how to find it. I didn't even know if I was a Christian. Before I had left Mr. Babbitt's church so abruptly, I begged him, "I need answers!"

"Be here next week," he said. "I will tell you about the Reformation."

294

CHAPTER 41
THE REFORMATION

WITHIN THE NEXT HOUR.

W*ebster's Dictionary* dropped from my hand with a thud upon my desk as I turned and hurriedly peeled off my blue pull-over sweater and tossed it upon the bed.

"Let's see, that's r-e-f."

I thought I knew what the Reformation was, but I had been misled on so many things, I wanted to make sure.

"R-e-f-o-r-m-a… There it is."

> A 16th century religious movement marked ultimately by rejection or modification of some Roman Catholic doctrine and practice and establishment of the Protestant churches.

Yep, the Reformation was the beginning of denominations as they split off of the Catholic Church, alright. But, since all those churches didn't exist until the 16th century, Mr. Babbitt surely isn't going to tell me the one, true, original church built by the apostles began in the Reformation, is he? Even if it did, how in the world could anyone know which one is it? He's always been so sensible before. Ho, boy. I don't know about this. I guess I'll just have to drift in limbo another seven days.

NEXT SUNDAY

A white sheet of posterboard covered half of the library's 4 x 8 foot table. Mr. Babbitt's King James Bible and a thick, black marker-pen laid on top. Not knowing where he wanted me to sit in this abnormal arrangement, I stood, waited, and wondered what he was up to.

Down the hallway, Mr. Babbitt's voice grew louder with each step his old legs took. When he came closer, his "talking" turned out to be his singing a religious song. In a medium bass tone, and dripping with faith and contentment, he soloed "I Want to be a Worker."

Mind-boggling! He is getting eaten up with cancer but he is as happy as a guy who won a million dollar jackpot. No, happier. And he is even singing about working for the Lord as a teacher. Well, I guess so; he's helping me see through the chaos man made of the church.

Mr. Optimistic entered the class with a smile on his face, as I expected, and a yardstick in his hand, which I never would have predicted. "Good morning, young Berean! Still eager for answers?"

"I'm hip!"

"You are hip?"

"Yeah. It means I'm good to go."

"Oh, I see. Teenage slang for an emphatic 'yes.' Well then, since you are hip to find out why there are so many denominations, we shall get right to it."

"And the yardstick is going to help?" My curiosity compelled me to ask.

"Indeed," he said as he stepped to the poster board and pointed with the yardstick to the table's middle chair for me to sit. "As I tell you the basic story of the Reformation with its break-offs from the Catholic Church, I will chart those new denominations. When completed, I think you will see for yourself something quite enlightening."

"Like you said, let's 'get right to it,'" I said with a level of excitement that soared off of the charts. I wanted answers!

Mr. Babbitt laid the yardstick upon the posterboard, placed both hands in his lap, and faced me. "The great falling away continued to grow unchecked in its religious monopoly for several centuries. Eventually, it became its own worst enemy. With the multiplied years of wicked popes and inhumane Inquisitions and bloody Crusades fresh in their minds, the laity now grew nauseous of the increase of corruption in the hierarchy. The love of money seemed to control the priests to epidemic proportions. They sold church offices and set aside canon law to favor those with enough money to sooth the priest's itchy palms. They even duped the laity with a new practice to give money to get loved ones out of purgatory."

I cast my eyes on the table and shook my head. "I had no idea."

"I would not expect you to," he said with noticeable sympathy. "This moral decay extended into their personal lives as they lived in open sin, kept concubines, and merely went through the formality of saying Mass."

"So the people finally had enough of the hierarchy's corruption, right?" I assumingly asked.

"That is hip!"

I laughed. He must have known I needed relief from the depressing thoughts. "Okay, so what happened?"

"By this time the Bible had been, to a certain extent, made available to the common man, and they read for themselves about the glaring false practices of Catholicism."

"Kind of like what I've been doing, huh?" Knowing I was not alone comforted me.

Mr. Babbitt then placed the yardstick across the length of the poster board, and, a few inches from the top, drew a horizontal line from edge to edge. "Gary, this line represents the true, original church Jesus built. At the left end is its beginning in 33 AD at Jerusalem, and at the right end is the Second Coming and the end of the world."

"So, it's a timeline of the church," I said to let him know I caught on to what he was doing.

He then drew a descending vertical line that began from that horizontal line at a spot a few inches from the left of the poster board and ended four or five inches from the bottom. From the end of that line, he drew a horizontal line to the right edge of the poster board. The configuration looked like a big "L."

"As he traced the "L" with the yardstick, he explained, "This is THE falling away, just as the Bible foretold."

"Catholicism," I choked.

"Yes." He then tapped at a spot three-fourths of the way across the horizontal part of the "L." "At this location is the emerging of the Reformation."

"Wow! The Catholic Church was the only church that existed for a *long* time."

"Well, almost," he muffled as though he did not say it to be heard.

Almost? What did he mean by that?

"Gary, what I am about to tell you is common knowledge and can be read in encyclopedias and books on church history. And I will present only the very basics of the beginning of but a few denominations just so you can get an idea why there are so many today."

"I gotcha. So, what's first?"

"Out of a reformation rumble that blew in the wind across several places in Europe in the early 1500's, a courageous German by the name of Martin Luther took a daring stand that seemed to set the example for others to follow. As an Augustinian friar, a lecturer in the Wittenberg University, a parish priest, and a doctor of theology, he was no insignificant Catholic. Yet, Luther diligently studied the Bible and noticed numerous points of contradictions between the teachings of the Bible and the practices of Catholicism. Luther openly and widely opposed the erroneous practices and, now notice carefully, he attempted to reform the Catholic Church by getting rid of the corruption."

"You mean, he wasn't trying to make a denomination?" I asked.

"No," he answered in half a blink of an eye. "He wanted to keep the Catholic Church, but eliminate the wrong."

"But," I objected, "the Catholic Church is the apostasy. The *whole thing* is wrong."

"You can see that. But Luther did not."

I watched in silence as Mr. Babbitt drew a vertical line up from the horizontal part of the Catholic Church line, and then a horizontal line to the right edge of the paper. "Of course, he was excommunicated. However, Luther had developed quite a following who then went with him and eventually formed the Lutheran Church—the first denomination." Then on this upside down "L" he wrote, "Lutheran Church, 1521."

"But," I inquired, "if Luther just wanted to change *some* things, wouldn't the Lutheran Church be a lot like the Catholic Church?"

"Good observation. Lutheranism maintained much of Catholicism, such as many of the practices in public worship and some of the sacraments. Luther only wanted to eliminate what he did not believe in, but keep what he believed was right. And that is what hap-

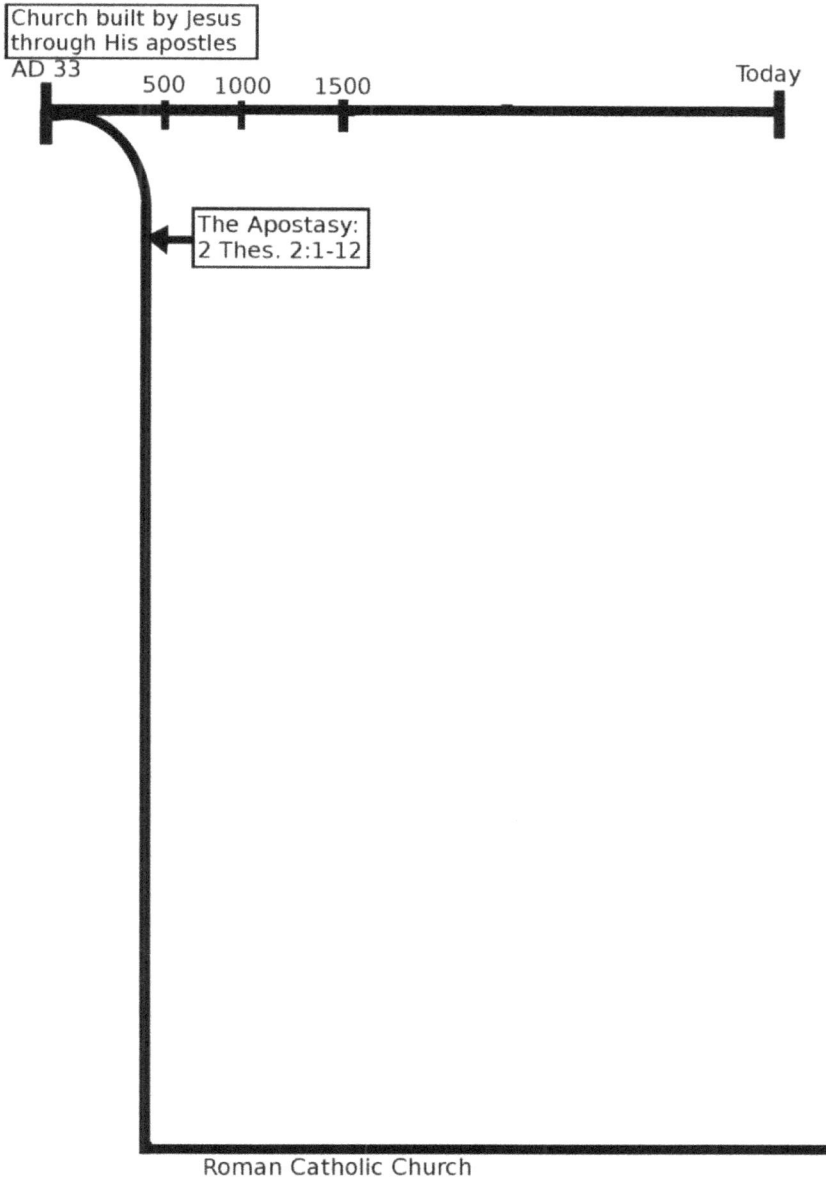

Church built by Jesus through His apostles

AD 33

500   1000   1500

Today

The Apostasy: 2 Thes. 2:1-12

Roman Catholic Church

pened with all the divisions I am going to tell you about."

"So, that's why it's called the *Reform*-ation, right?"

"Correct.

"There is one more historic effect of Luther you should know. Ever since the apostles, and for 1500 years, baptism was taught to be necessary for salvation. But Luther introduced the doctrine of salvation by faith only. Then, due to his popularity and efforts, his doctrine spread throughout Europe, influenced later reformers, and became the belief of most of those denominations and the subsequent generations of split-offs."

He laid down the yardstick and resumed unrolling the story. "Along the same time of Luther were two powerful reformers in Switzerland. Ulrich Zwingli, a priest, maintained the Bible to be the authority in religion instead of the Catholic Church, and he influenced many churches to remove various practices not found in the Bible. The other, John Calvin, taught a collection of doctrines so widely accepted that most denominations today, if not all of them, trace some of their fundamental doctrines to him. The followers of these two men established the Reformed Churches. Then, in 1560, many in this church, under the leadership of John Knox, split off and formed the Presbyterian Church."

"So, some of the denominations broke off of the Catholic Church, and others broke off of one another," I remarked as I watched him draw more "L's" on the graph.

Mr. Babbitt pushed on with determination. He desperately wanted me to learn about the Reformation and the reason why there are so many denominations today. And he did so in spite of a noticeable weakening in his strength.

Must be the cancer, I thought in helplessness, yet with deep appreciation of the man I once viewed as my antagonist. How wrong I had been.

"Along the same time as these men, and no doubt influenced by their teachings, sprang forth the Anabaptists. Among other practices of the Catholic Church, they rejected infant baptism and were baptized again. Soon, a Catholic priest joined them, but eventually separated to establish the Mennonite Church."

I did not interrupt Mr. Babbitt. He steadily filled my ears with the astounding story of the Reformation as his hands crafted before my eyes its historical picture.

"Also from the Anabaptists came the Baptist church in 1609, and in the years following, numerous groups split off of them: the Free-Will Baptists; the Primitive Baptists; the Southern Baptists and many others. And, it was the Baptist church from which the 7th Day Adventist Church came."

Although Mr. Babbitt drew neat lines, the chart began to look like a congested mess.

"Now Gary, here is an example of an outright selfish motive in establishing another church. In 1531, the King of England, Henry VIII, a Catholic, wanted a divorce from his wife so he could marry another woman. But the pope would not grant it. So Henry proclaimed England as separate from the authority of the pope, named the church the Church of England, and made himself its supreme head. Of course, the change in doctrines and practices from Catholicism was very small. After 150 years of the Church of England existing in America, they changed their name to the Episcopal Church.

"Within the Church of England during the mid-1700s, there arose a man, Charles Wesley, who strove to reform that church's errors. Unable to succeed, his followers broke off and began a new denomination—the Methodist Church. And then, in 1865, out of the Methodist Church came the Salvation Army.

"In America during the 1800s, a large number of people with a Pentecostal mindset came out of various denominations, especially the Methodist and Baptist. This resulted in many Pentecostal groups, including the Pentecostal Holiness, the Nazarene Church, the Assembly of God, and the United Pentecostal Church."

Mr. Babbitt looked over the chart in silence for a couple moments.

"Gary, I think this is as far as I need to go. But I do want you to know, these divisions and break-offs and formations of new denominations still continue, and now there are several thousand different denominations and the number keeps growing."

Mr. Babbitt laid down the yardstick beside the posterboard, set back in his chair, and allowed me time to mentally digest it all. The drawing looked like the huge oak tree in my front yard during winter—one trunk with several large branches that split off into smaller branches, then smaller and smaller until the entire perimeter spread into tiny twigs.

My, my, I thought, seething with disgust. *There's the Reformation, and there's the reformations of the Reformation. It created denomination upon denomination upon denomination. Different beliefs. Different organizations. Different practices. Just look at that confusing mess. It's as horrendous as Catholicism. And it's as wrong as Catholicism. They, likewise, are under the condemnation of Revelation 22:18-19. They, too, added differing man-made doctrines and ignored various Bible doctrines. And Matthew 15:9 applies to them too—vanity for teaching and practicing the commandments of men. Surely Mr. Babbitt is not saying all these denominations make up the one true church!*

I pointed to the chart and asked with timidity, "Is this the one true church?"

"Oh, no. Not at all," he responded without hesitation as he shook his head. "Look at that chart." He slightly tipped his head in its direction. "Tell me what you see."

"I see outrageous religious division. I see groups of people, each teaching doctrines different from all the others. I see terrible confusion."

"And you also see a condition that 1 Corinthians 1:10 condemns."

He did not have to say anything more—the pages were already flying.

> *Now I beseech you, brethren, by the name of our Lord Jesus Christ, that ye all speak the same thing, and that there be no divisions among you; but that ye be perfectly joined together in the same mind and in the same judgment.*

"Gary, look again at the chart and tell me, are they '*all speaking the same thing*'?"

302

THE REFORMATION

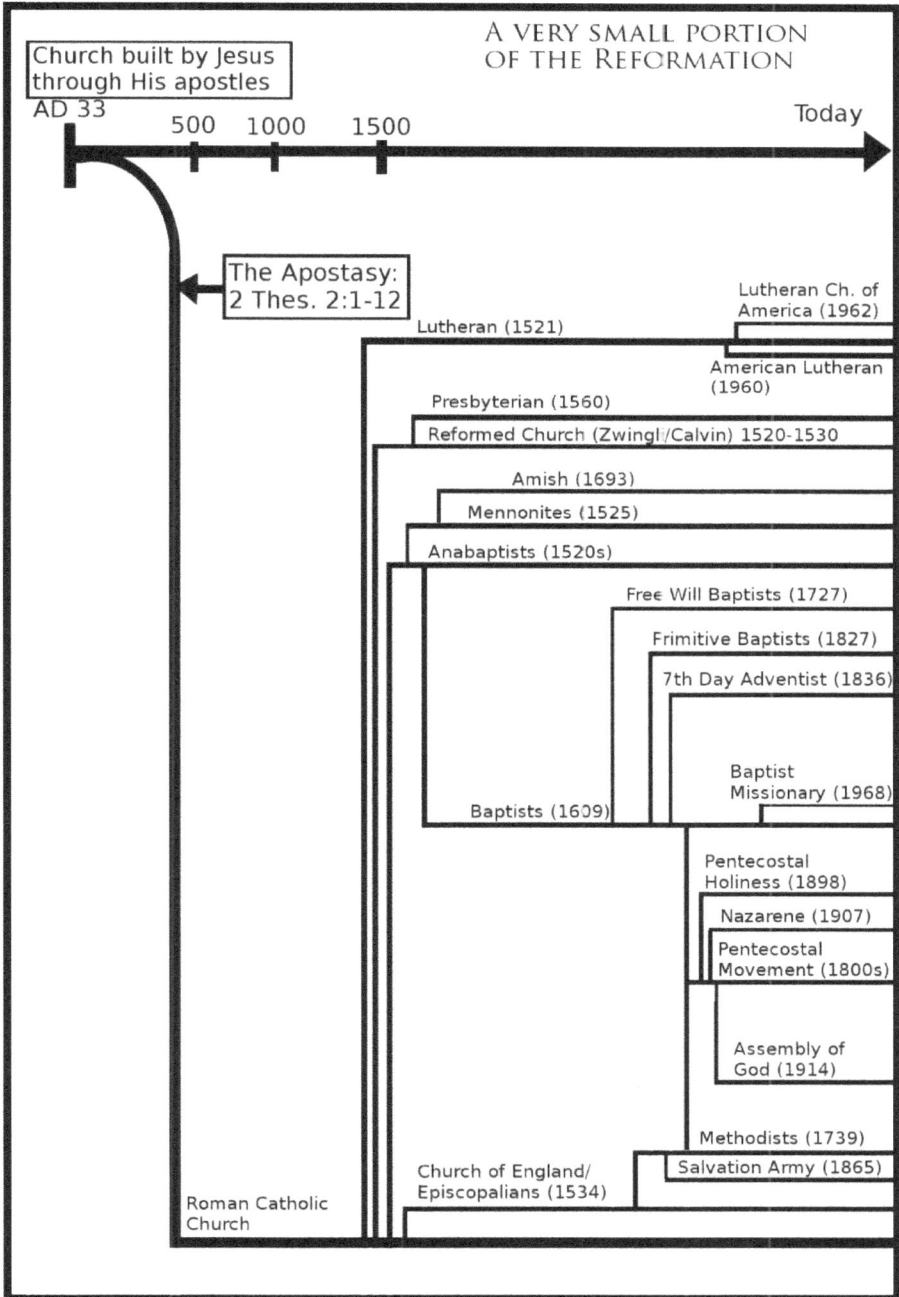

A VERY SMALL PORTION OF THE REFORMATION

Church built by Jesus through His apostles
AD 33
500 1000 1500
Today

The Apostasy: 2 Thes. 2:1-12

Lutheran (1521)

Lutheran Ch. of America (1962)

American Lutheran (1960)

Presbyterian (1560)

Reformed Church (Zwingli/Calvin) 1520-1530

Amish (1693)

Mennonites (1525)

Anabaptists (1520s)

Free Will Baptists (1727)

Primitive Baptists (1827)

7th Day Adventist (1836)

Baptist Missionary (1968)

Baptists (1609)

Pentecostal Holiness (1898)

Nazarene (1907)

Pentecostal Movement (1800s)

Assembly of God (1914)

Methodists (1739)

Salvation Army (1865)

Church of England/ Episcopalians (1534)

Roman Catholic Church

"Certainly not!"

"Is it a picture in which there are '*no divisions among you*'?"

"No way!"

"Are they '*perfectly joined together in the same mind and in the same judgment*'?"

"No, and no!"

"Well, then, does God's Word teach that denominationalism is accepted or condemned?"

"Condemned. No question about it. You're right, Mr. Babbitt, 1 Corinthians 1:10 condemns the denominating one from another."

He pushed on. "You also said you see in this chart 'terrible confusion.' Take a look at 1 Corinthians 14:33."

"Wow, Mr. Babbitt. Listen."

> For God is not the author of confusion, but of peace, as in all churches of the saints.

"Do you know what that means, Mr. Babbitt?!" *Yeah, right. Like he didn't already know.* "That means God did not make this…this confusing mess! He didn't produce the Reformation! It was all man's doings just like the apostasy. *Men* changed things with their additions and subtractions from the Scriptures!"

"And you are correct," he said with a soft sigh of sadness. It grieved him when people mishandled the Bible, and that, to their own ruin. "And Jesus says, '*Every plant which my heavenly Father hath not planted, shall be rooted up.*'"[1]

"'Rooted up?' You mean, destroyed?"

He nodded his head with remorse.

"But," I interjected, "a lot of my friends in these denominations say that all the denominations are each a part of the one big church."

"Yes. But they say that because that is what they have been told by others."

I grumbled to myself, *There's that domino effect again.*

"But that is not what Jesus tells them in John 17:20-21."

I hurried to it and read aloud.

Neither pray I for these alone, but for them also which shall believe on me through their word; that they all may be one; as thou, Father, art in me, and I in thee, that they also may be one in us: that the world may believe that thou hast sent me.

"Okay, I see that Jesus is praying for future disciples, even us today. And He prays that we'd be one. So, are all the denominations part of that one church?"

"The answer is in the verse, Gary. You can figure it out. Jesus is comparing the oneness of disciples with the oneness, or unity, of whom?"

"Let's see…with the oneness of the Father and Jesus."

"And what kind of oneness exists between the teachings of the Father and Jesus: disagreement, or perfect harmony?"

"I get it. Just as the Father and Jesus have perfect harmony in doctrines, so is the church to have such unity. So then, the one church is *not* made up of many denominations teaching thousands of disagreeing doctrines."

"No. The verse completely prohibits it. And there is something else you may have heard your friends say. It is claimed, in John 15:1-6, that the branches are different denominations that are abiding in Jesus, the vine. But it does not say that at all. It says, *'If a MAN'*—not a denomination—*'if a MAN abideth not in me, he is cast forth as a branch.'* Gary, the one church that Jesus built never has been, never will be, and is not today a collection of denominations."

I must admit, all of that scared me good. I mean, nothing was left! Not the Catholic Church. Not the denominations.

"Mr. Babbitt," I asked with a faint voice, "since the Catholic Church is the rejected apostasy, and since the Reformation with all its diverse denominations of confusion is condemned and shall be rooted up, what does that leave us?"

"See that first line I drew at the top of the chart? The one representing the church Jesus built by the apostles in the very beginning?"

"Yes."

"That church still exists."

My gloomy posture snapped straight up as I thundered, *"IT DOES?!!"*

"Indeed. Next Sunday, I will tell you about it."

CHAPTER 42
PULL OUT THE BLUEPRINT

SATURDAY-SUNDAY, MARCH 8

"**R**unners to your mark." *BANG!*

Eighteen pair of cleats jumped to a blur in front of the cheering spectators who rose to their feet in the Enid High School stadium. Track cinders flew as we dashed for our initial position in the mile-long race.

Stay near the lead. Keep from getting boxed in. Don't get tripped, I repeated to myself.

The race held special significance to me. My feet stepped in the long-gone footprints my dad made in this, his high school track. And, grandma was there.

One lap to go. I gave my body a systems check.

How's the legs?

We're okay. Still strong.

Lungs, how you doing?

We're good. We can handle this.

Overall energy, whatcha got?

Plenty in the tank. Use it!

So I did. Of the five runners in front of me, I passed three on the full straight-a-way. In the last curve, due to weeks of training against the wind for the final kick, I overtook one, then the other, and expanded the distance between us.

"Gary," grandma said after the little lady gave me a big hug, "you sure had me fretting and fit to be hog-tied when you passed up Thanksgiving dinner and lost all that weight during the holidays. But I now see you knew what you were doing."

"Well, grandma, twenty-six pounds in thirty days probably had everybody worried. But I promise, after track season, I'll have Thanksgiving every day for a week!"

I never forgot that day. But neither would I forget the next.

Mr. Babbitt slid the posterboard of his hand-drawn history of the church out from behind the bookshelf closest to the library's door and laid it upon the table.

The build-up of a week's anticipation for this moment tickled my stomach. Surpassing the excitement at the starting line of the mile-run, my emotions bounced out of control. And why shouldn't they? Mr. Babbitt had spoken the words I craved to hear, but thought I never would: "That church still exists." For seven long days, the thought sent my heart pounding: "That original church Jesus built by the apostles still exists unchanged today!" Yes, I was excited. With such a possibility, how could anyone not be?

"Gary, I do not suppose you forgot where we left off, did you?"

"Are you kidding?" I stretched my arm across the chart and tapped my index finger on the top line. "That church still exists!"

"Well then, let me show you how anyone can know 'that church still exists.'"

"But, you are going to prove it to me from the Bible, aren't you? I mean, in the Catholic Church…well, you know what I mean."

"Always, young Berean. Always. And God made it so easy to understand. Look at Matthew 16:18, a verse quite familiar to you. In it, Jesus made two promises to mankind. Read it for us would you?"

> *I will build my church; and the gates of hell shall not prevail against it.*

"Do you see His two promises?" he asked.

"Can't miss them. First, He promised He would build His church. But the second one, 'the gates of hell shall not prevail against it,' I don't understand."

"You will in a moment," he assured me. "Tell me, who made these promises?"

"Jesus."

"And who is Jesus?"

"He is the Son of God, Deity, God."

"Does God ever break His promise?"

"Course not." And I told him why; I knew that would be his next question. "If He did, then He either lied, which God does not do, or He's not powerful enough to follow through with what He said He would do, but nothing is too hard for the all-powerful God. So, God never breaks His promises."

"Exactly!" He confirmed as he hand-slapped the table-top. "So, when Jesus promised to build His church, it was a *certainty* that He would. And, of course, He did. Then what does this tell you about His second promise?"

"Same thing. What Jesus promised, He did. Period. It was as good as done. He is powerful enough to do what He said He would do, and He does not lie. So, the gates of hell will *not* prevail against the church. But, Mr. Babbitt, what does that mean?"

"Gates, in Jesus' time, symbolized strength or power. You see, the cities had walls around them for protection, and the weakest spot was the gate. So, the strength of the city was gauged by the strength of the gates. 'The gates of hell,' then, means the 'power of hell.' And 'hell,' or, as translated by some versions of the Bible, 'hades,' is the place where souls go after death. So, the phrase, 'the gates of hell,' means 'the power of death.'"

"I see. Jesus promised the church would never die out."

"Right! And since Jesus does not lie, and since He is powerful enough to do what He said He would do, then the church has never died out. That is why we know," he pointed to the top line on the chart, "that church still exists!"

I dropped my vision from Mr. Babbitt to the chart and stared at the long top line. The room seemed to turn brighter, but it was my eyes opening wider. *How simple is that?! Jesus left us with proof in the Bible. In spite of the great falling away that He knew was coming, and in spite of the formation of thousands of man-made denominations He already condemned, He knew His church would always be here, and He told us so.*

The thrill of that discovery launched me into a height of jubilation I never imagined possible. The hopelessness I felt about Christianity gave way to exhilaration. The most enlightening moment of my life inflated my heart to nearly bursting. *The original church Jesus built by the apostles still exists!*

Then I realized a problem.

"Mr. Babbitt," I said with apprehension, "with the world's phonebooks bulging with thousands of man-made churches, how am I going to find it?"

"Maybe you do not have to find it," he said with a twinkle in his eyes as though he had another fascinating thing for me to hear.

"Gary, suppose a man builds a house from a blueprint and then stores the blueprint. Several years later the man moves to another city and builds a second house from the same blueprint. Would not the second house be exactly like the original?"

"Well, yeah," I said with a shrug of my shoulders to indicate the answer was obvious.

Mr. Babbitt's eyes locked hard on mine. "And we can do the same with the church. As long as we have the blueprint, the Scriptures, we can build that original church wherever we are at, and in whatever century we live."

I did not say anything. I didn't know what to say. The blueprint allegory sounded good, actually. But it seemed a little bold.

"Gary, what do you know about Jesus' parable of the sower in Luke 8?"

"It's about a man who planted seed in four different kinds of soil. The seeds in three of the soils grew, but only one of them produced good plants."

"You remember it well. Then, when Jesus interpreted that parable, He told us in verse 11 *'the seed is the Word of God,'* and in verse 15 the plants in the good ground are people who became Christians. And notice what He says about those Christians: *'having heard the word, keep IT.'* That is, they keep *it*—the Word of God, and it *only*. They do not alter what He told them to practice. They do not add man-made teachings. Nor do they leave off anything He told them to do. Instead, they keep *the Word*, that is, they do *all* of what God tells them and *none* of what men tell them."

"In other words," I intruded again, "don't pull a Revelation 22:18-19 by adding to or taking away from His Word because when you do, you're keeping man's word, not God's."

"That is *exactly* what it means. Now, Gary, think. What would

310

happen if this seed, the Word of God, was planted into the hearts of several people in our town who then became Christians and who then *kept* the word, that is, they maintained their belief and practices in worship, organization, and doctrines just as the Word of God teaches?"

"Well, you'd have a lot of people in town getting saved."

"Well, yes, but since we are told in Acts 2:47, '*the Lord added to the church daily such as should be saved,*' then would not all those saved people—those saved people who then keep all of what God tells them and keep none of what men tell them—make up Jesus' true church in our town?"

"Of course!" I yelled as I jumped to my feet. "Mr. Babbitt! That is so sensible! Just do what God says to do to be saved, and then just do *only* what God says to do in the church. By doing that, you got the church!" I sat back down. "Yeah, I get it now. Just build by the blueprint. Go back before the Reformation with all its confusing denominations. Go back before Catholicism—the result of the apostasy. Go back before the great falling away. And go back *to the beginning* by sticking to the blueprint—the Bible, and *only* the Bible. Mr. Babbitt, this is so simple. Why have I not seen this before?"

"Because, I rather suspect, all you knew and believed possible was Catholicism and denominationalism. And because of that, this thought would never enter in your mind. But do not feel bad about yourself. Evidently, that is the way it is with most everyone."

"Another one of Satan's deceptions, I imagine."

"And a powerful one it is," Mr. Babbitt sighed.

He pulled his Bible directly in front of him, began turning the pages, and said, "Find in your Bible 2 Kings chapter 22. There is something you should see."

Unfamiliar with the Old Testament, it took me a moment to find it in spite of my feverous search. But patient Mr. Babbitt sat quietly until my last page settled.

"Gary, God recorded this account for us to learn from, and it applies to the very thing we are talking about. It happened about 600 years before the time of Jesus when the high priest found the long-lost book of the law which God delivered through Moses. A scribe

311

read the law to King Josiah who then reacted violently by tearing his clothes."

I just had to ask. "He tore his clothes? Why?"

"The Jews, when in tremendous remorse, did that when they heard terrible news. The king found out they were doing many religious practices forbidden by God's law, as well as failing to do the practices He commanded them to do."

"Man! That's just like what happened with the church!"

"You catch on quick. Yes, God's people in the Old Testament also had a falling away. And it happened because of the same reasons. Read verse 13 and 17 would you?"

> *Our fathers have not hearkened unto the words of this book, to do according to all that which is written concerning us.*

> *Because they have forgotten me, and have burned incense unto other gods, that they might provoke me to anger with all the works of their hands; therefore my wrath shall be kindled against this place, and shall not be quenched.*

"Yeah, I see," I said, still looking at the verses. "The people forsook God and did not worship the way *He* told them, and then they worshipped in the ways *they* thought up. That's just like the church in its falling away. Instead of God's way with elders for leaders, men invented the hierarchy. Instead of God's simple instructions for worship, men added all kinds of things. Instead of using the Bible as their only creed book, men brought in their creeds and Tradition."

"And, I am sure you noticed, God punished that apostasy of Judah, even though their apostasy included virtually the entire nation. And so will God punish in eternity those in that great falling away from the church, even though the number is so extensive."

"Boy! There's sure no safety in numbers when it comes to obeying or disobeying God."

"None at all," he agreed, shaking his head.

"Mr. Babbitt, I see another similarity of the two apostasies."

"Do tell."

"Since it shocked Josiah to learn that they practiced so many things contrary to God's law, then it is obvious he was completely unaware that he and all the people were nothing but an apostasy from the true Jewish religion. Mr. Babbitt, that describes *me*. I was completely unaware of the errors and the great apostasy until you showed it to me in the Scriptures. Also, since he said *'our FA-THERS have not hearkened unto the words of this book,'* then he and the people merely believed and practiced the way they did simply because some men years earlier made changes in the Jew's worship and religious beliefs. Then, by the time of Josiah, the nation was merely doing what their ancestors, parents, and everybody else was doing. Mr. Babbitt, that was just like me! And it's probably just like most everyone else in Catholicism. And denominationalism."

"Like I said, God records this account so we can learn from it," he reminded me. "And look what happened next. Josiah ordered the removal of every means of worship not found in the book of the law. Chapter 23:4-24 tells all about it, and it is summarized in verse 24. Would you read it for us?"

> *...all the abominations that were spied out in the land of Judah and in Jerusalem, did Josiah put away, that he might perform the words of the law...*

"You see, Gary, in order to get back to the way the Jewish religion was supposed to be, Josiah removed every practice that was not found in God's law."

"Yeah. I can see that. You got to clean house."

"But that is not all he did." Mr. Babbitt turned back a page in his Bible, and so did I. "Read 23:3."

> *And the king stood by a pillar, and made a covenant before the Lord, to walk after the Lord, and to keep his commandments and his testimonies and his statutes with all their heart and all their soul, to perform the words of this covenant that were written in this book.*

"So you see, Gary, not only did he remove everything they were doing religiously that was *not* found in God's law, he also began doing everything that *was* commanded."

"Wow, what a project."

"Yes, but they accomplished it. They wanted to. As the verse says, they did it with their heart and soul. They had heard from the book of the law that, ever since their leaders of earlier days went wrong, the entire mass of people was in the wrong and God's anger burned against them."

"Mr. Babbitt," I said sheepishly, "that's why I am trying to get right."

"I know," he said with a deeper compassion than ever before. "I also know many compelling causes might hold a person back. But, what God tells you about Josiah can help with that, too. Gary, it did not matter to Josiah how long they had been doing wrong, or how long they had not been doing right—he made the corrections. And it did not matter that his family and ancestors did wrong. It did not matter how many did wrong. And it did not matter what great religious leaders did wrong. Josiah sought one thing: get right with God and avoid His wrath of punishment. And he did it the only way possible. He used the book of God to eliminate everything it did not teach, and then practice everything it did."

"Mr. Babbitt, let's do that! Let's do like God shows us with Josiah! Let's pull out the blueprint, the Scriptures, and build a congregation of the true, original church!"

"We do not have to," he said calmly, much in contrast to my exuberance.

"Huh? But I thought…"

He cut me off. "It has already been done."

"REALLY?! WHERE?! WHEN?!" Both of my hands with fingers spread wide pressed upon the table as I leaned forward. "Tell me about it!"

Mr. Babbitt leaned back in his chair. "It has been occurring in our country since the late 1700s. Several preachers of different denominations—Presbyterian, Methodist, Baptist—who were isolated and unknown to each other, began to understand, proclaim, and follow God's lesson of Josiah. The number of people who agreed to this grew rapidly. They denounced denominationalism and Catholicism and severed ties with those religious bodies. Eventually, each of these isolated groups grew so large they became aware of each other and they united. Since then, that message has been proclaimed in thousands of cities and towns, and thousands upon thousands of people have embraced it. They rejected and left the denominations with their man-made teachings, and then used the 'blueprint' to establish a congregation of the Lord's true church in their own towns."

I sat astonished. The words, the most exhilarating I had ever heard, cast the past half year's mountain of disappointments and hopelessness out of my heart. It made perfect sense. It was so simple. It was Scriptural. I found the treasure!

"Mr. Babbitt, do you know where one of these congregations is at?"

His smiling face emitted a low, happy chuckle. "Gary, for the past few months, you have been assembling with one."

"I HAVE?!"

He nodded his head.

"You're not a denomination?!"

"Was the church Jesus built by the apostles a denomination?"

"Well, no. But you have a name on your sign."

"Listen closely. The church did not, and it does not today have a proper name. But, among other reasons, in order for any organization to own land and a building, the government requires every religious group to have a name. That is why you see on the sign, 'the church of Christ.' But, no, it is not our proper name. Rather, the phase comes from Romans 16:16 and simply means: the church that belongs to Christ."

"And all this time I thought the church of Christ was a denomination. But all along I've been meeting with the real New Testament church built by Jesus. Wow!"

I paused, partly because I do not think clearly when utterly astonished, and partly because I did not know exactly how to ask it. But he must have read my mind.

"Gary, let me remind you of the words of Acts 2:47. *'The Lord added to the church daily such as should be saved.'* You see, when you do what God—not man—but what *God* says to do to be saved, you are saved and God puts you into the church that belongs to

THE IVORY DOMINO

Christ.

"And *that* is what we will look at next week."

316

Chapter 43
Do the Math

T he symphony of early spring birds by my bedroom window welcomed me to the day. My eyes opened and, with the magic of dawn's light, the room softly glowed in tranquil gold. Comfortably laying in my cozy bed engulfed in sights and sounds of serenity, getting up was furthest from my mind.

"Ahhh. This is great," I unintelligibly mumbled. Then I thought, *and just imagine, this is nothing compared to heaven. No way do I want to miss it. And I certainly don't want to go into eternal hell.* My mind flashed back to the grueling agony of yesterday's mile-run at Duncan High School. I wouldn't even want *that* for eternity.

The sobering thoughts yanked me out of the morning grogginess. *But, if I were to die right now, where would I go? My infant baptism sure isn't taught in the Bible. Many of my friends say all I need to do is believe in Jesus. Which I do. But, just what does God say in the Bible? I want His answer. And I want to know it is **His** answer. He is the Judge at Judgment Day, not priests, popes, nor pastors.*

"Well, laying here isn't giving me the answer. I gotta get to Mr. Babbitt's class."

Mr. Babbitt's kind expression harbored a seriousness I easily detected. It stands to reason. Although all our previous discussions merited seriousness, this one did much more so. For him to show me from the Bible what to do to be saved, with the possibility of me rejecting it, weighed heavy on his mind. The past few months came down to this. And he knew it. So did I.

"Gary." He paused for a moment. "Jesus is going to judge you at Judgment Day, as He says in John 12:48, by the instructions in the New Testament. I am going to guide you so you can see what it says you must do to be saved. If you have not done what it says, *you* must decide if you are going to do it or not. But I tell you in advance, do not wait for me to high-pressure you, for I will not. Once you know what God says, you, on your own, need to act. Do you understand what I'm saying, young Berean?"

"Yes sir. If I don't do it, it won't get done. And my condition won't change."

He nodded his head with his seriousness still showing.

Mr. Babbitt opened his Bible and began where I least expected. "Revelation 22:18-19 teaches us how to answer our Bible questions. Listen to it one more time.

> *For I testify unto every man that heareth the words of the prophecy of this book, If any man shall add unto these things, God shall add unto him the plagues that are written in this book: And if any man shall take away from the words of the book of this prophecy, God shall take away his part out of the book of life, and out of the holy city, and from the things which are written in this book.*

"Gary, I am going to illustrate that for you. Suppose a teacher tells the students to add up the numbers of 1, 2, and 3. Which adds up to what?"

"Six."

He continued. "The first student, Al, wrote on his paper: $1+2+3+1 = 7$. Al's answer was wrong. Why?"

"He added an extra number to those the teacher gave."

"Another student, Tom, wrote: $1+2 = 3$. Why was his answer wrong?"

"He left off a number."

"A third, Ron, wrote: $1+2+3 = 6$. Why was Ron's answer correct?"

"He did not add an extra number to those the teacher gave, nor did he leave one off."

Then Mr. Babbitt asked, "Do you see how this illustrates what Revelation 22:18-19 is telling us?"

"Yeah! If I want to get the Bible's correct answer to my question, 'what must I do to be saved?' then I must not add any man-made doctrine, nor leave out anything God says to do. And then I

318

must put them all together to get the right answer from God."

He extended his hand toward me and tapped the table with his finger. "That is a crucial, God-given principle on how to learn what the Bible teaches. If those who profess to be Christians knew and practiced it, religious division would plummet.

"Now, let us first see how well you understand that principle by asking and answering this question: 'How must I pray so my prayer will be answered?' For sake of time, we will imagine the Bible has only three verses that give us the information. The first one is Matthew 21:22."

I found it and read, "*And all things, whatsoever ye shall ask in prayer, believing, ye shall receive.*"

"What does it say we must do so our prayer will be answered?" he inquired.

"Ask believing. We must ask in faith."

"Right. So, are we to now close our Bible and claim, 'That is our answer. That is all we must do, only believe?'"

"No," I said shaking my head.

"Why not?"

"Because the Bible might tell us something else we need to do in our praying. We need to look through all the Bible in case there are additional instructions on how to pray."

"Right again. And there are. Look in John 14:14."

When I located it, I read aloud. "*If ye shall ask any thing in my name, I will do it.*"

"What does this verse say about our praying?" he prodded.

"We must ask in His name. But what does that mean?"

"It means by Jesus' authority. We come to the Father in prayer by means of the privilege that Jesus provides for His disciples."

"I see."

"Gary, now we have two conditions for praying. But, what are we to do? Just take one and ignore the other?"

"No. We must do both."

"Correct. Now, the last verse is 1 John 5:14."

"Give me a second, Mr. Babbitt…here it is. '*This is the confidence that we have in him, that, if we ask any thing according to his will, he heareth us.*' This says we must ask according to his will."

"Yes. You see, sometimes the things we ask are not according to His will," he explained.

"You mean like asking for a million dollars, or, to never die?" I cringed as soon as the words left my lips. *Dummy!* I scolded myself. *With Mr. Babbitt's illness, how could I have said that!*

"That is right," he said without even a flinch of disturbance. "Now we have three different requirements for praying. So, are we supposed to take our pick? Can we just do one or two of the three?"

"Not according to Revelation 22. If we do, we'll be like Tom who left out a number from the three the teacher gave and ended up with a wrong answer."

"Indeed. If God gave an instruction, the instruction must be met, whether it is only one, three or more. Our question was, 'How must I pray so my prayer will be answered by God?' Gary, without adding to or taking away from the teaching of the Bible, what is the answer?"

"We must believe, *plus* ask in Jesus' name, *plus* ask according to God's will. We must do all three because each one of them is a requirement."

"Exactly. And it just so happens that God shows what happens when someone leaves off one of the conditions. Read for us James 4:3."

"It says, '*Ye ask, and receive not, because ye ask amiss, that ye may consume it upon your lusts.*'"

"They asked, but did they receive what they asked for?" he asked.

"No."

"Why not?"

"They asked according to *their* will, not God's. They left off a condition mentioned in one of those three verses."

"So you see, Gary, God tells us this: In order to receive God's blessing, whether it be His answering our prayers or His saving us from being lost, we must do *all* of what God instructs us to do without leaving off even one requirement."

"I get it, Mr. Babbitt. We *must* follow the teaching of Revelation 22. If we don't, we don't get saved, even if others tell us we are."

"Are you ready, then, young Berean?"

"You bet I am. Show me everything the Bible says I must do to be saved."

"Then turn to 1 Corinthians 1:21."

I found it and read, "*It pleased God by the foolishness of preaching to save them that believe.*"

"What does God inform you in this verse you must do?" he asked.

"Believe. God will save those who believe."

"Gary, do you believe that Jesus is the Son of God?"

"Yes. The Bible says He is; and the Father said '*This is my beloved Son*;' and He did miracles so we could believe He is the Son of God."

"So, what do we do now? Close our Bibles and say, 'Well, the Bible says we are to believe to be saved. So that is it. Just believe.' Is that what we should do?"

"I guess that *could* be all the Bible says to do. I don't know. But, like we did with prayer, we need to keep looking to see if there's something else He tells us to do."

Mr. Babbitt's curved up lips indicated he was pleased I understood how to put Revelation 22 into practice. "Before we look at the next verse, listen to this. Two robbers were caught. The first was sorry only in that he was caught. The second was sorry he committed the wrong and decided he would change his ways and turn from his life of crime. Gary, with regard to your sins against God, which of the two robbers do you feel like?"

"The second one, definitely."

"Good for you. Now read 2 Corinthians 7:10."

> *For godly sorrow worketh repentance to salvation not to be repented of: but the sorrow of the world worketh death.*

"Sorrow for sinning produces what?" he asked.

"Repentance. But, Mr. Babbitt, what exactly does that mean?"

"It means a person's sorrow for sinning leads him to change his mind about living contrary to God's laws."

"Like that second robber?"

"Yes. And what does the verse say repentance leads to?"

"To salvation."

"Indeed, repentance is needed for salvation. Now we have two things the Bible says saves us. What are we to do? Just take our pick of the two and ignore the other?"

"Gotta take both, Mr. Babbitt. Revelation 22, you know."

Mr. Babbitt smiled again. "So far, you believe Jesus is the Son of God, and, like the second robber, you have repented. Now read Romans 10:9-10. It gives you a third requirement."

> *If thou shalt confess with thy mouth the Lord Jesus, and shalt believe in thine heart that God hath raised him from the dead, thou shalt be saved. For with the heart man believeth unto righteousness; and with the mouth confession is made unto salvation.*

"This verse informs you of two things to do to be saved. One, you have already learned. What is the other?"

"It says I must confess with my mouth that Jesus is the Lord."

"Have you done that?"

"Often. Even a moment ago I said Jesus is the Son of God. But I'll say it again, Jesus is the Lord."

"Now, like with praying, we have three different conditions for salvation. Can we just do one or two of the three?"

"And, like praying," I replied, "if we leave off even one, we won't be saved. So is that it Mr. Babbitt? Believe, repent, and confess? Am I now saved?"

"You are. Unless the Bible teaches another requirement."

"Well, does it?"

"Take a look at Mark 16:16. Read it and see what it says."

I located it in no time. "'*He that believeth and is baptized shall*

DO THE MATH

be saved; but he that believeth not shall be damned.' So baptism is needed too. I've done that. Well, no, I haven't. Infant baptism isn't taught in the Bible. It's not what God tells us to do."

"Besides that," Mr. Babbitt added, "as you have just seen, before a person can be saved, he must believe, repent, and confess Jesus as Lord. But infants cannot do any of that. So infants cannot be saved by 'baptism only.'"

"Man, oh man! Have I ever been duped!"

"There are three more verses on baptism I want you to see. Read them and tell me what they teach about baptism. The first is Acts 2:38."

I turned to it and read:

> *Then Peter said unto them, Repent, and be baptized every one of you in the name of Jesus Christ for the remission of sins.*

"Can't miss that," I admitted. "A person must be baptized to get his sins forgiven."

"Indeed. Now 1 Peter 3:21."

> *The like figure whereunto even baptism doth also now save us (not the putting away of the filth of the flesh, but the answer of a good conscience toward God,) by the resurrection of Jesus Christ.*

"This one, like Mark 16:16, says baptism saves."

"And one more. Acts 22:16."

> *And now why tarriest thou? arise, and be baptized, and wash away thy sins, calling on the name of the Lord.*

"It says baptism washes away a person's sins. So the Bible has two verses that teach a person is saved when he is baptized, and two verses that teach his sins are forgiven when he is baptized. Mr. Babbitt, a person needs help to misunderstand those verses."

"Actually, the Bible has many more verses that teach baptism is a requirement for salvation. But God only has to say something once for it to be true."

"Mr. Babbitt, the Catholic Church is right about needing to be baptized to be saved, but the Bible says baptism is for believing adults, not infants."

"Correct. Gary, there is one more thing you need to see, but first let me ask, how were you baptized?"

"You know how we do it, Mr. Babbitt. The priest poured water on my forehead."

"Is that how God says to do it? Pouring?"

"Yeah. I guess. Well, to tell you the truth, I've never looked in the Bible to find out. I just accepted what the hierarchy told me and I assumed it was right. Besides, that's what we all did. Mom did it that way."

"Do you want to know what method of baptism God said to use?"

"Well, yeah! No sense in Him telling us to be baptized a certain way and then we do it a different way. We might *call* it baptism, but if we don't do it the way He told us, then in His sight we wouldn't be baptizing at all. And if we're not baptized, we didn't get saved!"

"How right you are. Now take a look at Romans 6:4."

When I found it I read with sheer astonishment.

> *Therefore we are buried with him by baptism into death: that like as Christ was raised up from the dead by the glory of the Father, even so we also should walk in newness of life.*

"A burial, Mr. Babbitt! God tells us to go under the water in a burial! Not pouring. Not sprinkling. So I didn't do what God said! My baptism wasn't even a Bible baptism! It wouldn't have saved me anyway!"

"I am sorry, but that is correct. It is just as Hebrews 5:9 says, Jesus gives '*salvation unto all them that obey Him*,' and pouring or sprinkling is not obeying Him. So anyone who received a so-called baptism by pouring or sprinkling was not, and is still not saved."

"Then sprinkling and pouring must be a man-made practice, huh?"

"I am afraid so."

My anger at those early Christians who began that false and

worthless practice flared up like a fuel-injected torch. For all those years, the possibility of not being saved never entered my mind. But all the time I was lost as lost could be and headed to hell. I was one of the blind being led by the blind and I had fallen into the ditch.[1]

"Gary, our question is, 'What must you do to be saved,' and you have seen for yourself what the Bible teaches. So what is its answer?"

"First, I have learned *how* to find the answer to that question. A person must find and do *everything* God tells us to do. Then and only then does a person do what *God* tells him to do to be saved. And so, then and only then is a person really saved."

"Correct. And what are those requirements?"

"A person must believe that Jesus is the Son of God. And he must repent—turn from his sinful ways. He must also confess that Jesus is the Lord. And then he must be baptized by a burial in water."

He then humbly asked with his eyes locked on mine, "Is the Bible's answer to the question, 'What must I do to be saved?' different from the answer the Catholic Church gives?"

"Mr. Babbitt, for the sake of my mother and my relatives, and for the sake of the sheer number of people in the Catholic Church, I wish it were the same, but the Catholic answer is not the Bible answer at all."

At that moment I knew for certain, I had not done what God requires for salvation. I merely did what feeble *men* said to do. Careless men who long ago got the church to follow falsehoods and change the practice. They committed an unimaginable crime against me, my family, the church, and God, and I was outraged and my thoughts boiled. *I mean, saved without believing in Jesus?! Yeah, right! Saved without repenting?! Oh, sure! Saved without confessing Jesus is the Lord?! You bet! Just take an infant who doesn't even know what is going on, pour water on his head and call it baptism, and presto change-o, you got a Christian?! Man, oh man! How woefully ignorant of the Scriptures we are! And that, to our own eternal destruction!*

Mr. Babbitt left me with one final thought. He spoke like a dying grandfather with compassion wrapped around each word. "Gary, I told you at the beginning of class, I would show you from the very book that will judge you at Judgment Day what you must do to be saved. You know you have not done what it says. Remember, I warned you not to expect me to pressure you, and I shall not. This has to be *your* choice. Yet, I hope you know how I feel about you and what I hope for you. You now have everything you need to know. I cannot do any more. The decision is yours and yours alone."

CHAPTER 44
THE BIGGER THEY ARE...

THAT AFTERNOON

"**A**re they still coming?" I asked Mr. Babbitt as he opened his front door.

"I am sure they are. They haven't called to cancel."

Earlier in the week, the preacher from a nearby large denomination, along with their guest speaker for their revival, approached the Babbitt's home as the two men knocked doors to invite people to their week-long series of sermons. Mr. Babbitt declined. He told them they did not correctly tell people what the Bible says a person must do to be saved which resulted in the people thinking they were saved when they were not. The revival preacher insisted for an appointment to discuss the matter, to which Mr. Babbitt asked permission for my presence.

"Remember, let me do all the talking. If you say anything, I will pull off my sock and stuff it in your mouth."

My laughter joined his chuckles as I held up my hands and said, "Okay, okay. I get the message." But I was thinking *Man! I was not going to say anything! I'm nerved-out about this!*

A bold rap at the door signaled their arrival. As the two men entered the living room and exchanged formalities with the Babbitt's, I measured them up.

The revival preacher, Mr. Sloan, clad in an expensive, shiny, dark-blue suit, stood three or four inches taller than Mr. Babbitt. An admirable, healthy looking man in his mid-fifties, neatly gelled his dark hair that showed a slight greying on both sides. With his strong, penetrating voice, he could have preached without a microphone. Confident and assertive, he controlled the setting just by his aura. I figured he must have been the life of every party, the chairman of every meeting, and the center-piece of every gathering, whether church, funerals, or weddings. *This guy will overpower Mr. Babbitt's mild disposition and weak physical condition,* I lamented.

The local preacher, Mr. Irwin, did not say much. He did not have the opportunity. But, at six foot, thin frame, late thirties, blond hair, a black pin-striped suit and focused eyes that portrayed constant concentration and an overdose of intelligence, he looked every part the preacher of a large denomination.

I hope Mr. Babbitt knows what he is doing, I thought as we made our way into his study and sat in the four chairs placed around his desk: Mr. Babbitt behind the desk; me on his left; Mr. Irwin across from me; and Mr. Sloan opposite Mr. Babbitt. While I struggled to keep my legs from nervous jitters and my stomach from throwing up, Mr. Babbitt sat as cool as milk in the refrigerator.

"So that I do not misunderstand you," Mr. Babbitt began ever so kindly, "exactly what is it you tell people they must do to have their sins forgiven and be saved?"

"Faith, man, faith!" Mr. Sloan thundered with authority. "A person must believe that Jesus is the Son of God. And when they do, they are at that moment saved."

"So, you teach salvation is by faith only?" Mr. Babbitt asked.

"Yes siree! We teach what the Bible teaches," boasted Mr. Sloan.

In large letters so all could see, Mr. Babbitt wrote across the top of his writing pad with a broad-tipped pen, "Salvation is by faith only," and then asked, "Now, my friend, how do you go about proving that?"

"How do I prove that?!" he roared as he threw his hands above his head. "Why, every Sunday school child knows how. The verses *fill* the New Testament. Listen up, man. I'll quote some for you.

> *For God so loved the world, that he gave his only begotten Son, that whosoever **believeth** in him should not perish, but have everlasting life. John 3:16.*

> *He that **believeth** on the Son hath everlasting life. John 3:36.*

> *Every one which seeth the Son, and **believeth** on him, may have everlasting life. John 6:40.*

*He that **believeth** on me hath everlasting life. John 6:47.*

*When Jesus saw their **faith**, he said unto the sick of the palsy, Son, thy sins be forgiven thee. Mark 2:5.*

*And he said to the woman, Thy **faith** hath saved thee; go in peace. Luke 7:50.*

*Whosoever **believeth** in him shall receive remission of sins. Acts 10:43.*

*Therefore being justified by **faith**, we have peace with God. Romans 5:1.*

*It pleased God by the foolishness of preaching to save them that **believe**. 1 Corinthians 1:21.*

*Whosoever **believeth** that Jesus is the Christ is born of God. 1 John 5:1.*

"And there plenty more, but these are enough to prove that man is saved by faith only."

"Mr. Sloan, I do not see it," Mr. Babbitt said with pure humility, but without a flinch.

"You don't see it?!" Mr. Sloan shot back in his amplified voice.

"No, and actually, neither do you."

I then knew why Mr. Babbitt wanted me there! He wanted a bodyguard!

Mr. Sloan was so flabbergasted he couldn't say a thing. At least not comprehensibly. He just mumbled and shifted back and forth in his chair like a coach struggling to keep from beating a dimwitted player.

"You see," Mr. Babbitt pointed at his clipboard, "you say, 'salvation is by faith *only*.' But none of those verses you quoted contain the word 'only.' So the verses do not say what you claim they do. Furthermore, not even one single verse of those 'plenty more' you alluded to has the word 'only.' And that is because there is no such verse in the entire New Testament that teaches your doctrine that says 'salvation is by faith *only*.'"

I could tell both preachers were scanning all their memorized verses for one that read "faith *only*," but they came up empty.

"It is like this," Mr. Babbitt explained. "The statement, 'we live by air,' means we must have air to live, but the statement does not mean we live by air *only*. We *also* live by food, water, and shelter. Likewise, the numerous times the Bible says we are 'saved by faith,' means we must have faith to be saved, but it does not mean we are 'saved by faith *only*.'"

"But," Mr. Sloan balked, "those verses say we are saved by faith. So if we are saved by faith, then we are saved by faith *only*."

"Sir, if you interpret the Bible that way, then you have an insurmountable problem. You see, 2 Corinthians 7:10 says we are saved by repentance: '*repentance to salvation.*' Now, if we use your manner of understanding a verse, then, since it says we are saved by repentance, then the verse means we are saved by repentance *only*. And you know that is false. Also, 1 Peter 3:21 says we are saved by baptism: '*baptism doth also now save us.*' Your reasoning would have us believing, since it says we are saved by baptism, then we are saved by baptism *only*. And that, too, is false. You see, if you interpret verses like you do, then you have the Bible teaching salvation by faith only, and salvation by repentance only, and salvation by baptism only. Mr. Sloan, you have the Bible contradicting itself! But God does *not* contradict Himself. That means the way you make those verses that say 'salvation by faith' to mean 'salvation by faith *only*' is wrong! That means you are teaching people a false, man-made doctrine that does *not* save! You have them thinking they are saved when they are not!"

I can see that, I thought. *Surely these two intellectuals can too.*

Mr. Babbitt pressed the point. "I asked you, 'How do you prove salvation is by faith *only*?' and you did not do it. And it is not because you are not smart enough. Certainly not! But it is because it cannot be done because the verses do not teach it."

It surprised me how simple Martin Luther's widely believed doctrine is proven false.

"Now Mr. Sloan, here is something else. Please tell me, if 'salvation by faith only' were true, would there ever be, in the New Testament, people who believed in Jesus, but were not saved?"

Visually unsettled, Mr. Sloan's cockiness waned. "Well, no."

"Correct," replied Mr. Babbitt as he opened his Bible. "Now the question is: Are there some who believed on Jesus but were not saved? Listen to John 8:30, *'As He spake these words, many believed on Him.'* Mr. Sloan, did these people believe on Jesus?"

"Yes."

"So, according to your teaching that 'faith only saves,' these people were supposed to be saved. However, later in verse 44, Jesus says to these same people, *'Ye are of your father the devil.'* Mr. Sloan, these people believed, but were not saved. And that shows 'faith only' does *not* save."

I glanced at both preachers. They stared down at the desk and said nothing. Mr. Babbitt had defanged and declawed the lions with his deep knowledge of the Scriptures.

"A moment ago, I said there is no verse that has the words, 'faith only.'" Mr. Babbitt spoke with the same gentleness and concern he always extended to me. "But actually, there is."

Both men simultaneously raised their eyes, then their heads.

"It is James 2:24."

> *Ye see then how that by works a man is justified, and not by faith only.*

"My friends, the only time the Bible mentions 'faith only' is when it declares that salvation is *not* by 'faith only.'"

The muscle bulge in Mr. Sloan's cheek exposed his clenched jaw.

"Notice, Mr. Sloan, Mr. Irwin, the verse does not say man is justified by 'works *only*' as some mistakenly claim, but 'by works,' meaning, works are *part* of what we must do to get saved. Also, it does not say 'we are not justified by faith,' which would mean faith has no part in salvation. Rather, it says we are not justified by 'faith *only*,' which means faith is not all that is needed. So you see, salvation includes *both*, faith *and* works. It is not one to the exclusion of the other, but both, just as verse 22 says:

> *Seest thou how faith wrought with his works, and by works was faith made perfect?*

"My friends, earlier you said, 'We teach what the Bible teaches.' But if you did, you would not be telling people to get saved by faith *only*. The Bible not only does *not* teach it, the Bible teaches *against* it."

A 250 pound linebacker at full speed could not have hit harder than did Mr. Babbitt's tender spoken words. And the two men sat stunned from the impact. They seemed bewildered, as though they never realized that all the verses they used to teach their doctrine, 'salvation by faith only,' does not say that at all. They appeared surprised to hear the Bible teach that we are *not* saved by 'faith *only*.' They looked dazed to learn about those believers who were *not* saved. Had they been just like me, believing what they believed just because others did, and others before them did, all the way back to Martin Luther's first preaching of faith only?

"Well," Mr. Sloan's voice broke the uncomfortable silence, "what works do you think are needed in order to get saved?"

That's a dodge! I struggled to keep my promise to refrain from speaking. *He's not even going to try to reply to what Mr. Babbitt put to him. But, I can't blame him, there is no reply.*

"I will be glad to answer your very important question," Mr. Babbitt replied.

My legs began jittering again, but cool Mr. Babbitt had not warmed a single degree. His humility and knowledge of the Scriptures, instead of Mr. Sloan's powerful personality, now controlled the discussion. Truth is determined by Scripture, not showmanship.

"We just read, in James 2:22, it takes both, faith *and* works to obtain salvation. Likewise, Galatians 5:6 tells us that which avails is 'faith working.' Now, one of the best verses describing that faith and that work which gives us salvation is Mark 16:16:

> *He that believeth and is baptized shall be saved.*

"Hold it right there!" Mr. Sloan regained some of his flattened assertiveness. "That verse does not teach baptism is necessary for salvation!"

Mr. Babbitt did not even blink. "This verse teaches belief is necessary for salvation, does it not?"

"It most certainly does."

"Why?"

"Because belief comes first, and salvation then follows."

"Oh," Mr. Babbitt said as he regained control of the conversation and attempted to help the two men see what they overlooked. "So 'believeth' is present, and 'shall be saved' is future. And the present must happen before what happens in the future?"

"You got it man," Mr. Sloan confirmed. "'Believe' is present, so it must come before 'shall be saved' which is future."

"Well, what about 'is baptized'? Is it past, 'was baptized;' future, 'shall be baptized;' or present, 'is baptized'?"

A deathly quiet fell over the room again. The two disciples of Luther got the point. I did too. "Is baptized," just like "believeth," is also present, and present *must* take place *before* that which is future. And that means, just as "believeth" must occur *before* being saved, so must baptism!

Mr. Sloan, shattered by that un-get-over-able point, yet, not wanting to renounce the doctrine he had believed for so long, stammered as he searched for something to say. "But, uh, baptism is not needed because the rest of that verse says, *'but he that believeth not shall be damned.'* See there! Baptism is not needed because it does not say 'he who is not baptized shall be condemned.'"

"Why should it?" asked Mr. Babbitt without a shred of nervousness in his voice. "If someone does not believe, he is *already* condemned, which is precisely what John 3:18 tells you: *'he that believeth not is condemned already.'* So the second part of the verse does not need 'is not baptized' in order to be condemned—he is condemned *already*.

"Besides, if a person does not believe, he sure is not going to be baptized. Here, maybe this sentence will help you understand: 'He that inserts the key into the lock and turns the key shall unlock the door; but he that does not insert the key shall not unlock the door.' You well know, the second part of the sentence does not need to say 'and does not turn the key' because if the key is not first inserted into the lock, the second action, turning the key in the lock, cannot be done. So that popular objection about the rest of the verse is silly."

For a few moments Mr. Sloan returned, as he often did, to squirming in his chair with a low grumble. Then he barked, "No matter. My New American Standard Bible has a footnote for verse 9 which says; and I quote: 'Some of the oldest manuscripts omit from verse 9 through 20.' So there you have it! Mark 16:16 is really not even part of the Bible!"

What?! Now *my* chair got the buff-job. But Mr. Babbitt continued to sit calmly.

"Mr. Sloan, just what are those manuscripts that do not have those last verses of Mark?"

"Well, I do not know. But I do not need to. The footnote is enough."

Mr. Babbitt locked eyes with Mr. Sloan for a lengthy moment before he spoke, but still with kindness. "I recommend you research things before you blindly swallow them and then get others to believe it. In contrast to the *thousands* of manuscripts which *do* contain Mark 16:9-20, the number of manuscripts upon which this irresponsible footnote rests are but two, the Vaticanus and the Sinaiticus.

"Furthermore, my friend, if you say Mark 16:9-20 is not part of the Bible just because the Vaticanus does not have it, then you must also claim and teach that 1 Timothy, 2 Timothy, Titus, Philemon, Hebrews 9:15 to the book's end, and Revelation—a total of 40 and 1/2 chapters—are not part of the Bible. Why? Because the Vaticanus likewise *does not have them*! Mr. Sloan, do you claim and teach that?!"

Mr. Sloan squirmed, but this time without grumbling.

"I did not think so."

Wow! This is incredible! I thought as I noticed my legs no longer jittered. *This big bag of wind can blow these things uncontested and unquestioned into trusting ears, but when he's up against someone who can push back, the bag bursts and we find it is empty!*

334

"And the Sinaiticus," Mr. Babbitt pressed on. "If you insist the Sinaiticus is the authority to determine what belongs in the Bible, then you must also take, as part of the Bible, six complete apocrypha books and most of two others![1] Why? Because the Sinaiticus, your authority for what belongs in the Bible, *has them!* Mr. Sloan, do you claim and teach that those eight unauthentic books are part of the Bible?"

Mr. Sloan did not even squirm this time.

"Not that either, I see." Mr. Babbitt paused, and then resumed, "Mr. Sloan, Mr. Irwin, there is one more thing you ought to know. Due to the writing material being so extremely scarce in the 4th century when these two manuscripts were written, the scribes used up the writing space on each page as much as possible. They even went so far as to leave out the space between the words so as to not waste room. But, in spite of being so stingy with space, the Vaticanus and Sinaiticus both, at the end of Mark 16:8, left a large amount of blank space—a space exactly large enough to hold those last twelve verses!"

Mr. Babbitt took a large book from off his desk, turned to a pre-marked page, and held it up for all to see. It was pictures of the Vaticanus and Sinaiticus, both opened at Mark 16, and each with the long blank space just as Mr. Babbitt described.[2]

"Mr. Sloan, the blank spaces do not tell us they rejected Mark 16:9-20. Rather, the blank spaces tell us they *accepted* it! The scribes knew it belonged there, but apparently did not have it at the time they were writing and left room intending to add it later."

The two stone statues said not a word. They both now knew the footnote was worthless.

"Mr. Sloan, Mr. Irwin, Mark 16:16 is *indeed* a verse from God that *plainly* teaches people that they must be baptized *before* they can be saved. But you take it away from them. You take away from the Word of God."

And I know what that means, I said to myself. *Revelation 22:18—you take away from God's Word, God takes heaven away from you.*

"But," Mr. Sloan objected with a mere shadow of his previous confidence, "the thief on the cross was not baptized, and he was saved."

"How do you know he was not baptized?" Mr. Babbitt fearlessly asked.

"Good Lord, man! He could not get off his cross!"

And peering straight into his eyes, Mr. Babbitt asked, "How do you know he was not baptized *before* he was put on his cross? Have you not read Matthew 3:5-6 and John 3:26, which say:

> *Then went out to him [John] Jerusalem, and all Judea, and all the region round about Jordan, and were baptized of him.*

> *Behold, the same [Jesus] baptizeth and all men come to him.*

"My friends, how do you know the man on the cross was not among those multitudes? You do not. And so you cannot claim the man on the cross was not baptized! Actually, since he knew about Jesus' life and mission and His coming in His kingdom,[3] the evidence indicates he *had* been among the great numbers who heard Jesus and were baptized.

"And besides all this, it does not even matter whether or not he was baptized. When they were on the cross, they were still under the Law of Moses which did not require baptism. Jesus' law, which requires baptism, did not come into effect until *after* the death of Jesus, just as Hebrews 9:17 says:

> *For a testament is of force after men are dead: otherwise it is of no strength at all while the testator lives.*

"So, to claim we do not need to be baptized today because the thief was not baptized is ludicrous. "

Mr. Sloan's shoulders sagged. His confidence crumbled. His pomp plummeted. No more objections came from his mouth. He caught on that the meek old man would show them wrong.

Out of the quiet, Mr. Babbitt spoke from the depth of his compassionate heart, "Mr. Sloan, Mr. Irwin, surely you see your problem. You are telling people 'salvation comes by faith *only*.' But

336

there is not one verse on faith that has the word 'only.' Fellows, you are teaching a doctrine the Bible does not teach. Rather, as you have seen for yourselves, the Word of God declares we are *not* saved by 'faith only,' and you saw the example of believers who were *not* saved. On the other hand, Mark 16:16, which is indeed part of the Bible, distinctly shows both, belief and baptism, must occur *before* and in order to obtain salvation. My friends, you need to seriously reconsider what you yourselves did to be saved, and what you now tell others, because this same Bible will be opened at Judgment Day to determine your eternal destiny according to whether or not you did what it says."

"Mr. Babbitt, even if you are right in saying a person must be baptized to be saved, I was baptized a few weeks after I believed. Also, all our people are eventually baptized. So that means we would be saved, and you are fussing for nothing."

"My friend, think back to your baptism. Were you told to be baptized so you could be saved?"

"Well, no," he answered with reluctance.

"No, you were not. You were *told* your baptism would not save you; you *believed* your baptism would not save you; and you were baptized, but *not* for the purpose of getting saved. Therefore, when you were baptized, you were not saved; you never have been."

Mr. Sloan squirmed. He knew what I knew: Mr. Babbitt was right. Then he resorted to what everyone does when they are in the wrong: "Well, you know we are all entitled to our own interpretations."

To which Mr. Babbitt missed not a beat, "But not to our MIS-interpretations. Nor are we free from their consequences. Otherwise, Paul would not have corrected Peter,[4] or the Galatians,[5] or the Corinthians,[6] or numerous others. "

Stifled at every step, Mr. Sloan rose, placed his hand over his physical heart, and said, "I know I was saved without baptism because the moment I believed, the Holy Spirit gave me a feeling in my heart to tell me I was saved."

"Mr. Sloan, by claiming that, you make God out to be a liar. On one hand, by means of your feelings, you have God telling you that you are saved *without* baptism, but on the other hand, by means of the God-inspired Scriptures, He tells you that you are saved *by* baptism. You see, you have God telling you a contradiction. So, one is false. It is a lie. So, either God lies, or God does not prove things by giving people feelings. But you well know from Titus 1:2 God does not lie. So these feelings you were told to expect when you believed were probably an auto-suggested psychological effect. But whatever they were, they definitely were not communication from God."

Without saying anymore—I think he was afraid to—the two passed through the living room, extended cordialities to Mrs. Babbitt, and left, but without the haughtiness in which they came.

Mr. Babbitt closed the door, turned, and somehow gave me a pleasant smile from his disappointed face.

"Mr. Babbitt, why wouldn't they admit they were wrong? Why wouldn't they change? I mean, we're talking eternity here."

"Gary, it could be one of many reasons," he said as he reclined from weariness into his creaking antique rocking chair. Jesus said in John 12:43, some men *'love the praise of men more than the praise of God.'*"

"You mean, like, they didn't want to look bad in front of each other?"

"Yes, and it can go deeper than that. If they admitted their error, they would lose their preaching jobs; they even would have been cast out of their denominations. They also might lose the admiration of their family. Or, they just might be one of those who hate to admit they are wrong."

"But, but…" I struggled to express my thoughts. "We're looking at heaven or hell here!" You gotta do whatever it takes to escape going to hell and avoid missing heaven!"

"Yes, and Mrs. Babbitt and I will pray for them. But, right now, our concern is for you. You have learned so much these past few months. And, today in class and in this study with those men, you learned what God says a person must do to be saved. Gary, *you* have the decision to make."

CHAPTER 45
"YOU HAVE THE DECISION TO MAKE"

THAT EVENING

"Why did I let you two talk me into this?" I grunted as I pinned Kandy face-down on the floor while Chuck and Danny gave her a birthday spanking.

"Hurry! The tiger is breaking loose!" She freed an arm and began to beat my leg.

"Whoa girl! Don't break my leg. I still have a lot of races to run."

Dad and Mom sat on the brownish-orange sofa and laughed at the frolics of their four children.

"And one to grow on." The two little gigglers simultaneously slapped her a good one and then jumped up and down in uncontrolled excitement. But when I let her up, they darted out of the room. I wondered if I too should run, but her semi-concealed smirking face indicated she enjoyed the family attention.

Wrestling Wonder Woman and indulging in her chocolate cake and vanilla ice cream served as a momentary relief from the echo of Mr. Babbitt's words, "You have learned what you must do to be saved; now you have the decision to make." But the words would never go away. Not really. Even if I ignored them until they grew cold, they would still be there even though I would not hear them anymore. There will always be Judgment Day. There will always be eternal hell. And there is still the one and only way God tells us to avoid it. And I knew how. So, what was my problem? What held me back?

During the past two months, the members of the church where Mr. Babbitt attended grew accustomed to seeing me at their 6 PM worship. Today was no different. After all, even though Mr. Babbitt's lessons and Mr. Young's sermons revealed far more Bible teachings in six and a half months than I heard in all my life, I wanted to know more. I discovered the instructions from God are not dry and restrictive; they are refreshing and life-enhancing.

But this time, keeping my mind in worship proved challenging. Mr. Babbitt's words proved too forceful a statement to suppress: "You have learned what you must do to be saved; now you have the decision to make."

During the past few months I knew I must follow the truth no matter where it led. The conviction of doing whatever it took to avoid hell and get to heaven still drove me. And now I knew where that truth led. I needed to be baptized as a believing adult in order to get my sins forgiven and get saved. But now that it came time to actually do what that six-month search discovered, several ropes lassoed me and held me back.

But the Catholic Church is the oldest, I whimpered.

But the oldest what? I shot back. It's the oldest man-made church. It's the great apostasy, remember? It is vain and Jesus is going to destroy it when He comes. You want to be a part of that?

As the church sang songs, I continued to argue with myself.

Yet, it is the largest, yanked another rope.

You know good and well truth is not determined by number, I squabbled back. *Noah was right; the millions were wrong. Lot was right; Sodom and Gomorrah were wrong. The Scriptures are right, no matter how few may stand with it; man-made doctrines and their churches are wrong, no matter how many may be in them. No, man's multitude does not change the Lord's laws.*

Then the scare-word jumped out of the shadows. *But I would be excommunicated!*

After my senses returned, I thought, *So what? I'd just be excommunicated from the apostasy. Actually, I'm getting out of apostasy and into the church! I'm not getting kicked out of the true church Jesus built by the apostles, I'm getting put into it! I'm not losing, I'm gaining! I'm not being lost, I'm being saved!*

I pulled out of my self-debate long enough to notice a couple of men serving the Lord's Supper.

So, I welcome the excommunication. I will be put out of the

*enormous multitude that fell away from the real church by its man-
made doctrines and practices issued by its man-made councils of its
man-made hierarchy—a hierarchy led for hundreds of years by
popes steeped in immorality, inquisitions, and crusades! I want out
of the ungodly apostasy that horribly misinterprets Matthew 16:18
to mean Peter is the rock, and then lies about a non-existent succession of popes from 600 AD back to Peter and covers it up with forgeries, and then invents the make-believe authority of Tradition to
teach those practices that are not taught in the Bible. And then they
have the nerve to tell the laity not to read the Bible, but rather just
listen to what the clergy tells them. What a racket! If that doesn't
wave the red warning flags of error, deception, and cover-up, nothing does! Yeah, they can excommunicate me if they want; it doesn't
mean a thing!*

The quietness of the auditorium grabbed my attention. I raised
my vision off of the back of the pew in front of me to see Mr. Young
stepping up to the pulpit. From the very start, Roy's sermon sounded
like something Mr. Babbitt set him up to preach. But that was okay,
I appreciated their efforts to help me. And what he said made a lot of
sense. Well, it should, it came from the Bible.

One of his points focused upon Matthew 28:19-20.

> *Go ye therefore, and teach all nations, baptizing them in
> the name of the Father, and of the Son, and of the Holy
> Ghost: Teaching them to observe all things whatsoever I
> have commanded you: and, lo, I am with you always even
> unto the end of the world.*

He explained the passage teaches, that after being baptized, the
new Christian is then to begin to learn and do all Jesus commands in
His Word, the New Testament. Roy emphasized the verse's word
"all" to mean just that—*all,* not some. The thought of learning and
obeying everything in the New Testament overwhelmed me as an
impossible task, but Roy relieved me with other verses which indicate the growth is expected to be a gradual development.[1] Yet, a determined and continual development nonetheless.

He also highlighted the important passage of Titus 2:11-14.

> *For the grace of God that bringeth salvation hath*

appeared to all men, teaching us that, denying ungodliness and worldly lusts, we should live soberly, righteously, and godly, in this present world; Looking for that blessed hope, and the glorious appearing of the great God and our Savior Jesus Christ; Who gave himself for us, that he might redeem us from all iniquity, and purify unto himself a peculiar people, zealous of good works.

Roy pointed out that verse 12 instructs the Christian to stop doing ungodly and sinful things, and instead, live righteously and godly. Of course, the only way to know which is which is to learn the Bible. Then verse 14 tells the Christian he is to be active in good works. Roy mentioned several of the good works taught in the Bible. They fell under two categories; loving God, and loving others.[2] He emphasized that, in loving God, the Christian will gladly obey Hebrews 10:25.

Not forsaking the assembling of ourselves together, as the manner of some is; but exhorting one another: and so much the more, as ye see the day approaching.

All of that makes sense. Anybody who truly repents in order to be saved is going to change his ways. I knew that a penitent person would no longer want to do what the Bible says do not do, and he would desire to do what is good and right. And, even if God did not command us to be in the worship assembly, this penitent person would still want to be in the assembly anyway to worship Him instead of being elsewhere worshipping himself—which is exactly what he would be doing if he skipped out to enjoy things of this world. It is not only about becoming saved, it is about becoming a Christian. It is a new mind and a new way of life.

Roy's last point, whether intentional or not, hit me right between my ears. Yes, specifically me—someone in a man-made church who is considering the baptism the Bible teaches. He explained, since only those who believe in Jesus, repent of sin, confess Jesus as Lord, and are baptized for the forgiveness of sins are those who are saved and added by God to His church as taught in Acts 2:38, 41, and 47, then everyone who has not done even one of those requirements is not saved nor are they in the church of Jesus. Even large groups of such people—the apostasy and denominations—are lost and outside the Lord's church. So, when a person in a man-made church learns the truth and is baptized correctly, he or she is now a member of the true church and is to worship and work with them. However, if the new Christian goes back to his man-made church made up of non-saved people, his baptism would be for nothing, as Roy pointed out from the Scriptures.

> *Be ye not unequally yoked together with unbelievers: for what fellowship hath righteousness with unrighteous-ness?...Wherefore come out from among them, and be ye separate," saith the Lord. 2 Corinthians 6:14-17.*

> *And have no fellowship with the unfruitful works of dark-ness, but rather reprove them. Ephesians 5:11.*

So, I summarized in my mind, *be baptized to get saved; be added by God to His church with whom I worship and work; continue to learn and obey the Bible; be active in good works; and look forward to eternity in heaven. What a great deal God gives us!*

However, spiraling up from the depth of my subconscious came the strongest lasso of all. *But what about Mom? What about my grandfather and grandmother, and my aunts, uncles, and cousins? I would be betraying them and our ancient family religion!*

But the more I thought about it, the more I realized the only way I would betray them is if I knew the truth but did not tell them! *What if we were all in a house that was on fire? I could stay in there and be destroyed with them, or, having found a way out I could silently escape alone and betray them, or, I could escape and warn the others with what I discovered. The first two choices are unthinkable! In real life, everybody does the third one. How much more, then, ought I do so with their eternity at stake?! If one of them had learned what I have, I would certainly want him to tell me! They are just like me six and a half months ago, completely unaware of the early apostasy and that we are in it today. No! I will not betray them! I will do what the Bible says to do to be saved, and I will tell my family these truths and hope they respond as I am about to.*

Roy's sermon was coming to a close. Soon he would offer the opportunity for baptism. Excitement rippled through my chest and shoulders. Thrill whirled up and down my arms and legs. Delightful thoughts flashed within my head. *Salvation! I am about to be saved from my sins! Heaven will be mine, not hell! I am quitting the vain and dooming doctrines and practices of men. I am not joining a condemned man-made denomination; rather, God is adding me to the very church Jesus built! I am getting into Jesus' church and out of the apostasy!*

I quickly recalled how often I viewed myself as a domino at the end of a long train of dominoes standing on end, one behind another with a slight space between. A slight push on the first topples the next, which topples the next, and the next, and the next, until all have imitated what the first one did. It grieved me that people are the same way in religion. But I cannot point my finger at anyone; the domino effect victimized me too. I simply took my turn at doing and believing what the ones before me did. I merely assumed we were right. I did not question anything. Understandably, I just trusted in what those I loved and respected told me, just as they had trusted in those they loved. The tragedy is, those who pushed the first domino of so much of our beliefs and practices were men, not God. Religious dominoes: the malicious, soul-enslaving trap of the devil.

The song leader approached the pulpit to lead the church in singing a song during which anyone desiring baptism could let Roy know. I visualized myself as my brothers' ivory domino at the end of their long train of black dominoes. In the distance I saw the dominoes toppling one after another. The point of impact rapidly advanced toward me. I mentally heard the clacking of the plastic pieces. Closer it came. Much closer. Three left. Two. One.

But the ivory domino would not fall.

I stood as the congregation rose to sing. I glanced back at Mr. Babbitt, but he looked straight ahead. It caused me to remember what he told me, "I am not going to pressure you. I have done all I can. You have learned what you must do to be saved. Now *you* have the decision to make."

Thank you for all you did for me, Mr. Babbitt. I have made my decision.

And I stepped into the aisle…

EPILOGUE

I was baptized that evening, March 15, 1970. Shortly thereafter, the cancer ended Mr. Babbitt's life.

After much thought, I resolved to use my life to help others know about these critical but concealed truths about the church and salvation. I attended the Elk City School of Preaching, graduated from Oklahoma Christian College in 1975 and the Harding Graduate School of Religion in 1979.

Chuck and Danny were baptized when teenagers. Many years later, the three of us lowered our wheel-chair bound mother into Chuck's pool where I baptized her. Bruce left the Catholic Church, disturbed by issues he himself had begun to notice, but maintained his love to God as he also pursued the truth in the Scriptures.

Sheila, my high school friend, and I attended the same college, where she met her husband-to-be, and I re-met the Parker girls' lovely cousin, Sheila Gamble, my future life-long wife. We all remained friends through college, graduate school, and to this very day.

But, this book is not about me. It is about you. Before you began to read this book, you were probably just like I was: content and secure with my church and beliefs, but wrong, fatally wrong, and without knowing it. I did not know about the gradual and comprehensive apostasy that turned into the Catholic Church, nor how its by-product, the divisive and confusing denominations, fit in. I did not know—I did not even conceive—that the very church Jesus built in the first century exists today; and, although I had a Bible, I did not know I had not done what it says to do to be saved. I would have viewed anyone a heretic who told me that what I did to be saved did not save me at all and that I was not in the church Jesus established.

What I just confided in you about myself probably describes you. That is why this book is about you. Now that you have completed the book, you yourself have gone from where I was— uninformed of these things—to where I am now.

Whether you are in the Catholic Church, or denominationalism, or something else, I urge you to come out of it as I did. Millions have already heard this message and have denounced man-made doctrines and churches. So get with the person who encouraged you to read this book. He or she will help you get baptized and become acquainted with the wonderful people in the church. Neither the facts presented in this book nor the Scriptures cited are ever going to change. Every day Judgment comes closer. You have learned what you must do to be saved. I have done all I can. Now *you* have the decision to make.

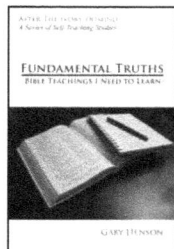

END NOTES

CHAPTER 2. THE WAGER

[1] The diocese (an area of churches) whose presiding bishop is the archbishop (whose authority extends over other dioceses and their bishops in his province).

CHAPTER 3. THE LEGITIMATE REASON

[1] See: *Haley's Bible Handbook*, Henry H. Haley, Zondervan Publishing House: Grand Rapids, Michigan, 1965. P. 409.

[2] Psalm 41:9 with Luke 22:47-48.

[3] Zechariah 11:12 with Matthew 26:15.

[4] Zechariah11:13 with Matthew 27:5.

[5] Zechariah 11:13 with Matthew 27:7.

[6] Psalm 35:11 with Matthew 26:60.

[7] Isaiah 50:6 with Matthew 26:67.

[8] Psalm 22:16 with John 20:25-29.

[9] Isaiah 53:12 with Mark 15:27.

[10] Psalm 22:18 with John 19:23-24.

CHAPTER 4. YOU WIN SOME; YOU LOSE SOME

[1] *The Daily Oklahoman*, published by the Oklahoma Publishing Company, September 20, 1969. Pages 13-14.

CHAPTER 14. WHAT'S GOOD FOR THE GOOSE IS GOOD FOR THE GANDER.

[1] John 8:32

CHAPTER 17. BETWEEN A ROCK AND A HARD PLACE

[1] The RSV Interlinear Greek-English New Testament. Grand Rapids, Michigan: Zondervan Publishing Company, 1968.

[2] W.E. Vine, Vine's Expository Dictionary of New Testament Words.

[3] Vine's, vol. 3, p.302.

[4] Easton's Bible Dictionary.

[5] Ibid.

[6] *Essentials of New Testament Greek*, Ray Summers, Nashville: Broadman Press, 1950.p. 22-23.

CHAPTER 18. "PROVE ALL THINGS"

[1] Acts 15: 1-23.

[2] 1 Thessalonians 5:21.

[3] John 8:32.

[4] Name has changed to: Southern Nazarene University.

CHAPTER 19. STRAIGHT FROM THE HORSE'S MOUTH

[1] *The Catholic Encyclopedia*, ed. Herbermann, Pace, Pallen, Shahan, Wynne. Special edition under the offices of the Knights of Columbus Catholic, i.e., Truth Committee. NY: The Encyclopedia Press, Inc. 1907.

[2] Catholic Encyclopedia, VIII. 426.

[3] John 18:36.

[4] Catholic Encyclopedia, VIII. 36.

[5] *History of the Christian Church*, Philip Schaff (Grand Rapids, MI: Eerdmans; 1910). 4:287.

[6] Catholic Encyclopedia, II. 429.

[7] Schaff, 4:298-9.

[8] Catholic Encyclopedia, II. 661-662.

[9] Catholic Encyclopedia, VIII. 429.

[10] Schaff, 6: 145.

[11] Schaff, 6:158.

[12] Catholic Encyclopedia, VIII. 9-10.

[13] Schaff, 6:429.

[14] Catholic Encyclopedia, VII. 452.

[15] Catholic Encyclopedia, XII. 129.

[16] 1st Corinthians 14:33.

[17] Catholic Encyclopedia, I. 289.

[18] Catholic Encyclopedia, VI. 213.

[19] Schaff, 7:8.

[20] Schaff, 7:258.

[21] Schaff, 4:284-285.

[22] Catholic Encyclopedia, VIII. 426.

[23] Catholic Encyclopedia, VIII page 426.

[24] Schaff, 4:297.

[25] Catholic Encyclopedia, IX. 165.

[26] Schaff, 7:8.

[27] Catholic Encyclopedia, I. 292.

[28] Catholic Encyclopedia, VIII. 429.

[29] Catholic Encyclopedia, VIII. 562.

[30] Schaff, 6:614.

[31] Isaiah 47:13.

[32] Catholic Encyclopedia, VI. 786.

[33] Revelation 19:6; Daniel 4:17, 35; 5:21; Psalm 83:18.

[34] Acts 2:23; Isaiah 46:10.

[35] Matthew 28:20.

CHAPTER 21. A DATE WITH VACANDARD

[1] Catholic Encyclopedia, VIII. 26.

[2] Vacandard, Preface ix.

[3] Schaff, VI.2.

[4] Schaff, VII. 56.

[5] Schaff, II. 78.

[6] Schaff, VI. 533-4.

[7] Vacandard, 132.

[8] Catholic Encyclopedia, VIII.34.

[9] Vacandard, 119.

[10] Vacandard, 147.

[11] Schaff, V. 888.

[12] "The devil, so Gregory asserted, was appearing in the shapes of a toad, a pallid ghost and a black cat." (Schaff, VI. 517.) "The Pope [Innocent VIII] admitted that men and women could have immoral relations with demons, and that sorcerers by their magical incantations could injure the harvests, the vineyards, the orchards and the fields." (Vacandard, 199.) "Pope after pope issued orders not to spare those who were in league with the devil, but to put them to torture and cast them into the flames." (Schaff, V. 888.) "Among the documents on witchcraft, emanating from papal or other sources, the place of pre-eminence is occupied by the bull, *Summis desiderantes* issued by Innocent VIII, 1484. This notorious proclamation, consisting of nearly 1000 words, was sent out in answer to questions proposed to the papal chair by German inquisitors, and recognizes in clearest language the current beliefs about demonic bewitchment as undeniable. It had come to his knowledge, so the pontiff wrote, that the dioceses of Mainz, Cologne, Treves, Salzburg and Bremen teemed with persons who, forsaking the Catholic faith, were consorting with demons. By incantations, conjurations and other iniquities they were thwarting the parturition of women and destroying the seed of animals, the fruits of the earth, the grapes of the vine and the fruit of the orchard. Men and women, flocks and herds, trees and all herbs were being afflicted with pains and torments. Men could no longer beget, women no longer conceive, and wives and husbands were prevented from performing the marital act." (Schaff, VI. 520.)

[13] Schaff, V. 517.

[14] Vacandard, 239-241.

[15] Vacandard, 244.

[16] Schaff, V. 527.

[17] Vacandard, 128.

[18] Vacandard, 143.

[19] Catholic Encyclopedia, VIII. 31.

[20] Schaff, VI. 547.

[21] Schaff, VI. 530.

[22] Acts 17:31; 2 Timothy 4:1, 8; Romans 9:14.

[23] Catholic Encyclopedia, VIII. 32.

[24] Vacandard, 226.

[25] Vacandard, 152-153.

[26] Vacandard, 153-154.

[27] Vacandard, 192.

[28] Schaff, VI. 548-549.

[29] Schaff, VI. 530.

[30] Schaff, V. 531.

[31] *Catholic Encyclopedia*, VIII. 33. Vacandard, 158. Schaff, VI. 2.

[32] Catholic Encyclopedia, VIII. 32.

[33] Vacandard, 232-233.

[34] Matthew 28:20.

[35] Numbers 23:19.

[36] Psalm 147:4-5.

[37] Catholic Encyclopedia, VIII. 34.

[38] Catholic Encyclopedia, VIII. 33-34.

[39] Schaff, V. 531.

[40] Catholic Encyclopedia, VIII. 33.

[41] Vacandard, 109.

[42] Schaff, VI. 530.

[43] Catholic Encyclopedia, VIII. 33.

[44] Vacandard, 56-57.

[45] Schaff, VI. 543.

[46] Vacandard, 210.

[47] Schaff, V. 531.

[48] Schaff, VI. 548-549.

[49] Vacandard, 201.

[50] Schaff, II. 78.

[51] Vacandard, 198-199.

[52] Schaff, VI. 531-532.

CHAPTER 22. GOD GETS A WORD IN

[1] Acts 9:1-9.

[2] Revelation 22: 18-19. For I testify unto every man who hears the

words of the prophecy of this book: If anyone adds to these things, God will add to him the plagues that are written in this book; and if anyone takes away from the words of the book of this prophecy, God shall take away his part from the Book of Life.

[3] Catholic Encyclopedia, VIII. 28.

[4] Catholic Encyclopedia, VIII. 26.

[5] Catholic Encyclopedia, VIII. 26.

[6] Catholic Encyclopedia, VIII. 26.

[7] Catholic Encyclopedia, VIII. 26.

[8] Catholic Encyclopedia, VIII. 26.

[9] Catholic Encyclopedia, VIII. 27.

[10] Catholic Encyclopedia, VIII. 27.

[11] Vacandard, 208-209.

[12] Vacandard, 239.

CHAPTER 23. FOOTBALL FINALE

[1] *The Daily Oklahoman,* Saturday, October 25, 1969. Page 15.

[2] Ibid., Saturday, November 1, 1969. Page 14B.

[3] Ibid., November 8, 1969. Page 15.

[4] Ibid., Saturday, November 15, 1969. Page 14.

CHAPTER 24. "ONWARD CHRISTIAN SOLDIERS"?

[1] *Catholic Encyclopedia,* "Crusades," IV. 543.

[2] Ibid., IV. 543.

[3] Ibid., IV. 543-557.

[4] Ibid., IV.

[5] Ibid., IV. 546.

[6] Ibid., IV. 546.

[7] Ibid., IV. 556.

[8] Matthew 26:52.

[9] John 18:36.

[10] Catholic Encyclopedia, IV. 546.

[11] Ibid., IV. 546.

[12] Ibid., IV. 546.

[13] Ibid., IV. 547.

[14] Ibid., IV. 548.

[15] Ibid., IV. 548.

[16] Ibid., IV. 549.

[17] Ibid., IV. 549.

[18] Schaff, V. 238.

[19] Schaff, V. 127.

[20] Schaff, V. 511-512.

[21] Mark 16:15-16.

[22] Schaff, V. 288.

[23] *Cyclopedia of Biblical, Theological, and Ecclesiastical Literature,* John McClintock, and James Strong. Originally published by: Harper and Brothers, New York, 1867-1887 (In Twelve Volumes). II. 595.

[24] Joshua chapters 8 through 12.

[25] Joshua 10:42.

[26] Schaff, V. 290.

[27] Joshua 1:1-9.

CHAPTER 25. CLASH OF THE TITANS

[1] *A Debate Over the Roman Catholic Religion*, Alexander Campbell and John B. Purcell, Cincinnati: stereotyped and published by J. A. James & Company, 1837. Page 17.

[2] Ibid., p. 18.

[3] Ibid., p. 22.

[4] Matthew 12:22-24.

[5] *A Debate Over the Roman Catholic Religion*, p. 37.

[6] Ibid., p. 28.

[7] Ibid., p. 151.

[8] Ibid., p. 32.

[9] Ibid., p. 28.

[10] Ibid., p. 22.

[11] Ibid., p. 28.

[12] Ibid., p. 28.

[13] Ibid., p. 22.

[14] Ibid., p. 37.

[15] Ibid., p. 43.

[16] Ibid., p. 153.

[17] Ibid., p. 28.

[18] See chapter 18.

[19] 1 Thessalonians 5:21.

CHAPTER 26. ABRACADABRA

[1] Catholic Encyclopedia, VI. 135.

[2] *Stevens –Beevers Debate on the New Testament and Roman Catholicism,* Eldred Stevens and Eric Beevers, Ph.D. Williams: Nashville, 1953, p. 5.

[3] Ibid, pp. 200-202.

[4] Catholic Encyclopedia, VI. 136.

[5] Catholic Encyclopedia, XII. 768.

[6] Catholic Encyclopedia, III. 484.

[7] Catholic Encyclopedia, IV. 781.

[8] Catholic Encyclopedia, I. 636.

[9] Catholic Encyclopedia, XV. 106.

[10] Catholic Encyclopedia, V. 773.

[11] Catholic Encyclopedia, V. 777.

[12] Catholic Encyclopedia, V. 777.

[13] Catholic Encyclopedia, I. 446.

[14] Catholic Encyclopedia, IX. p.224-5.

CHAPTER 27. HOCUS POCUS

[1] Matthew 15:9.

[2] *Stevens –Beevers Debate on the New Testament and Roman Catholicism,* Eldred Stevens and Eric Beevers, Ph.D. Williams: Nashville, 1953, p. 200.

[3] Full quote of *Catholic Encyclopedia* supplied for the reader.

[4] Stevens –Beevers Debate, p. 201-202.

[5] Catholic Encyclopedia, IV. 41.

[6] Catholic Encyclopedia, VII. 327.

[7] Ibid. 334.

[8] Catholic Dictionary, p. 402.

[9] Revelation 22:18.

[10] John 8:30-31.

[11] Catholic Encyclopedia, XIV. 378.

[12] Catholic Encyclopedia, VI. 135.

[13] Catholic Encyclopedia, XII. 184-186.

[14] Catholic Dictionary, p. 403.

[15] Catholic Encyclopedia, XV.391.

[16] Catholic Encyclopedia, I. 62.

[17] Catholic Encyclopedia, XII. 576-577.

[18] 1 Timothy 4:2.

[19] Catholic Encyclopedia, I. 629-630.

CHAPTER 29. THE BABYSITTER

[1] Catholic Encyclopedia, IV. 517.

[2] Ibid.

[3] Ibid.

[4] Catholic Encyclopedia, III. 484.

[5] Catholic Encyclopedia, III. 264.

[6] Catholic Encyclopedia, VII. 667.

[7] Catholic Encyclopedia, XII. 737.

[8] Catholic Encyclopedia, XII. 414.

[9] *The Baltimore Catechism*, #3, Q.560. [cf., *Catechism of the Catholic Church*, Doubleday: New York, 1994, page 30 (#78).]

[10] Catholic Encyclopedia, X. 657.

[11] Catholic Encyclopedia, I. 776.

[12] Catholic Encyclopedia, VI. 217.

[13] Deuteronomy 32:4.

[14] Catholic Encyclopedia, X. 6.

[15] Catholic Encyclopedia, XII. 184-186.

[16] Catholic Encyclopedia, XV. 391.

[17] Catholic Encyclopedia, I. 64.

[18] Catholic Encyclopedia, XI. 164.

[19] Catholic Encyclopedia, VII. 788.

[20] Catholic Encyclopedia, IX. 244.

[21] Catholic Encyclopedia, XII. 576-577.

[22] Matthew 15:9.

[23] 1 John 3:4.

[24] Revelation 22:18-19.

CHAPTER 30. DEAD MEN SPEAK

[1] Campbell, Alexander, *The Millennial Harbinger*, volume VIII, pages 20-22. (As quoted in: Wilson, L.R., *Roman Catholicism*, Nashville: The Freedom Press, 1965, pages 28-29.)

[2] Titus 1:2.

[3] Irenaeus, *Against Heresies*, book 1, chapter 8, section 1.

[4] Irenaeus, *Against Heresies*, book 2, chapter 27, section 2.

[5] Catholic Dictionary, page 647.

[6] Campbell-Purcell Debate, page 23.

[7] Catholic Encyclopedia, X, "Music: Ecclesiastical Music."

[8] 1 Corinthians 9:5.

[9] 2 Timothy 3:16-17; Revelation 22:18-19; etc.

[10] Ephesians 3:3-4.

[11] Matthew 15:9.

CHAPTER 33. ON MY OWN, ALMOST

[1] Revelation 22:18-19.

[2] Colossians 3:17.

[3] Ephesians 3:3-4.

[4] Matthew 7:21-23.

CHAPTER 34. NO PAIN; NO GAIN

[1] Matthew 25:41.

[2] Matthew 25:30.

[3] Jude 13.

[4] As told by my guide at the Cave of the Winds, Colorado Springs.

[5] Revelation 21:8.

[6] Matthew 13:50.

[7] Matthew 5:29.

[8] John 12:48.

CHAPTER 35. MISERY LOVES COMPANY

[1] *Fiddler On The Roof* is a musical with music by Jerry Bock, lyrics by Sheldon Harnick, and book by Joseph Stein.

[2] 2 Timothy 3:15-17.

[3] Revelation 22:18.

[4] John 18:36.

[5] Matthew 15:9.

CHAPTER 37. WHEN ALL ELSE FAILS, READ THE INSTRUCTIONS

[1] Philippians 1:21.

[2] Galatians 2:11-14.

[3] 1 Corinthians 1:10.

CHAPTER 38. THE GREASED SLIDE

[1] Paul Harvey was a popular American radio broadcaster for the

ABC Radio Networks from the 1950's through the 1990's. *Paul Harvey News* was carried on 1,200 radio stations, 400 Armed Forces Network stations and 300 newspapers.

[2] *Cyclopedia of Biblical, Theological, and Ecclesiastical Literature,* John McClintock, and James Strong. Originally published by: Harper and Brothers, New York, 1867-1887.

CHAPTER 41. THE REFORMATION

[1] Matthew 15:13.

CHAPTER 43. DO THE MATH

[1] Matthew 15:14.

CHAPTER 44. THE BIGGER THEY ARE...

[1] 1 Maccabees; 4 Maccabees; Wisdom of Solomon; Ecclesiasticus: Tobit 2:2ff; Judith 1:1—11:13; 13:9-15; Epistle of Barnabas; Shepherd of Hermas.

[2] *A Review of the New Versions*, Foy E. Wallace Jr., Fort Worth, Texas: Noble Patterson Publisher, 1973. Appendix.

[3] Luke 23:41-42.

[4] Galatians 2:11-14.

[5] Galatians 1:6-9.

[6] 1 Corinthians, all sixteen chapters.

CHAPTER 45. "YOU HAVE A DECISION TO MAKE"

[1] 1 Peter 2:2; Hebrews 5:12-14.